OPERATIONS IN WAZIRISTAN

1919–1920

Compiled by the General Staff
Army Headquarters
India
1923

The Naval & Military Press Ltd

Published by
The Naval & Military Press Ltd
5 Riverside, Brambleside, Bellbrook
Industrial Estate, Uckfield, East Sussex,
TN22 1QQ England
Tel: +44 (0) 1825 749494
Fax: +44 (0) 1825 765701
www.naval-military-press.com

In reprinting in facsimile from the original, any imperfections are inevitably reproduced and the quality may fall short of modern type and cartographic standards.

OPERATIONS
IN
WAZIRISTAN
1919-1920

(Second Edition)

Catalogue No. O. W. 4 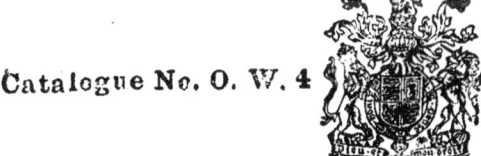 Case No. 28-Books-M. O. 3

Compiled by the General Staff
Army Headquarters
India

1923

DELHI
GOVERNMENT CENTRAL PRESS
1923

The Illustrations, Panoramas and Maps, other than Maps Nos. 4, 5 and 6 given in the Contents, have not been included in this edition.

(B 25/1036A)Q 31505—1972 1375 4/24 H & S, Ltd **Gp. 25**

CONTENTS.

	PAGE.
GLOSSARY	ix

CHAPTER I.

INTRODUCTORY.

Geographical—Inhabitants—Characteristics of Mahsuds and Wazirs.—Blood feuds.—Fanaticism.—Lack of unity between Mahsuds and Wazirs.—Fighting strength and armaments.—Tactics of tribesmen ... 1

CHAPTER II.

POLITICAL.

Afghan claims to Waziristan 1884-92.—Policy of British Government 1892.—Opening of Gomal route 1890.—Tribal allowances.—Durand Agreement 1893.—Occupation of Wana 1893.—The Mullah Powindah.—Reconsideration of Policy after signing of Durand Agreement.—Occupation of the Tochi Valley 1894.—Formation of Tribal Militias.—Policy in 1899.—Its test during the Afghan War 1919 7

CHAPTER III.

OPERATIONS AGAINST THE WAZIRISTAN TRIBES PREVIOUS TO 1914.

Operations against Mahsuds, 1860.—Attack on Palosina Camp 22nd-23rd April.—Action of Barari Tangi, 2nd May.—Mahsud Blockade 1879.—Operations against Mahsuds 1881.—Afghan intrigues 1892.—Boundary intrigues 1892.—Boundary Commission 1894.—Attack on camp by Mullah Powindah.—Punitive Operations 1894.—Attack on Political Officer's escort Upper Tochi 1897.—Mahsud Blockade 1900-01.—Expedition against Kabul Khel Wazirs 1902 ... 12

CHAPTER IV.

OPERATIONS AGAINST WAZIRISTAN TRIBES BETWEEN 4TH AUGUST 1914 AND 11TH JUNE 1917.

Incursions by Afghan tribesmen 1914-15.—Attitude of Mahsuds 1914-17.—Mahsud situation at beginning of 1917.—Negotiations with Mahsuds.—Attack on Sarwakai Post in March.—Route to Wana cleared by moveable column.—Attack in the Gwalerai Algad 1st May.—Attack on Tormandr Post, 6th May.—Action near Palosi Ziarat, 9th May.—Punitive operations sanctioned.—Attack near Chota Gwalerai Pass, 16th May.—Proposed plan of operations.—Comparison of Gomal and Shahur routes.—Gomal posts rationed.—Attitude of the Amir.—Capture of Tut Narai Post, 31st May.—Distribution of troops in the Tochi.—Attack on piquetting party near Khirgi 7th June 30

CHAPTER V.

OPERATIONS IN THE SHAHUR AND KHAISARA VALLEYS BETWEEN 12TH JUNE AND 17TH AUGUST 1917.

Preliminary reconnaissance from Jandola.—Passage of Shahur Tangi, 14th and 15th June.—Advance to Barwand 19th June.—Attack on piquet Barwand, 19th June.—Attack on Nanu Village, 21st June.—First overtures for peace.—Situation on 22nd June.—Advance to Narai Raghza, 23rd June.—Action near Shrawanai Pass, 24th June.—Arrival of peace emissaries.—Withdrawal to Ispana Raghza.—Value of Aeroplanes.—Terms given to Mahsuds.—Hostilities suspended, 27th June.—Mahsud hostages and surrender of rifles—Withdrawal to Manzal.—Full jirga interviewed at Sarwakai, 10th August.—Terms complied with.—Peace announced, and force returns to Jandola.—Climatic conditions and health of troops ... 51

CHAPTER VI.

Events leading up to campaign 1919-20.

Plan of campaign in Waziristan during Afghan War 1919.—Situation in North Waziristan May 1919.—Evacuation of Upper Tochi Posts 23rd May.—Withdrawal of garrisons of Spinwam and Shewa, 24th and 25th May.—Situation in Miranshah.—Attitude of Northern Waziristan Militia.—Attacks on Tochi Posts.—Situation in South Waziristan in May.—Attitude of Southern Waziristan Militia.—Evacuation of the Wana Agency in May.—Situation in the Tochi at end of May.—Attitude of Mahsuds.—Formation of Tochi Relief Column, 30th May.—Tochi Posts relieved.—Punitive measures against Lower Daurs.—Situation in the Derajat.—Relief of Jandola, 9th June.—Afghans in Wana.—Raid on Drazinda, 11th June.—Preparations for an advance into Khost.—Attack on Bannu aerodrome, 14th July.—Attacks on road piquets in the Tochi, July and August.—Action at Zarkani, 19th September.—Actions near Manjhi, October.—Air raid on Wana, 9th October.—Attacks on convoys near Girni and Khajuri, 21st October.—Maliks visit Kabul.—Summary of offences by Mahsuds and Wazirs, May to November 1919.—Necessity for punitive operations.—Factors governing policy to be adopted.—Policy decided on.—Terms to Wazirs and Mahsuds.—Measures taken on sanction of operations ... 66

CHAPTER VII.

Operations of the Tochi Column.

Distribution of troops November 1919.—Concentration of Tochi Column, 8th November.—Advance to Datta Khel, 12th November.—Tochi Wazirs accept our terms, 17th November.—Mahsuds reject terms 11th November.—Withdrawal of Tochi Column to Dardoni, 26th November.—Troops transferred and Derajat Column formed 93

CHAPTER VIII.

Operations of the Derajat Column.—First phase.

Factors governing choice of Takki Zam route.—Measures adopted to secure L. of C. west of Khirgi.—Preliminary preparations for advance over Spinkai Raghza, 11th-13th December.—Air Operations.—Equipment of Derajat Column.—Strength and armament of opposing forces.—Headquarters of Derajat Column moves to Jandola.—Attack on piquets at Jandola, 17th December.—Advance to Palosina, 18th December.—Description of country round Mandanna Hill.—Action near Mandanna Hill, 19th December.—Operations to establish piquet on Mandanna Hill, 20th December.—Operations to establish piquet on Black Hill, 21st December.—Permanent piquet established on Black Hill, 22nd December.—Negotiations for settlement.—Jirga at Jandola, 29th December.—Original terms enhanced.—Submission of Maliks.—End of first phase ... 97

OPERATIONS IN WAZIRISTAN 1919-1920.

CHAPTER I.

INTRODUCTORY.

Geographical.—Waziristan lies on the western border of the Indian Empire, and forms the connecting link on the Afghan frontier between the districts of Kurram and Zhob. For political and administrative purposes it is divided into Northern and Southern Waziristan, its shape resembling a rough parallelogram, 5,000 square miles in extent, practically the whole of which is a tangled mass of mountains and hills of every size, shape and bearing. At first sight the mountains appear to run irregularly in all directions, but a study of the map will show that there are well defined ranges protecting the interior of the country and making penetration into it a matter of extreme difficulty.

The general trend of the main watercourses is from west to east, and the country gradually rises by a series of parallel ranges from the Derajat plain to the watershed which divides the basin of the Indus from that of the Helmand. The streams vary greatly in width and are generally flanked throughout their length by high hills, but occasionally these narrow valleys open out and cultivation takes the place of rocks and stones. Here and there, by cutting through ranges of hills at right angles to their courses, they have formed gorges which are locally known as 'tangis' and these are usually held by the tribesmen to oppose an enemy's advance. The beds of the watercourses are thickly strewn with stones and boulders. In dry weather a stream of water usually trickles down them, and has to be crossed and recrossed frequently; but after rain they fill very rapidly, and become dangerous torrents.

The two chief highways of Waziristan are the Tochi and the Gomal Valleys, the former giving access from the Bannu district to the Afghan district of Birmal, and the latter connecting the two British districts of Derajat and Zhob, and forming the principal route used by Powindah caravans in their annual migration from Afghanistan to India. There are no well-defined lateral communications between the Tochi and Gomal Valleys, but the following routes are possible alignments for metalled roads*:—

    (a) Datta Khel to Wana, *via* Shawal-Dhana.
    (b) Datta Khel to Wana or Jandola, *via* Tut Narai-Razani-Razmak, Makin and thence either,
        (i) *via* Kaniguram—Lare Lar to Wana : or
        (ii) *via* Tank Zam to Jandola and thence *via* Shahur Tangi and Sarwakai to Wana.
    (c) (Continuation of Thal-Idak road) Idak to Wana or Jandola, *via* Star Sarobi-Upper Khaisora Valley to Razani and thence as in (b).
    (d) Wana, *via* Spin to Khajuri Kach and thence down Gomal to Murtaza.

Inhabitants.—Waziristan is essentially a barren country, and the poorness of the soil has hitherto proved an insuperable obstacle to a large increase in the population. The chief inhabitants are the Darwesh Khel Wazirs, the Mahsuds, the Daurs, and the Bhittannis. The two last named tribes can be dismissed in a few words. The Daurs inhabit the banks of the Tochi River from Ghazlamai village to Khajuri Post, and are reputed to be morally the lowest of the Afghan races. Nevertheless they are diligent, hardworking, and patient cultivators, and though unwarlike by nature, have often resisted successfully attempts by their neighbours to oust them from their rich lands.

The Bhittannis are a tribe inhabiting the borders of the Dera Ismail Khan and Bannu districts and who dwell partly in independent territory. The independent Bhittannis though hereditary enemies of the Mahsuds have more than once foregone their time-honoured feud, and combined with their more warlike and rapacious neighbours in attacks and raids in British territory. Now, however, they have practically identified themselves with British interests and for some years have not given serious trouble.

---

*The following motor roads are now (1923) under construction :—
    (a) Idak to Jandola *via* Isha-Tal-Dizh Narai-Asad Khel-Razani-Razmak Narai-Makin-Sorarogha.
    (b) Jandola to Sarwakai *via* Shahur R.

Tradition, the truth of which is very doubtful, assigns a common origin to the Darwesh Khel Wazirs and Mahsuds, but the name Wazir is applied exclusively to the former branch.

The original home of the Wazirs and Mahsuds is said to have been in the Afghan border district of Birmal and that these races began to move eastward at the close of the 14th century, first occupying the area north of the Tochi river and then spreading southward to the Gomal.

*The Wazirs are largely a nomadic race and have comparatively few permanent villages or settlements. They are divided into two main classes, the Utmanzai† and the Ahmadzai.‡ The former occupy the Tochi Valley and areas adjoining it, moving up to the higher hills in the summer and returning in the winter to the foothills and valleys. The majority of the Ahmadzai migrate every autumn with their flocks to the grazing lands on the western borders of the Bannu District, returning in the spring to their summer settlements in the Wana and Shakai plains.

The three main branches of the Mahsuds are the Alizai, Shaman Khel, and Bahlolzai, each of which is sub-divided into numerous sections and sub-sections. The settlements of these sections are so greatly intermixed that it is impossible to define clearly the localities occupied by the main branches of the tribe. As a result of this intermingling, sectional feuds are almost unknown and therefore in dealing with the Mahsuds, the possibility of a combination of all the sections against a common foe must always be considered.

Characteristics of Mahsuds and Wazirs.—Relying on the inaccessibility of their country, the Waziristan tribes have for centuries defied the power of the rulers of India and Afghanistan, and on more than one occasion in the past they engaged and defeated the invading armies of the Moghuls. Their character, organization and instincts have made them independent and strongly democratic, so much so that even their own maliks (or elders) have little real control over the unruly spirits. Any man may rise by courage and wisdom to the position of *Malik*, but

---
* For main sub-divisions of Mahsuds and Wazirs see Appendix "L."
† Known as the Tochi Wazirs.
‡ Known as the Wana Wazirs.

many who have attempted an undue assumption of authority have been assassinated. True sons of Esau, the Waziristan tribesmen carry their lives in their hands and finding that the natural resources of their country do not favour them enough, they eke out their existence by plundering their more peaceful neighbours. This mode of life has produced in their men a fine physique and a free and independent manner, and in their women a remarkable power of resisting fatigue and of nurturing their children under the most adverse conditions and circumstances.

Both Waziris and Mahsuds are notorious for their raiding propensities, and for the rapidity with which they remove their plunder to the security of the inner hills of their country.

Blood feuds.—The Waziristan tribes do not in theory carry out a blood-feud to the bitter end as do other frontier Pathans, for the death of the offender generally extinguishes the feud; but if the offender escapes the life of a relation may be taken instead, and as this may in turn be avenged, the feud tends to become interminable as is the case among the Afridis. On the other hand, a murder may be compounded on payment of a sum which usually varies between Rs. 700 and Rs. 1,000. Professional assassins are sometimes employed to deal with a murderer, the fee being from Rs. 60 to Rs. 150.

Fanaticism.—Mahsuds and Wazirs are not as a rule very much under the influence of their Mullahs and are consequently less fanatical than many tribes on the frontier. On the other hand there have been many instances of murders of British officers or officials by individual fanatics or "ghazis," who were in some cases trusted and apparently devoted employees of the officer they murdered.

Lack of unity between Mahsuds and Wazirs.—The chief weakness of the Waziristan tribes lies in their lack of unity. The Mahsuds and Wazirs have long been at feud, and a whole-hearted combination of the two is therefore unusual. On the other hand, the democratic character of the tribes, especially of the Mahsuds, has the disadvantage from our point of view that their *jirgas*, or assembly of tribal leaders, have little restraining influence over the more lawless elements, and are therefore not truly representative of tribal opinion; in other words, a *jirga* can produce no reliable guarantee that the terms they have accepted will be carried out. This was well illustrated during the 1919-20 campaign, and placed us at a considerable disadvantage in our negotiations with the Mahsuds. It is important to remember, however, that a wave of fanaticism or the rise to power of some commanding personality may at any time cause Mahsuds and Wazirs to sink their differences and effect a formidable combination against us. It must not be forgotten also that when the Government of India undertake operations against an offending tribe, neighbouring sections are often placed in an unenviable position; if they decide to stand aloof, they run the risk of losing their property or lives unless strong enough to defend them, while if they agree to help their co-religionists, they will probably become the objective at some later date of another punitive expedition. They generally elect to brave the remoter retribution, and for this reason it is impossible to foresee the exact limits to which a tribal rising may extend.

Fighting strength and armaments.—The fighting strength of the Waziristan tribes has been appreciably reduced by the campaign of 1919-20 but it is as yet too early to calculate accurately the extent of their loss. Moreover, the fighting strength of a frontier tribe is to be measured not so much by heads as by rifles, and there can be no doubt, as will be explained in a later chapter, that the Mahsuds and Wazirs are still well supplied with arms, in spite of the severe casualties they have suffered and the large number of rifles they have been forced to surrender. At the present time the Wazirs can probably still arm effectively about 10,000 out of a total strength of 23,000 fighting men, and the Mahsuds about 12,000 out of a total fighting strength of 16,000; and this takes no account of smooth-bores and other obsolete weapons, of which there are sufficient to arm the remainder of the tribe.

Tactics of tribesmen.—Moreover, the Wazirs and Mahsuds operating in their own country, can be classed among the finest fighters in the world, and at the present moment they include in their numbers upwards of three thousand men who have served in our regular army or militia and who have an intimate knowledge of our habits and tactics. The tribesmen have been described as the best umpires in the world, for they seldom allow a tactical error to go unpunished. History furnishes numerous examples of the price which has to be paid when fighting against them for the neglect of ordinary precautions, such, for instance, as a failure to piquet heights, the daily adherence to a fixed method of carrying out protective measures, a loss of touch with detached parties, or the miscalculation of time and space.

The tribal system of intelligence is also very good. All movements of troops are closely watched, and at the first threat of an advance into their country the implicated sections hasten to bury their grain and send their women, children and cattle into the fastnesses of the upper hills, or to the settlements of sections with whom we have no quarrel.

Owing to his activity on the hillside and general watchfulness, it is exceedingly difficult to outflank the tribesman or to cut off his retreat, while if vigorously pursued and unable to get clear away, he will hide his rifle and appear as a peaceful villager. He is an expert at attacking small parties and convoys, and when the troops begin to withdraw it is astonishing how large numbers of the enemy will appear in places which had seemed to be deserted, and with what determination the rear-guard will be hurried. In the past the Mahsuds have been conspicuously successful in capturing small, isolated posts, their usual procedure being to send an emissary to induce the commander to detach a large part of the garrison in pursuit of an imaginary raiding gang. One of their greatest triumphs was the seizure of Kashmir Kar Post in 1901 which was largely due to one of their number having spent several weeks disguised as a shepherd learning the habits of the garrison.

This success was eclipsed by the capture of Tut Narai Post in the Upper Tochi on 31st May 1917 by a gang of Abdullai Mahsuds who employed the ruse of sending two of their members disguised as women to attract the attention of the militia garrison. The gang decamped with 59 rifles and about 12,000 rounds of ammunition.

CHAPTER II.

POLITICAL.

From the time of our earliest dealings with the Wazirs and Mahsuds these tribes have presented a difficult problem and one which still awaits a satisfactory solution.

Afghan claims to Waziristan, 1884-1892.—The Political history of Waziristan, especially in its earlier stages has always been closely interwoven with, and to some extent over-shadowed by that of Afghanistan. Since the middle of the nineteenth century the British Government has from time to time been involved in military operations with the Waziristan tribes, but the first event of purely political importance with which we are concerned occurred in 1884, when the Amir of Afghanistan made an attempt to establish his supremacy over the Wazirs, and, though it met with little or no support from the tribesmen, our policy with regard to Waziristan had not reached a sufficiently advanced stage to enable us to dispose of the question finally. Four years later the Amir was informed that it was not our intention to occupy Wana. This somewhat vague intimation led him to suppose that the Afghans were free to go there, and they accordingly did so. Previous to this the Amir had on more than one occasion asserted that Waziristan belonged to him, but his claim was not definitely repudiated until 1892, when he was informed that, although he would not be called upon immediately to evacuate Wana, we did not admit his right to occupy it, and he was forbidden to advance further into Waziristan pending a settlement. At the same time he was reminded that we had always insisted on the independence of the Wazirs and upon our right to deal directly with them, that we should continue to do so and that he must not attempt to bring them under his authority. This pronouncement was unpalatable to the Amir, who in reply objected to our having any dealings with the Wazirs and claimed the whole of Waziristan in his dominions. This claim, which had no foundation in fact, was disallowed.

Policy of British Government, 1892.—The position of Waziristan was thus clearly defined to the Amir as being one of complete independence, qualified by our right to hold direct relations with its inhabitants. About this time a proposal was made that we should hand over the suzerainty to the Amir, allow the tribesmen to pay him tribute, and at the same time exercise some sort of control over them ourselves and bind the Amir to abstain from all actual interference with the tribes. Lord Lansdowne, however, disliked the idea of this arrangement which would have given both ourselves and the Amir concurrent rights in the same country, and it was rejected. Nor did the Government of India view with more approval a suggested solution of the question involving a partition of the Wazir tribes between ourselves and the Amir. This scheme by which the whole of the Darwesh Khel would have been transferred to Afghanistan was considered as presenting insuperable difficulties and was also dropped.

It had always been the policy of the British Government to abstain as far as possible from interference with the internal affairs of the independent tribes living beyond our Indian border. All that Government wanted was to gain the confidence of the tribesmen and to definitely establish the fact that Afghanistan had no right whatever in Waziristan.

Opening of Gomal Route, 1890.—When the Gomal route was first opened in 1890 a system of tribal allowances was inaugurated, the main considerations on which they were granted being as follows: (1) general good behaviour; (2) the prevention of raids and other offences across the border of British India; (3) the surrender for trial and punishment of tribesmen for offences against us; (4) the furnishing of tribal escorts to Officers visiting any part of their country under orders of Government; (5) the rendering of services, for which they received allowances, in any part of their country most convenient to Government. The subsidizing of the tribesmen formed part of a policy to supplement the scanty resources of the Wazirs and Mahsuds and to assist in providing them with an honest means of livelihood. It was in the complement of this policy, namely, in the employment of the tribesmen and enlarging the scope of their energies, that the Government hoped to find the real remedy.

Durand Agreement, 1893.—In 1893 the negotiations of the previous year reached a final settlement and by the Durand Agreement, signed in Kabul in November, the

Amir definitely renounced all claim to Waziristan (the Birmal tract excepted) and agreed to the request of the British Government that the boundary line between India and Afghanistan should be deliminated.* A Commission was accordingly appointed in October of the following year to demarcate the Western boundary of Waziristan from Domandi, on the Gomal, northwards.

Occupation of Wana, 1893.—It was considered that this was a suitable opportunity to accept the invitation of the Wazirs of Wana, given two years previously, to occupy their country, thereby preventing future aggression on the part of either the Afghan authorities or the Powindahs and securing the Gomal route against the depredations of the Mahsuds. To do this it was decided to establish a military post in Wana with outposts along the line of the Gomal Valley. No sooner was Wana occupied than a Mahsud attack on the camp occurred and the third Mahsud expedition of 1894-95 was the immediate result.

The Mullah Powindah.—This attack was organized by a fanatical priest of the Shabi Khel, Alizai section of the Mahsuds, known as the Mullah Powindah, who had already achieved notoriety as a leader of the faction, hostile to the *maliks*, which may be termed the "Young Mahsud" Party. From this date the Mullah steadily increased his influence with the tribe and up to his death in 1913 was a constant thorn in the side of the Indian Government.† He was as bitterly opposed to the British as he was to the control of the tribe by their *maliks*, and all efforts to uphold the authority of the latter against his faction failed. Efforts to drive him from the country proved of no avail and Government, making a virtue of necessity, tried a policy of conciliation. In 1900 his official status was recognised and in 1906 a grant of land was sanctioned for him in British territory. This privilege was however cancelled in 1907 as a result of his continued hostility and Government adopted the policy, which had better results than any previous efforts to lower his prestige, of ignoring his existence in all official dealings with the Mahsuds. On his death his son, Mullah Fazl Din, was nominated as his successor by the tribe, and, although

---

*The Durand Line.
†The Mullah was nicknamed the "Pestilential Priest" by Lord Kitchener.

he never achieved anything approaching his father's influence, he was prominent as a leader of the opposition both in the 1917 and 1919-20 expeditions.

Reconsideration of Policy after signing of Durand Agreement.—The signing of the Durand Agreement necessitated a reconsideration of our policy regarding the Wazirs and Mahsuds, and it was recognised that in the course of time the whole of their country up to the Afghan border must come more and more under our control. On the conclusion of the Mahsud operations in 1894 it was deemed advisable, for the greater security of that part of the frontier, to take advantage of the repeated offers of the Daurs of the Tochi and to occupy their country. Posts were therefore established along the valley of the Tochi as far as Sheranni and occupied by troops and local levies. The districts thus occupied in Wana and Tochi were termed " Protected Areas " and were administered by Political Officers, while a loose form of political control based on tribal allowances was exercised over the Wazirs and Mahsuds outside these areas.

Formation of Tribal Militias.—With the object of relieving regular units of the Indian Army of the task of garrisoning outlying posts, and of purely police duties on the frontier, and in view of the fact that neither the Tochi nor the Gomal routes were regarded as being suitable as main lines of advance into Afghanistan, it was decided in 1899 to call on the inhabitants of the various localities to take part in their own defence, and at the same time to establish a lien on their loyalty, by enrolling them in Militias and Levies to supply the local garrisons. Though not a military body, since they were under the control of the civil administration, these militias were trained and equipped on military lines by officers seconded from the Indian Army.

Policy in 1899.—The policy in 1899, then, was briefly as follows :—On the North and South of Mahsud country, the " Protected Areas," long narrow strips of country under the direct control of our political officers, stretched out towards the Afghan border. In these areas were various posts garrisoned by tribal militias, led by British officers but directly under the Civil administration, and with backing of regular troops in Bannu and Dera Ismail Khan. The *raison d'etre* of these militias was to prevent incursions by tribesmen from the interior into the Bannu and Derajat areas, and definitely to obtain the loyalty of a number of their young men by providing congenial employment for them. Over the remainder of the country a loose form of political control was exercised, which consisted mainly in affording moral support to the *maliks*, and, by the payment of tribal allowances for good behaviour, to ensure the tribesmen could support themselves without increasing their income by raiding in British territory.

There is no doubt that this policy was open to serious objections both from a Political and Military point of view, and a study of the next chapter will show that on many occasions military operations were necessary to enforce it. It was, however, considered at the time the best solution of an extremely difficult problem and in spite of many suggestions for its revision* it was adhered to with slight modifications for the next twenty years.

Its test during the Afghan War 1919.—During the Afghan War in 1919 the loyalty of the Militias, which had successfully stood the test of the Great War, was put to a heavy strain by our withdrawal from the Upper Tochi and from Wana. This, combined with the call of Islam, proved too much for them and the defection of large portions of their trans-frontier elements not only reduced the value of these corps but proved a potential source of danger to us. Mahsud and Wazir raiding parties swept over the border tracts of the Derajat and Zhob, and even penetrated into the Punjab, robbing and murdering peaceful villagers, especially Hindus, and their activities increased rather than diminished after the signing of peace with Afghanistan.

This continued and gratuitous provocation could no longer be tolerated and it was decided to send a Military expedition into the heart of Waziristan to quell the hostile elements and to restore order.

---

*One of the most discussed suggestions was the occupation of Waziristan up to the Durand Line.

CHAPTER III.

OPERATIONS AGAINST THE WAZIRISTAN TRIBES PREVIOUS TO 1914.

The great majority of the disturbances in Waziristan have been caused by the Mahsuds, against whom the six principal series of operations have been mainly directed. Sections of the Darwesh Khel Wazirs have on occasion given trouble, but have generally proved less obstinate. This can be accounted for partly by the fact that many of them hold land in the plains, and as their hill settlements are more accessible than those of the Mahsuds they have to be more circumspect than the latter in their dealings with us.

Operations against Mahsuds, 1860.—The first important expedition occurred in 1860, the immediate cause being a Mahsud attack on the town of Tank, which was completely crushed by the skill and energy of an Indian Officer. Colonel Paget's description of this brilliant* little cavalry affairs is as follows : " Emboldened by years of immunity, and believing that they could successfully oppose any attempt to penetrate their mountains, the Mahsuds had on March 13th, 1860, without provocation or pretext of any kind, come out into the plains to the number of some 3,000, headed by their principal men with the intention of sacking the town of Tank, which stands on the plains some five miles from the foot of the hills. The Nawab's agent, having obtained previous intimation of their gathering, on the 12th informed Saadat Khan, the Indian officer in command of the troop of the 5th Punjab Cavalry† (now the 25th Cavalry, Frontier Force) then holding Tank. This Indian officer at once summoned the sowars from the neighbouring regular outposts, besides collecting twenty of the Nawab's horsemen and some irregular horse; so that the force at his disposal was one hundred and fifty-eight sabres of the 25th Cavalry and thirty-seven mounted levies. On the morning of the 13th

---

* " Record of Expeditions against the North-West Frontier Tribes " by Paget and Mason *See* also "Campaigns on the North-West Frontier." by Captain H. L. Nevill, D.S.O., R.F.A.

† When a unit still exists, its present designations will be given; this arrangement will, it is thought add interest to the narrative, the old designations being practically unknown to the present generation of readers.

the whole party moved out towards the mouth of the Tank Zam, on arriving near the entrance of which they found the Mahsuds drawn up about half a mile on the plain side of the defile. The Mahsuds immediately opened fire on the cavalry, on which Ressaldar Saadat Khan ordered his detachment to retire with the intention of drawing the enemy further into the plain. The stratagem was successful and the enemy followed with shouts of derision; but when they had come nearly a mile the cavalry turned and having first cut off their retreat to the hills, charged in the most dashing manner. The Mahsuds, personally brave and invariably of vigorous, muscular frames, wanted the power of combination to resist effectually the charge of our cavalry. Cut down and ridden over, they fled in confusion, the men in front forcing back the men behind till all became a helpless rabble, struggling, striving, straining to regain the safety of the mountain defile. The result was that about three hundred Mahsuds were killed, including six leading *maliks*, and many more wounded. Our loss was one Jemadar of levies killed, two non-commissioned officers, and eleven sowars of the 25th Cavalry, and three of the levies wounded." The principal chief of the whole Mahsud tribe was killed in this encounter.

The unprovoked nature of this attack led to the despatch of an expedition, and Brigadier-General N. B. Chamberlain was accordingly ordered to assemble a force to enter the Mahsud hills and there exact satisfaction for the past and security for the future. The force, which numbered about five thousand of all ranks, included detachments from the following units :—

21st, 22nd, 23rd and 24th Mountain Batteries (Frontier Force), whose guns were at this time carried on elephants; Guides Cavalry, 23rd Cavalry (Frontier Force) and 15th Lancers; 1st Sappers and Miners: Guides Infantry; 20th Infantry and 21st Punjabis; 32nd Pioneers; 54th Sikhs; 55th, 56th and 57th Rifles (Frontier Force) and 5th Gurkha Rifles (Frontier Force). Before advancing, a proclamation was addressed to the Mahsud Chiefs announcing the objects for which the force was about to enter their hills; to tell them that, within a fixed period, they were free to attend the camp and hear the demands of the British Government; and that, on their failing to appear or comply with the demands, they would be treated as enemies and punished accordingly. No reply having been received to the proclamation, General Chamberlain moved forward on the 17th April with the whole of his force, augmented by sixteen hundred levies, to the mouth of the Tank Zam and camped on the present site of Khirgi post. On arrival at Jandola, a portion of the force was sent up the difficult defile known as the Shahur Tangi to operate against certain hostile sections of the tribe in the neighbourhood of Haidari Kach and Barwand. No opposition was encountered and an important fort was destroyed; but during the absence of this column, the remainder of the force had been seriously attacked in its camp at Palosina near Jandola. On the night of the 22nd/23rd April, a body of 3,000 Mahsuds making a sudden rush, overpowered and nearly destroyed the camp piquets immediately in their line of attack; here the majority of them stopped, but 500 of the bravest of them dashed into the camp sword in hand, and penetrated into the areas occupied by the Guides and the mounted levies. For a time the confusion was general, but eventually a counter-attack by the 25th Punjabis, 54th Sikhs and the Guides was organised, the camp cleared and the enemy pursued for fully three miles over the hills. Ninety-two Mahsud corpses were found in and around the camp and forty more in a *nala* on their line of retreat; our own casualties, many of which occurred among unarmed followers, amounted to 37 killed and 132 wounded.

Attack on camp at Palosina, 22nd-23rd April 1860.

Action of Barari Tangi, 2nd May 1860.—Three days later, the column from Haidari Kach rejoined the force headquarters, and a move up the Tank Zam was begun. Some negotiations took place with a party of Mahsud *maliks* before the Ahnai Tangi was reached, but they led to nothing and the force moved forward towards the Barari Tangi on the 2nd May. The Barari Tangi is a narrow cleft cut by the Tank Zam through a range of mountains crossing its course at right angles, both banks of which are perpendicular cliffs eighty to one hundred feet in height. A strong obstacle in the shape of large rocks and felled trees had been placed in position by the Mahsuds, completely closing the river bed. The enemy's position was one of great strength. A double row of *sangars*, admirably sited for flanking fire, had been constructed on either side of the defile, and above these again were numbers of sharpshooters whose fire would also tell on a body advancing by the only line of approach to the main position. A precipitous ridge also afforded the enemy a safe line of retreat—always an important consideration in Mahsud tactics—enabling him to inflict injury on an attacking force up to the last moment and then to get away without fear of being cut off.

The interesting action which followed will well repay careful study, especially in the light of our most recent experience on the same ground; but space does not permit of more than a brief outline of it here. The troops advanced in two columns, that on the right being entrusted with a frontal attack on the left of the main position. The leading line consisted of two companies of the 21st Punjabis, who succeeded in establishing themselves without great difficulty within a short distance of the enemy's *sangars,* situated on the crest of a rugged, steep ascent, the last twelve or fifteen feet of which were practically inaccessible. Here a check occurred, the men seeking shelter from the enemy's fire and from the rocks and stones hurled down upon them from above. The Mahsuds, emboldened by the check leaped from their breastworks and rushed down upon the 21st Punjabis sword in hand causing a panic which for a time threatened to become general. The leading companies fell back upon their support, and, the latter having also given way, the enemy continued his advance upon the mountain guns and the 55th Rifles in reserve. The latter unit stood its ground firmly, and the Mahsuds, coming under heavy rifle and gun fire, retreated up the hill, hotly pursued by the 55th Rifles, who took the main breastwork. The other troops now rallied and the left of the position was won.

Disheartened by the loss of their left, the Mahsuds offered only a feeble resistance to the advance of our other column which advanced steadily from ridge to ridge with the loss of only two men. In the centre, as soon as the barricade at the mouth of the gorge had been removed, the 20th Infantry and 5th Gurkha Rifles moved forward and completed the capture of the whole position. No further opposition was offered and camp was pitched on the Bangiwala Kach, three miles beyond the defile. Our loss in this affair was thirty killed and eighty-six wounded, while the enemy left thirty-five dead bodies on the ground.

There is no need to describe in detail the remainder of the campaign. Our troops visited Kaniguram and Makin without succeeding in bringing the Mahsuds to terms; and then, the state of our supplies rendering it necessary to bring the operations to a close, the force was withdrawn to Bannu *via* Razani and the Khaisora Valley. Although the expedition did not result in the submission of the Mahsuds, its success was considerable. The loss inflicted on them was estimated at over a lakh of rupees; their chief town Kaniguram had been occupied and spared only on payment of a fine; Makin, their next most important town had been completely destroyed; their hitherto unknown country had been surveyed and mapped; and whenever they had met our troops, they had been signally defeated.

Mahsud Blockade, 1879.—The next twenty years was a period of almost continual unrest on the Waziristan border, and several minor expeditions had to be undertaken. In 1879, a body of Mahsuds, estimated at between 2,000 and 3,000 men, raided the town of Tank, plundered and burnt the *bazaar*, and carried off a large quantity of private property. This event was the signal for general disorder, and for some time predatory bands of marauders continued to raid, plunder, and destroy along the border, enjoying a considerable measure of immunity as the result of our pre-occupation in Afghanistan. All we were in a position to do at the time was to institute a blockade, a form of reprisal which is very difficult to enforce and which must in any case be a slow process.

Operations against Mahsuds, 1881.—On the termination of the Second Afghan War, however, Government was able to take the matter in hand. In 1881 a proclamation was published and widely circulated, which, after reciting the engagements under which the Mahsuds had bound themselves to abstain from aggression in British territory, offered to them a final opportunity for peaceable submission and invited them to depute delegates to arrange for the terms of settlement. Meanwhile orders were issued for the concentration of a force at Tank under the command of Brigadier-General T. G. Kennedy, C.B., and of a reserve brigade at Bannu under the command of Brigadier-General J. J. H. Gordon, C.B. The former consisted of 12 guns, 270 sabres and 3,660 bayonets, and included detachments from the following units: 22nd, 23rd and 24th Mountain Batteries (F. F.), 21st Cavalry (F. F.), 51st and 54th Sikhs (F. F.), 55th, 56th and 57th Rifles (F. F.), 20th Infantry and 21st Punjabis and 32nd Pioneers. The Bannu Column numbered 8 guns, 330 sabres and 3,380 bayonets, and included a battery of Royal Field Artillery, the 4th Battalion Rifle Brigade, the first time British troops had been employed in Waziristan, detachments from the 21st Mountain Battery (F. F.), 18th Lancers, 14th Sikhs, 20th Infantry, the 21st and 30th Punjabis and the 58th Rifles (F. F.).

Neither column was seriously engaged, and the total battle casualties incurred during the expedition amounted to only 32. The Tank Column marched to Kaniguram, *viâ* Jandola, Barwand, and Kundiwam, the only action of importance being at Shah Alam, between Kundiwam and Kaniguram, where the enemy had to be ejected from a strong position on a densely wooded hillside. When the troops had deployed for attack and were halted while a reconnaissance of the position was being made, the Mahsuds suddenly charged the 51st Sikhs, but the attack broke down before the fire of this battalion, and suffered considerably. The Bannu Column marched *viâ* the Khaisora Valley and Razani to Razmak, where communication was established with the Tank Column at Kaniguram; and then, after a short stay in the heart of the Mahsud country, each column returned to its base. During the return march the Bannu Column paid a visit to the Shaktu Valley, the inhabitants of which had hitherto held aloof from all negotiations, thinking themselves secure on account of the difficulty of penetrating to their settlements and because they were left unmolested in the campaign of 1860. They now submitted without a struggle, and the presence of their *maliks* in the British camp reassured the people, most of whom had never before seen a European.

Although the expedition had been successful up to a point and the boldest of the Mahsuds had been taught that no natural difficulties of their country could protect them from punishment, yet the demands of the Government had not been fully complied with, and the blockade was therefore continued. Even before the troops had left the Mahsud hills, some leading spirits among the anti-peace party sought the intercession of Afghanistan, and the appearance of the Amir's agent at Kaniguram tended considerably to thwart the efforts of the party who favoured a settlement with the British Government. However, such was the pressure of the blockade that the welcome accorded to the Amir's emissary was but a cold one and he departed suddenly for Khost and thence to Kabul, accompanied by a few leading Mahsuds. The absence of these latter and the reaction consequent on the hopes raised by interference from Kabul retarded a final settlement with the tribe. Ere long, however, the Mahsuds discovered that papers had been received by the Amir purporting to offer him the sovereignty of their country and freedom to enlist troops from their hills. This discovery alarmed and irritated a people both proud and jealous of their independence, and the feeling that their freedom was involved produced a reaction in favour of concluding peace direct with the British Government. The surrender of six prescribed ring-leaders had been laid down as an earnest of their submission, and these were now brought in. The Mahsuds having thus accepted a humiliation as great as a Pathan clan can suffer, thereby proving an honest desire and intention to submit, the blockade was raised and they were once more at liberty to renew trade and intercourse with markets in British territory.

Afghan intrigues, 1892.—Save for a few minor incidents, the next ten years was a period of comparative peace on the Waziristan border, but in February 1892, the Amir of Afghanistan again began to intrigue with the tribesmen.

In May a force of Afghan Cavalry and Infantry arrived at Wana under Sirdar Gul Muhammad Khan, and matters began to take a serious turn. In July the Government of India addressed a warning to the Amir, informing him that no encroachment in Wazir territory would be tolerated, pending a settlement of the frontier; the substance of this letter was at the same time communicated to the Mahsuds and Wazirs, who were told to refrain from acts of aggression against Afghanistan. The activities of Gul Muhammad, however, created considerable unrest, and it was found necessary to concentrate a force at Khajuri Kach as a precautionary measure; but in September the Amir withdrew his troops and the attitude of the tribesmen improved.

In October, 1893, a Mission under Sir Mortimer Durand went to Kabul at the invitation of the Amir, and an agreement was signed by which the latter relinquished all claims to Waziristan.

Boundary Commission, 1894.—In accordance with this agreement; preparations were made early in 1894 for demarcating the new boundary. As the attitude of the tribesmen was uncertain, it was decided to place a large force on the frontier during the delineation, and it was also considered a favourable occasion on which to accept an invitation, recently received from the Wana Wazirs, to take over and administer their country. It was finally decided that the British and Afghan Commissioners should meet and start work at Domandi on the Gomal, and a proclamation was issued to the Wazirs describing the line agreed upon and informing them that the Government had no intention of interfering with their internal affairs, but only desired to establish peace. Large *jirgas* assembled to discuss the situation, and for the most part appeared to be prepared to receive the Commission in a friendly spirit.

The escort to the Commission consisted of one Squadron, 21st Cavalry (F. F.), 23rd Mountain Battery (F. F.), 20th Infantry, 53rd Sikhs (F. F.), and 1st Gurkha Rifles. Wana, which was to be the headquarters of the Commission, was reached on October 25th, *viâ* Spin and Karab Kot. Some sniping into camp occurred during the march, but the attitude of the inhabitants was generally friendly, and a large *jirga* of Wana Wazirs, which came into Wana during the afternoon, appeared pleased at the arrival of the troops. For political reasons, the camp was pitched at the eastern end of the Wana plain and was surrounded by a chain of piquets posted merely for purposes of observation and not intended to hold their own against a serious attack. In the latter event, they were instructed to fall back on their supports and then to the camp perimeter, which was to be the main line of defence; three of the twelve piquets were detailed for the defence of the political camp situated at some little distance from the main camp.

On the 28th, news was received that a certain number of Mahsuds headed by the Mullah Powindah were trying to create dissensions and prevent a representative jirga coming in. It was reported that the Mullah had succeeded in collecting about 800 men, that he proposed to visit Kaniguram for the purpose of increasing his force, and that he intended to attack the camp at Wana or harass convoys. On the evening of the 1st November news was brought in that the Mullah had arrived at Torwam with a following of a thousand men; piquets were consequently doubled and the troops ordered to be under arms at 4 A.M. The next day messengers arrived from the Mullah, but they were informed that no dealings could take place with him except through the *jirga*. The camp defences were strengthened and the same precautions taken as on the previous night.

Attack on camp near Wana by Mullah Powindah, 3rd November 1894.—The night of the 2nd November, which was very dark, passed quietly till 3-30 A.M., when the whole camp was suddenly roused by three shots, followed by wild yells and the beating of drums. At the same time a desperate rush of some five hundred fanatics was made straight into the left flank and rear of the camp, held by the 1st Gurkha Rifles. So rapid was the rush that before the Gurkhas could turn out of their tents, the leading men of the enemy had climbed over the defences and penetrated into the middle of the camp.

It appears that under cover of darkness the enemy had crept up two large ravines, and, rushing two piquets in their line of advance, one of which had fired the three alarm shots, had charged straight down on the camp. At the same time a large body of Mahsuds continued their course down the ravine and had split up into two parties, one of which joined the main attack on the left flank of the camp, while the other, continuing down the ravine, broke up against the rear-guards. Many of this party made their way into camp behind the hospitals, where they did much damage among the transport animals, and some of them succeeded in reaching the cavalry lines, where they got to work cutting free the horses in the hope of causing a stampede.

Meanwhile, the Gurkhas had stopped the main rush from passing down the centre street of the camp, and the regimental reserve was fighting hand to hand with the enemy. They were soon reinforced by two companies of the 20th Infantry and a company of the 53rd Sikhs (F. F.), and the enemy was systematically driven out of the camp at the point of the bayonet. He made two more but less determined attempts to gain a footing within the perimeter, but these were steadily met, and our infantry got in several effective volleys with the help of star shell.

At daybreak the enemy's fire slackened, and as he was now evidently in retreat, the cavalry was ordered to pursue. Within a few minutes of this order being received, the squadron had started and was quickly followed by a mixed detachment of artillery, sappers, and infantry. After covering about three miles the cavalry came in sight of the enemy, but the ground was here so bad that it was impossible to move out of a trot. On gaining better ground, however, they charged and recharged the tribesmen with great effect.

In addition to our losses in officers and men at Wana, amounting to 45 killed and 75 wounded, the enemy succeeded in carrying off a large number of rifles and Rs. 2,600 in cash. More than a hundred transport animals were also killed or wounded. The enemy's loss was estimated at about 350 killed.

Punitive operations, 1894.—The attack at Wana made a punitive expedition inevitable, and three mixed brigades were accordingly assembled at Wana, Jandola and Bannu, respectively, the whole under the command of Lieutenant-General Sir William Lockhart, K.C.B. The 1st Brigade consisted of the original Commission escort, reinforced by the 2nd Battalion, Border Regiment. The 2nd Brigade included the 28th Mountain Battery, a squadron each from the 21st and 22nd Cavalry (F. F.), No. 5 Co., 1st Sappers and Miners, the 33rd Punjabis, 38th Dogras, 57th Rifles (F. F.) and the 1st Battalion, 5th Gurkha Rifles (F. F.). The 3rd Brigade consisted of the 21st Mountain Battery (F. F.), the 23rd Cavalry (F. F.), the 51st Sikhs, 56th Rifles, and 59th Rifles, all of the Punjab Frontier Force.

It is unnecessary to describe in detail the operations of these three brigades, as no fighting of importance occurred, our battle casualties amounting to only 23 all told. Suffice it to say, that the whole of Waziristan was completely overrun from end to end, all sections of the Mahsuds implicated in the Wana attack were punished, much damage was done to towers and defences and a large quantity of forage and grain and over 1,000 animals were captured. The Government terms were fully complied with, and the demarcation of the boundary successfully accomplished.

Nevertheless, crimes of violence continued to be of frequent occurrence during the next few years. In 1895, an officer of the 59th Rifles was stabbed near Boya, and his syce and orderly dangerously wounded; a lance-naik of the 56th Rifles was shot dead at Miranshah; a party of Daurs tried to enter the post at Miranshah and succeeded in stabbing two sepoys; an officer of the 23rd Cavalry was very severely wounded near Boya; and a sowar of the same regiment on grass-cutting guard was also shot dead near the same place. These and other offences necessitated a show of force in the Tochi Valley, which henceforward became a permanent location for regular Indian troops.

Attack on Political Officer's escort in Upper Tochi, 1897.—The next episode of importance was an unprovoked and unexpected attack on a Political Officer's escort at Maizar in the Upper Tochi Valley in 1897. The Political Officer had proceeded to Maizar with a mixed escort to settle a dispute among the local tribesmen regarding the incidence of a fine imposed for the murder of a Hindu clerk. The tribal *maliks* met the party and escort in an apparently friendly spirit, and, pointing out a site to halt at, offered to provide a meal for the Mussalman sepoys of the escort. The party were thus lulled into a false sense of security. Suddenly a hubbub began in a village close by, and the villagers, who had been listening to the pipes of the 51st Sikhs which were playing in camp, drew off. A man was observed to wave a sword from the top of a tower and two shots were fired in quick succession from the village, the second of which wounded a British officer. Firing now commenced from other neighbouring villages, as the result of which another British officer was wounded. The guns of the escort opened fire with case at 100 yards range; two of their officers were quickly wounded but the gunners continued to fight their guns with great gallantry. As only sixteen rounds per gun, however, had been brought with the escort, ammunition soon ran short.

and orders were given for a retirement to the ridge. Meanwhile a general stampede had occurred among the baggage animals, and when the retirement was ordered most of the reserve ammunition and other equipment had to be abandoned.

The enemy now appeared in force on all sides, but the retirement, which began under such very trying circumstances, was carried out with great deliberation and gallantry. All the British officers were wounded, two of them mortally; but all continued to carry out their duties and lead their men. The gallantry of three *subedars* of the 51st Sikhs and 55th Rifles was especially noteworthy. Getting together a party of their men, they made a most determined stand by the wall of a garden, whence they covered the first withdrawal. Here they remained themselves until the enemy closed with them, and one of them was killed. Under cover of this stand the wounded were carried and helped away, the guns withdrawing to a low *kotal* about 300 yards distant. Here a fresh stand was made, the guns firing blank to check the enemy, as all the service ammunition had been expended. One of the battery officers now received a third, and this time a fatal wound, and another, who had fainted from loss of blood and had been fastened on to the Political Officer's pony when the retirement began, was found to be dead on arrival at the *kotal*. The retirement was continued by successive units, the enemy coming on in increasing numbers, and endeavouring to envelop the flanks, but on arrival at the Sheranni plain, reinforcements from Datta Khel joined the party and the enemy was at last beaten off.

Immediately after the outbreak at Maizar, the local Wazirs had despatched messengers to other sections of the tribe for assistance, and they also approached the Afghan authorities. For a long time it was uncertain what effect these appeals would have, and a strong force under Major-General Corrie Bird, C.B., was therefore assembled at Bannu to deal with possible eventualities. The force consisted of two mixed brigades, the first including one squadron, 21st Cavalry (F. F.), 23rd Mountain Battery (F. F.), No. 2 Company, 1st Sappers and Miners, 2nd Battalion, Argyll and Sutherland Highlanders, 51st Sikhs (F. F.), 55th Rifles (F. F.), and 33rd Punjabis;

and the second, one squadron 21st Cavalry (F. F.), four guns of the 26th Mountain Battery, 3rd Battalion, Rifle Brigade, 14th Sikhs, 6th Jat Light Infantry, and the 25th Punjabis. Practically no opposition was encountered during the march to Sheranni and Maizar, both of which were found deserted. All the defences at these two places were destroyed, and visits were paid to neighbouring valleys known to have been implicated in the outrage.

In the meantime the Tirah campaign had begun, but, contrary to expectations, the operations against the Afridis and Orakzais did not cause any special restlessness in Waziristan, save that they delayed a settlement with the perpetrators of the Maizar attack. However, as the winter of 1897 approached, the prospect of losing their spring crops reduced the tribesmen to a more submissive mood, and at the end of October the head of the offending section gave himself up as an earnest of good behaviour in the future. The total casualties at Maizar, in addition to the loss of the British officers already mentioned, had been 21 killed and 28 wounded, while our losses in the subsequent operations were 6 killed and 8 wounded. The most noteworthy aspect of the campaign had been the unusual amount of sickness among the troops. The climate of the Tochi valley is at all times trying, but the rapid concentration at Bannu in the middle of the hot weather had, no doubt, affected the constitutions of the men and rendered them more disposed to contract disease, and less able to shake it off, than would usually be the case. The principal diseases were diarrhœa and dysentery, which took an epidemic form and became very severe.

Mahsud Blockade, 1900-1901.—No sooner had the Government of India settled with the Tochi Wazirs than the Mahsuds again began to give trouble, and the punishment of this tribe had to be undertaken for the fourth time. During 1898 and 1899, raids were of frequent occurrence, and in January 1900, the levy post at Zam and the Public Works Department bungalow at Murtaza were both attacked. In October, the police post at Nasran, eleven miles north of Tank, was surprised by Mahsuds, two sepoys being killed and ten rifles stolen; and, though the raiders were intercepted and part of the booty recaptured, this was only accomplished at the cost of the life of the British officer in command of the pursuit party. A Mahsud *jirga* was accordingly summoned to Tank and a fine of Rs. 1,00,000 for past offences was imposed, the *jirga* being informed that if Rs. 50,000 were not paid up within fifteen days, a blockade would be imposed. At the conclusion of the fifteen days' grace, the *jirga* returned and asked for a further period of two months in which to consider the terms; this was refused, and the blockade came into operation on December 1st.

The following preliminary measures were taken to ensure the effectiveness of the blockade. On the east, small moveable columns were located at Jani Khel and Zam, and a cordon of posts established between Bannu and Dera Ismail Khan; in the south, the Gomal line was reinforced by putting regular garrisons into Murtaza and Manjhi, two temporary posts were established at Tormandu and Khwuzma Narai, and the existing posts at Khajuri Kach, Sarwekai, Haidari Kach, and Jandola were strengthened. A new post was also established in the Spin plain. South of the Gomal, the battalions stationed at Fort Sandeman and Loralai respectively were moved up to form a cordon of posts on the Zhob-Waziristan border. The troops originally employed on the blockade consisted of the 21st and 25th Cavalry (F. F.), eight guns of the 22nd, 26th and 27th Mountain Batteries, 17th Infantry, 23rd Pioneers, 27th and 28th Punjabis, 35th and 45th Sikhs, 123rd Outram's Rifles, and half a battalion each of the 109th Infantry and 124th Baluchistan Infantry.

These measures were so far effectual that the Mahsuds began to make overtures regarding the payment of the fine, and for some time payment proceeded regularly, but in January 1901, a series of fresh offences began which made further negotiations impossible. A mail runner was murdered near Nili Kach, and the mail was looted near Sarwekai; a British officer had his baggage looted and his two servants killed near Murtaza; three sepoys of the 45th Sikhs on " grazing guard " were killed near Jandola; the militia post at Kashmir Kar was attacked, one havildar, three sepoys and three workmen being killed, and thirty rifles stolen. These and various other offences compelled the Government of India to introduce a new procedure into the ordinary methods of a purely passive blockade.

Hitherto the tribesmen had invariably received notice prior to the commencement of active operations affording them the opportunity of coming belatedly to terms. It was now, however, decided that, while the blockade should continue as before, it should be varied and accompanied by sharp attacks lasting two or three days at a time and undertaken by small mobile columns acting simultaneously and by surprise. To enable this to be done the following additional units were employed: 29th Mountain Battery, 27th, 28th and 29th Punjabis, 32nd Pioneers, 38th Dogras, 55th, 56th, and 58th Rifles (F. F.), 1st Battalion, 2nd Gurkha Rifles, and 1st Battalion, 3rd Gurkha Rifles.

The first series of these operations commenced on the 23rd November and was directed against the Mahsuds of the Khaisara and Shahur Valleys, combined with demonstrations from Jandola into the Tank Zam and from Datta Khel against the north-west portion of the Mahsud country, the general object being to demolish all defences, capture prisoners and cattle, and to destroy grain and crops. Four columns, each consisting almost exclusively of infantry and varying in strength from 900 to 1,250 men, started from Datta Khel, Jandola, Sarwekai and Wana; all were opposed, and each suffered some loss, but the combined operations were very successful, due in large measure to the Mahsuds having been lulled into a false sense of security by the inactivity of the blockade.

Moreover, no sooner were these operations at an end than a further series was projected. On this occasion the Mahsuds, being on the alert, carefully watched the movement of the troops, and there was little chance of taking them by surprise. A column of 2,500 rifles and 4 guns left Jandola on the 4th December and bivouacked at Dwe Shinkai. Next day it withdrew to Guri Khel, the rearguard being so heavily pressed across the Umar Raghza that it had to *lager* for the night on the hills to the north. During the 6th, on which date the rearguard rejoined the main body, the enemy made frequent attacks on the piquets but were invariably repulsed, on one occasion at the point of the bayonet by a company of the 29th Punjabis. During the withdrawal to Jandola on the 7th, the enemy showed increased activity and the 29th Punjabis again distinguished themselves by repulsing a determined attack and inflicting on the enemy a loss of 40 killed.

The third phase consisted of combined operations by columns from Jandola and Sarwekai respectively which joined hands at Dwe Shinkai and then carried out a series of raids up the Shinkai Valley in three columns. Only slight opposition was encountered. The Mahsuds, however, still evinced no inclination to submit, and a fourth series of operations was consequently planned against them. For this three columns were formed, based respectively on Jandola, Jani Khel, and Datta Khel, and varying in strength from 2,500 to 1,400 men, the objective being the punishment of Mahsud sections inhabiting the Shaktu, Sheranna, and Shuza valleys and the capture of a large number of cattle known to be grazing on the slopes of the Baba Ghar. The operations of these columns were uniformly successful. Standing camps were now established at Zam, Miranshah and Baran, whence it was intended to resume punitive measures as soon as the troops had enjoyed a much-needed rest. By this time, however, the Mahsuds had lost heavily in men and cattle, and had thoroughly realised that the innermost parts of their country could be reached and traversed by our troops. They consequently opened negotiations for peace and the removal of the blockade, and after the usual delays paid up the fine in full, restored all the rifles they had captured, and gave hostages for the return of all plundered cattle. Our total battle casualties during this campaign amounted to 32 killed and 114 wounded, those of the Mahsuds being estimated roughly at 126 killed and 250 wounded. In addition, 215 Mahsud prisoners were taken, 64 towers were destroyed, 153 villages had their defences levelled, and over 8,000 head of livestock were captured.

Expedition against the Kabul Khel Wazirs, 1902.— The severity of the punishment inflicted on the Mahsuds by these operations did not, however, impress all sections of the Wazirs, and before the end of the year, an expedition had to be set on foot against the Kabul Khel—a branch of the Darwesh Khel Wazirs who inhabit the wedge of hilly country lying between the Kohat and Bannu districts, east of the Kurram river. For some years a number of outrages had been committed in this neighbourhood, and in each case the perpetrators were known to have taken refuge in the village of Gumatti, about $8\frac{1}{2}$ miles from Bannu. This village was accordingly surprised and surrounded at dawn on the 6th February 1899, by a small column of troops from the Bannu garrison. Seven of the outlaws were captured while trying to escape, but the remainder took refuge in two strong towers from which it was found impossible to dislodge them; and as a direct assault would have incurred a loss quite out of proportion to the object in view and the column had to return to Bannu the same day, it was obliged to withdraw without accomplishing its object. Three days later another column from Bannu found the village deserted, and blew up the towers without encountering any opposition. The outlaws, who had now lost all hope of pardon, continued their depredations on the border until, in 1902, the state of affairs had become so intolerable that an expedition had to be sent into the district. The troops employed were drawn from the 21st, 22nd and 27th Mountain Batteries; the 21st, 23rd and 25th Cavalry (F. F.); the 51st, 53rd and 54th Sikhs (F. F.), and the 56th, 57th and 58th Rifles (F. F.), and the 22nd Punjabis, together with detachments from the Kurram and North Waziristan Militias. Four columns were formed and operated from Thal, Idak, Barganatu and Bannu respectively, only the latter encountering more than slight opposition. This column found itself confronted at Gumatti by a strong, fortified enclosure, thickly surrounded by trees, and held by six outlaws. The mountain guns had no effect on the defences, even at 400 yards range, and Colonel Tonnochy, the officer commanding the column, was ordering them to advance still closer when he fell mortally wounded. Two unsuccessful attempts were made to breach the walls with gun-cotton, and it was at last decided to carry the place by escalade. This was accomplished by a storming party of the 53rd Sikhs (F. F.), though all three British officers were either killed or wounded. All six outlaws were killed, our own loss amounting to four killed and fifteen wounded. The total loss inflicted on the enemy by the four columns which rounded up the district amounted to 20 killed, 303 prisoners, 66 towers destroyed, and 5,288 head of cattle captured.

In connection with this expedition, an incident occurred which, though it had no bearing on the course of the operations, deserves special mention as a fine example of a forced march carried out at very short notice. It had been arranged that the whole of the prisoners and cattle collected by the Thal and Idak columns at Spinwam should, on the dispersal of the force, be taken to Idak; and in view of their large numbers, it had been decided to order out 100 men from Idak to meet the Idak column on its return and assist in the task. A message was accordingly despatched on the 22nd November directing the officer commanding at Datta Khel to send 100 rifles to meet the Idak column about half way from Spinwam on the following day. The message did not reach Datta Khel till after 3 P.M., on the 22nd, and 100 rifles of the 56th Rifles (F. F.) left that place two hours later. Marching all night, they reached Miranshah (25 miles) by 1-20 A.M. on the 23rd and Idak at 5 P.M. on the same day, having covered 49 miles in just under 24 hours. Only one man, a bugler, fell out during the march.

Following the Kabul Khel expedition comparative peace reigned on the Waziristan border for some years, although in 1904, the murder of the Political Agent at Wana, and, in 1905 of the Commandant of the South Waziristan Militia and the Brigade Major at Bannu, necessitated the infliction of heavy fines and the dismissal of all Mahsuds from the South Waziristan Militia. In 1911, a force of about 2,000 Mahsuds invested Sarwekai, at the same time cutting the telegraph lines and completely isolating Jandola and Wana: but the unexpected and rapid move of the Derajat Brigade from Dera Ismail Khan to Spinkai within striking distance of the enemy brought about his dispersal before any serious damage had been done. Our posts at Spinwam on the Kaitu and at Spina Khaisora in the Upper Tochi were similarly attacked without success in 1913, but no further important operations were undertaken against the Waziristan tribes prior to the outbreak of the Great War.

CHAPTER IV.

Operations against the Waziristan tribes between 4th August 1914 and 11th June 1917.

On the whole the situation on the North-West Frontier remained remarkably quiet during the Great War, and it was only against the Mahsuds that operations on an important scale had to be undertaken. The position during this period was one of considerable difficulty. The border tribes were naturally excited by the entry of Turkey into the war; they were encouraged by the preaching of a few prominent mullahs to look towards Kabul and prepare for *Jihad*; they heard the wildest rumours about the military situation in India and abroad; and as the war wore on pro-Turkish emissaries worked incessantly among them to foment a general rising. The then Amir, Habibullah, however, declined to depart from his declared policy of neutrality and discountenanced the efforts of his more fanatical subjects to bring about a *Jihad*.

It was an essential part of the Government's policy at this time to avoid any unnecessary complications on the frontier, the two main reasons against the employment of military force being, firstly, that it would entail the diversion of troops much needed elsewhere, and secondly, that it might lead to an outbreak all along the Border.

It was not therefore until the truculent attitude of the Mahsuds had rendered military intervention absolutely necessary in the interests of general peace that a punitive expedition against them was sanctioned.

The close of 1914 was marked by the outbreak of a series of raids. It was supposed that Government was not in a position to undertake reprisals, and there was a rumour abroad that the frontier posts were about to be evacuated.

Incursions by Afghan tribesmen from Khost, 1914-15. —At the end of November a Khostwal *lashkar* crossed the border from Afghanistan and looted the *sarai* at Miranshah before being driven off by the Northern Waziristan Militia. The Bannu moveable column advanced to Idak and other precautionary measures were taken but the prompt action of the Militia had had its effect and the *lashkar* withdrew to Khost.

In January 1915 another unsuccessful attack by Khostwals was made on Spina Khaisora in the Upper Tochi and on 24th March a *lashkar* estimated at 10,000 Zadrans and other Khost tribes crossed the frontier and advanced the following day to the neighbourhood of Miranshah Post. A column of the Northern Waziristan Militia with a section of mountain artillery moved out from the post and by means of a night march succeeded in taking up a position across the enemy's line of retreat. On the morning of the 26th the enemy who was in *sangars*, was attacked by a force consisting of—

2 squadrons 25th Cavalry (F. F.).

29th Mountain Battery less one section.

10th Jats.

52nd Sikhs (F. F.).

under command of Brigadier-General V. B. Fane, C.B., and driven in headlong flight across the Durand Line harassed *en route* by the Militia detachment. The enemy losses were estimated at 200 killed and 300 wounded.

This action proved a very salutary lesson to this part of the frontier, and no incident of any importance occurred in the Tochi for over two years.

Attitude of Mahsuds, 1914-17.—The Mahsuds showed no inclination to aid these *lashkars* from Khost, although they were smarting under the stoppage of their tribal allowances and restrictions imposed on them for their failure to surrender certain individuals demanded by Government for their connection with the murder of Major G. Dodd, C.I.E., Political Agent, Wana, who died at Tank on 14th April 1914.

The anti-British party led by Mullah Fazl Din, son of the notorious Mullah Powindah, was eager to begin hostilities but the majority of the tribe was restrained by the *maliks* from following its lead. In October however, Fazl Din's party asserted itself and a great increase in raids was the result. During the following month a gang of about 80 Mahsuds attacked the road piquets between Khajuri Kach and Tanai inflicting a loss of 5 killed and 10 wounded, and a few days later a party of the Southern Waziristan Militia was ambushed near Tormandu Post losing 10 killed, 3 wounded and 13 rifles.

In spite of these outrages it appeared that the bulk of the Mahsuds were anxious for a settlement with Government, but certain irreconcilable sections notably Fazl Din's section, the Shabi Khel, and the Abdur Rahman Khel continued almost nightly to raid the border villages in order to implicate the rest of the tribe. The hostile forces at work were too strong for the party in favour of peace. Fazl Din exchanged visits with Lala Pir, a fanatical mullah of Khost, and a member of the Turkish Afghan party toured the frontier spreading mendacious stories of overwhelming Turkish victories in Mesopotamia and promising an early invasion of India.

Mahsud situation beginning 1917.—To understand the subsequent events it is necessary to remember two determining factors; the difficulty in which Mullah Fazl Din found himself, and the implications of our own policy at the beginning of 1917.

It was to the interest of those *maliks* in the tribe who were friendly to us and whose sections desired intercourse with British territory, to break down the influence of the Mullah whose continued hostility was the chief obstacle in the way of a settlement. This they were in a fair way to accomplish.

Our policy was to avoid for the present the final settlement of the Mahsud problem. We had received grave provocation, but it was not convenient, at a time when troops were needed for the Great War to exact in full measure the penalties due. The hostile sections of the tribe, with the exception of the Abdullai, had no access to British territory and could not be affected by anything less than a punitive expedition. It seemed advisable to take no action beyond entering the case against the guilty sections for future retribution, and meanwhile to depend upon the restraining influence of the friendly sections to prevent collision with the tribe as a whole.

Negotiations.—In accordance with this policy the *maliks* of the friendly Manzai sections were warned to use their influence with the other section of the Alizai clan, the Shabi Khel, the chief supporters of the Mullah, since they too would be held responsible for outrages committed by the Shabi Khel. The Manzai *maliks* then held a *jirga* at Dwa Toi on the 18th January at which all the leading Shabi Khel *maliks* and Mullah Fazl Din were present, and announced their intention of attacking the Shabi Khel unless they made a temporary settlement with Government, or at least promised to desist from further outrages. The Shabi Khel asked for time to consider the matter.

Meanwhile Government had sanctioned a scheme for employing Mahsuds on the repair of the road between Mad Hassan and Spinkai. This road had existed for some years and was acknowledged by the Mahsuds to be well outside the limits of their territory. It was proposed to give contracts to the three main Mahsud clans who would arrange to supply the labour required. The scheme was received favourably by the *maliks* but was bitterly opposed by the Mullah who used the not unreasonable argument that better roads make invasion easier. As the Shabi Khel were still discussing the proposal put forward by the Manzai, it was considered undesirable that their decision should be prejudiced by the Mullah's arguments misleading though they were, and the scheme was abandoned and all work stopped on 18th February.

The Shabi Khel resolved against compliance with the terms for a temporary settlement, and the recalcitrant sections prepared for active hostilities. It should be remembered that during the spring there are more Mahsuds in the south of the country than at any other time of the year. The Nana Khel of the Baddar and the Upper Khaisara bring their flocks to graze in the Shahur valley, and the normal population of these parts is increased three-fold. It is therefore comparatively easy to raise a *lashkar* if sufficient temptation can be held out to these tribesmen.

Mullah Fazl Din decided that the time for action had come. He announced publicly that he intended to attack British territory as a reprisal for our breach of faith in attempting to repair the Mad Hassan-Spinkai road. Consequently on 26th February he collected at Marobi a few hundred Shabi Khel and some Abdullai, and on the 27th moved to the Spli Toi reaching Barwand on the 28th. On the march he was joined by large numbers of the Nana Khel who have always taken the lead in hostile movements against us.

At Barwand the *lashkar* now numbering about 1,500 men was joined by the Wazir Mullah Hamzulla and some

Shakai Wazirs. An attempt made to induce the Manzai *maliks* to join the *Jihad* failed, and these *maliks* returned to their homes.

As soon as the news of these movements was received the posts were warned, and Major Hughes—Southern Waziristan Militia with 70 men reinforced the garrison at Sarwekai bringing its strength up to 250 rifles.

On the evening of 1st March the post was cut off entirely from telegraphic communication.

In the next few days, during which the attack on the post developed, communication between Tanai and Sarwekai could only be made by heliograph *viâ* Dargai Oba.

The *lashkar* at Barwand was joined on 1st March by parties of Bahlolzai, so that its strength now stood at about 3,000.

The attack on Sarwekai Post, March 1917.—Sniping into Sarwekai began at 2 P.M. on the 1st March. This post stands on a spur of Kundi Ghar at a height of 3,940 feet, the spur rising to the north-west in a series of steps, the nearest of which, Garesi Sar, commands the post at a range of 1,400 yards. The road from Dargai Oba crosses a nullah full of thick dwarf palm and then zigzags up to the post.

To the south-east on the road to the Khuzma Narai is a tower, connected with the post by a trench. On the north there were formerly two other similar towers, but these have been demolished, and their sites are known as those of No. 1 and No. 2 tower respectively. To the north of these sites a long nullah winds down to Barwand, distant about 5 miles. There are many nullahs and much broken ground in the neighbourhood of the post and it is easy for a force to collect without being seen by the garrison. Sniping from Garesi Sar and the slopes about it is an ordinary occurrence, and can be usually disregarded.

On this occasion, however, the post was sniped on three sides from sangars within a few hundred yards; a party was sent out to drive the enemy off, but when heavily fired on, was ordered to retire. This was about 4 o'clock in the afternoon.

Major Hughes now decided to seize, during the night, three sangars on Garesi Sar, from which the Mahsuds at a range of 1,400 yards had been firing at the post. Accordingly 100 rifles under an Indian officer proceeded at midnight and occupied them with practically no opposition. At 7-30 A.M. a party of 150 Mahsuds attacked the sangars but were driven off with loss. As it was necessary to carry up food and water to the party on Garesi Sar, and the rationing parties were invariably fired on, it was decided to withdraw it to the post. With the object of covering the withdrawal, Major Hughes proceeded with 50 rifles to take up a position in support. The withdrawal commenced and was followed up immediately by the enemy, the covering party under Major Hughes becoming heavily engaged. Much hand-to-hand fighting ensued, but by 5 P.M. the survivors succeeded in reaching the post having suffered casualties amounting to twenty-one killed (including Major Hughes), ten wounded and eleven prisoners. The enemy casualties were some fifteen killed and twenty wounded.

Major Davis commanding the Southern Waziristan Militia learning of this action, moved out with 150 rifles on the 3rd March from Wana and establishing heliographic communication with Sarwekai learnt that the garrison had sufficient rations and stores for a prolonged resistance. The enemy continued sniping at the post up to the 8th March on which day they dispersed.

On receipt of the news of this affair the General Officer Commanding Derajat Brigade ordered the moveable column to proceed from Tank and to march *viâ* the Gomal route to Sarwekai where it arrived on the 9th March. On the following day the force advanced to Barwand in three parallel columns with a view to driving off parties of the enemy who were reported in that vicinity. Only slight opposition was encountered. *Kirris* and enemy property at Barwand were burnt and the column withdrew suffering two wounded casualties. The column returned on the 11th March to Khajuri Kach where it remained in a standing camp until the 3rd April when it began its withdrawal to Tank, which was carried out without incident. Meanwhile the 44th Infantry Brigade with the 23rd Mountain Battery had arrived in the Tank area as a reserve.

The minor raiding which had been going on for some time now culminated in an attack near the Gwalerai Narai on the convoy from Khajuri Kach. The presence of enemy gangs had already been reported and consequently the escort had been strengthened. On the 9th April the convoy started from Khajuri Kach for Nili Kach. When in the vicinity of mile-stone 38, fire was suddenly opened on two piquet groups going into position, killing or wounding every man. An attempt was made to re-establish the piquets but the increased volume of fire forced the piqueting troops to withdraw. Our total casualties were 18 killed and 2 wounded.

The 44th Brigade, which had meanwhile been withdrawn from the Tank area, had already reached Kalabagh and Darya Khan when orders were issued for the 1/4th Gurkha Rifles and one section 23rd Mountain Battery to return to Tank. Two companies of the 1/4th Gurkha Rifles with the section 23rd Mountain Battery remained at Tank while the other half battalion joined the moveable column at Murtaza, where it had moved from Tank on the 10th April.

A general rising of the Mahsuds was not anticipated, and it was not intended to take offensive action at present. It was, however, necessary to keep open the communications to our various posts, and, as far as possible, to suppress raiding. With these objects in view the Derajat Brigade was strengthened by the 1/4th Gurkha Rifles, one section 23rd Indian Mountain Battery, 107th Pioneers and No. 7 Company Sappers and Miners. The two latter units were intended for the improvement of communications and the construction of a bridge across the Gumal near Murtaza.

The moveable column at Murtaza under the command of Brigadier-General Baldwin, D.S.O., was now composed of—

> One squadron, 11th K. E. O. Lancers.
> 30th Mountain Battery.
> 11th Rajputs.
> 21st Punjabis.
> 67th Punjabis and
> 2 Companies 1/4th Gurkha Rifles.

Moveable column clears route to Wana.—The Mahsuds who had attacked the convoy on the 9th were reported to be still in the Spinkai area. This decided General

Baldwin to clear the route up to Wana and with this object in view he began his advance on the 17th April and arrived at Khajuri Kach on the 18th without opposition. On the 20th the column moved to Tanai and the next day at 7 A.M. started for Wana. The route from Tanai crosses an open plain for a mile and then enters the Sanzala Nala which it ascends on the right bank under low hills for another mile to Zaranni Oba where it turns west up the gorge of the Sanzala; it then crosses a ridge and emerges at the Karab Kot tower six miles from Tanai. In advancing through this defile the column encountered opposition, but owing to the skilful handling of the piqueting troops and the close support of the guns, the route was cleared for transport by 10 A.M. The strength of the Mahsuds was estimated at 400. Our casualties amounted to 14 wounded.

The column reached Wana on the 21st without further opposition and on the 24th returned to Tanai where it halted until the 2nd May, being well situated to support either Wana or Sarwekai.

Attack in the Gwaleri Algad, 1st May.—On the 1st May a convoy of 80 camels left Nili Kach for Khajuri Kach escorted by a force composed of 378 rifles from the 21st Punjabis, 2/67th Punjabis and 94th Russell's Infantry.

At 11 A.M. the piqueting troops for four piquets were fired on and all, except one man shot down. The supports were attacked heavily and forced to withdraw. Meanwhile the convoy had begun to stampede and it was decided to return to Nili Kach, which was reached without further molestation.

The piqueting troops from Khajuri Kach who had moved out to meet those from Nili Kach reached Gwaleri Kotal without incident, and hearing firing at 11 A.M. pushed on and came across some 400 Mahsuds carrying away their wounded and loot; these were fired on. Hurrying to the scene of the action, the Khajuri Kach party came upon our dead and wounded, who were sent through to Nili Kach. Our casualties during the day had been severe, and amounted to 2 British officers, 2 Indian officers and 51 Indian other ranks killed and 1 British officer, 2 Indian officers and 50 Indian other ranks wounded.

News of this action reached General Baldwin at Tanai the same afternoon, and he at once despatched a small column to intercept the raiders on their return journey. The column, however, arrived too late to achieve its object. On the same date the main column moved from Tanai, and arrived at Nili Kach on the 3rd May.

The success of the attacks just described encouraged the Mahsuds to further acts of aggression and small gangs were constantly crossing the border and plundering the villages of cattle and other property. Considerable bodies of Mahsuds were also reported to be abroad and several attacks on our posts were attempted.

Attack on Tormandu Post, 6th May.—On the night of the 6th-7th May, a party of Mahsuds attacked the Tormandu tower. An iron platform and shield had been constructed for the assault, but the garrison was on the alert, the attack was beaten off and the device abandoned. On the 7th, the wing of the 1/4th Gurkhas at Tank was ordered to join the moveable column at Nili Kach, and a company of the 54th Sikhs (F. F.) was despatched to Murtaza to protect the parties of Pioneers working between that place and Spinkai, the remainder of the regiment staying at Tank.

Action near Palosi Ziarat, 9th May.—On the evening of 9th May, Major L. P. Collins, D.S.O., 1/4th Gurkha Rifles, who was in command at Sarwekai received information from the Political Agent who was present in the post that a strong party of Mahsuds was at the Khuzma Narai with the intention of returning to the Shahur.

As Major Collins had received orders to intercept parties of raiders he decided after consulting the Political Agent to hold the route by which the Mahsuds were most likely to return. Two miles east of Sarwekai is the well-known land-mark of Palosi Ziarat, situated at the head of the Danawat Algad which runs towards Haidari Kach, and at the foot of Mamrez Sar which rises to a height of 4,077 feet, some 600 feet above it. Two miles again south-east of the Ziarat is the Sheranna Algad. This was the region, east and south of Palosi Ziarat which Major Collins decided to piquet in order to intercept the Mahsuds on their return journey. His force consisted of 250 rifles 1/4th Gurkha Rifles, 80 of the 11th Rajputs and 120 of the Militia. With these he moved out from Sarwekai at

1 A.M. on the 10th and posted one piquet on Mamrez Sar and four others west of the Sheranna, while it was still dark.

Soon after dawn smoke was seen issuing from a nullah about one thousand yards distant from the most southerly piquet and Subedar Mohibbullah, I.O.M., of the Militia with 50 Gurkhas and 50 Militia was detailed to get above this spot and drive the Mahsuds towards the line of piquets behind which was the reserve. At 7 A.M. the Subedar succeeded in surprising and opening fire on a party of the enemy who were cooking their food.

The Mahsuds were caught completely off their guard—no ordinary occurrence—and at first lost heavily, but there was no panic amongst them and in an incredibly short time they were counterattacking with extraordinary ferocity. The rest of the *lashkar* reinforced by a party of Shahur Shaman Khel, now joined in the attack on the piquets. Fierce fighting ensued, during which our force gradually withdrew, hard pressed by the enemy. A further reinforcement, in the shape of 100 Dhurs, Nekzan Khel, under Ghulam Khan, was seen from Sarwekai to be coming from the direction of Barwand, evidently with the intention of cutting in between the retiring troops and the post, but it was dispersed by the artillery of the garrison, and the retirement was further facilitated by a piquet of 50 rifles sent out on the right flank from Sarwekai to the Waragha Tangi Sar. The post was reached about noon and as soon as the firing died down search parties were sent out and were successful in collecting a certain number of the wounded. The strength of the enemy, who were almost exclusively armed with small bore rifles, was estimated at between four and five hundred, and their losses were ascertained to have been over 70 killed or died of wounds, amongst them being their notorious leader, Sher Dil. Our casualties were 2 British officers, 1 Indian officer, and 36 rank and file killed, 3 Indian officers and 60 rank and file wounded, 70 Indian rank and file missing.

Though our losses in this engagement were severe, those inflicted on the enemy were also heavy and it was reported that the Mahsuds regarded the encounter in the nature of a defeat, and paid a tribute to the steadiness and valour displayed by the Gurkhas in the hand to hand fighting that took place.

As the whole of the Mahsuds were now openly against us it was clear that our defensive policy would have to be abandoned and a punitive expedition undertaken. The Shaman Khel and Manzai sections, who hitherto had not been unfriendly asked for a guarantee that they would not be held in any way responsible for any future misdeeds of hostile sections, but this, of course, was impossible.

Punitive operations sanctioned.—Punitive operations having been decided on, the force shown in Appendix "A" was concentrated in the Derajat Area. The garrison of the Tochi Area was also reinforced, the whole being known as the Waziristan Field Force and coming under the command of Major-General W. G. L. Beynon, C.B., C.I.E., D.S.O.

For Political duties the following officers were appointed to the force :—

Sir John Donald, K.C.I.E., C.S.I.	Chief Political Officer to the Waziristan Field Force.
Major F. H. Humphreys	In charge of North Waziristan.
Major R. J. W. Heale	In charge of the Bhittannis.
J. A. O. Fitzpatrick, Esq., C.I.E.	In charge of Wana and the Mahsuds.

With regard to the policy to be adopted, it was recognised that a final settlement with the Mahsuds could not be effected without either occupying their country in strength for a considerable period, or by instituting an extended blockade. But such measures as these were out of the question during the Great War, being too costly in men and money. There remained an act of temporary but not ineffectual retaliation for our recent losses and the present defiance, which would perhaps at the same time afford a warning for the future. This was a punitive expedition into the rich Khaisara valley, which was expected to produce the desired effect without exciting any feeling of alarm in Khost or Afghanistan generally, which had hitherto remained quiet and refrained from interference. By devastating the Khaisara we should be punishing the sections mainly responsible for the mischief done. With this end in view, operations were finally sanctioned.

A force consisting of two brigades, each with a mountain battery and a company of sappers and miners, was to concentrate at Wana, carry out punitive raids in the Khaisara valley, and return to Wana where it would remain until the effect on the Mahsuds could be judged. The posts of Sarwekai, Khajuri Kach, Nili Kach and Murtaza were to be garrisoned by a battalion each, while two battalions and some cavalry were to hold Jandola and the Derajat posts.

Four additional battalions were added to the Bannu Brigade in the Tochi, where operations were to be of a defensive nature only.

The rising of the river Indus and the floods occurring in the Gomal greatly hampered the concentration of troops and accumulation of supplies. The Mahsuds, however, still continued their activities and on the 13th May raided two tongas, 7 miles from Tank. This gang was engaged next morning in the hills, 4 miles west of Rori village by a detachment of six sowars of the 11th Lancers and thirty rifles of the 54th Sikhs from Rori post who inflicted casualties.

Attack near the Chota Gwaleri Pass, 16th May.—A convoy with much needed supplies for Wana and Sarwekai had been delayed by floods which had made the Gomal unfordable. On account of the large number of camels, it was decided to move the convoy in two echelons, and on the 15th May the first of these, escorted by the 21st Punjabis and the 11th Rajputs, with two sections of mountain artillery, under Brigadier-General Baldwin, started from Nili Kach and reached Khajuri Kach without incident. The second echelon, escorted by the 1st Nepalese Rifles, two companies of the 1/4th Gurkha Rifles, and a section of mountain artillery under the command of Lieutenant-Colonel Sealy, 1/4th Gurkha Rifles left Nili Kach the following day, troops from Khajuri Kach co-operating in the piqueting duties from that post to the Gwaleri Pass.

The advanced troops from Nili Kach reached the summit of the Chota Gwaleri Pass at 8-15 A.M. without encountering opposition, but on the vanguard moving forward up the main *nala* bed it was ambushed and all but two of its number shot down. Large numbers of Mahsuds were then observed on the hills in the vicinity. Artillery fire was opened on these causing them to scatter only to reappear later and fire on the main body which now had reached the slopes of the Chota Gwaleri. Reports were received at the time that the enemy was moving in rear of the convoy. Numbers of them could also be seen east of point 4601 (see Map No. 4) from which position they were maintaining a desultory fire. Lieutenant-Colonel Sealy decided that it was not possible to get the convoy through, and at noon began the return march to Nili Kach, but owing to the difficulty in collecting the dead and wounded the echelon did not reach the post until 8 P.M. Our casualties were 17 killed, 9 wounded, and 4 missing.

Our losses on this occasion were attributable directly to the premature advance of the vanguard along the nala bed before the establishment of at least two essential piquets on features commanding the route. The sudden onslaught of the tribesmen threw the supporting troops into confusion and before a counter-attack could be organized the Mahsuds had stripped the dead and wounded and retired under the fire of their covering parties.

Meanwhile the troops at the Gwaleri Pass endeavoured without success to engage the retiring enemy. Attempts to establish communication with the troops from Nili Kach also failed.

The news of the return of the second echelon to Nili Kach soon reached General Baldwin and the Headquarters of the Waziristan Force, and instructions were issued for both echelons to remain where they were until the arrival of reinforcements which were being sent up.

Brigadier-General Southey commanding the 43rd Brigade at Tank was ordered to proceed with the 54th Sikhs, the 107th Pioneers, and one section 23rd Mountain Battery as reinforcements to Nili Kach, and from that place, with the assistance of Lieutenant-Colonel Sealy's troops, to attack the hostile *lashkar*, reported as numbering about 2,000, and to clear the Gwaleri Pass. The crossing of the Gomal, still swollen by floods, delayed General Southey, and it was not until the 20th that he arrived at Nili Kach. The next day the column left for Khajuri Kach where it arrived without having encountered any opposition. General Baldwin's force co-operated from Khajuri Kach, as also did 5 aeroplanes based on Tank. The convoys now pushed on to Wana and Sarwekai under escort of General Baldwin's troops, General Southey remaining at Khajuri Kach. Both places were rationed with a further month's supplies, and the escort returned, after leaving the 1/4th Gurkha Rifles at Sarwekai. During the advance of the rationing convoys a half-hearted attack had been made on Wana Fort on the 18th, but the enemy withdrew to Inzar Narai after three hours' desultory sniping. Sarwekai post was also sniped on the 21st and 22nd, but without effect.

Reports now came in from political sources that the *lashkars* had dispersed and that most of the tribesmen were busy sowing rice and maize and harvesting barley, and that the reaping of wheat was to begin shortly. A lull in hostilities therefore seemed probable, and the general feeling among the Mahsuds was said to be in favour of an early agreement with Government.

Proposed plan of operations.—For the proposed operations into the Khaisara valley it was necessary to have a reserve of at least three weeks' supplies at Wana, but the difficulties of concentration both of these supplies and the troops on account of the rising of the Indus and the continual floods of the Gomal, made it necessary to reconsider the line of advance. It had been intended that the striking force should advance to Wana *via* the Gomal route. On account of the delay which had been caused, and of the uncertainty as regards the Gomal river, it was now proposed to concentrate all troops at Jandola and to advance to Wana *via* the Shahur, still maintaining the Khaisara valley as our objective. From a political point of view this was less desirable, as the Shahur route led us very near the border line of certain sections of the tribes who were reported wavering between hostile neutrality and active hostility, but this objection was no longer valid for even the Manzai section had taken part in the attack on the convoy on the 16th instant. Furthermore, it was important that the advance should take place without further delay, so that the standing and newly harvested crops could be destroyed before they had been threshed and buried.

The advantages and disadvantages of the two routes, briefly stated, are as follows:—

Comparison of Gomal and Shahur routes.—The Gomal route is outside Mahsud territory and is less liable to attack than the Shahur. There is a motor road from Tank to Murtaza, and, if a bridge were constructed over the Gomal at the latter place, mechanical transport could go straight through to Nili Kach. As a set-off against these advantages, however, the Gomal is constantly in flood; the country is difficult, affording great opportunities for a few riflemen to hold up whole convoys; also, the stages are long and the climate is unhealthy.

The Shahur route, on the other hand, except for three miles through the Shahur Tangi, is easier to protect; the stages are shorter, which is a consideration during the trying heat of summer and though floods do occur they only close the route for a few hours and are not so frequent or prolonged as those in the Gomal. Further, a concentration of troops at Jandola would have a steadying effect on the Bhittannis and would strengthen them in their resistance to attempts by Mahsud raiders to cross their hills. Finally, it was calculated that by using the Shahur route, the punitive operations into Khaisara could be carried out some ten days earlier than *via* the Gomal.

The disadvantages of this route are that it runs through Mahsud territory, and though it is more easily defensible it is also more liable to attack. Moreover, it had to be borne in mind that no stage of the Jandola route, *via* Chasan Kach and Khirgi, was practicable for wheels and consequently that camel transport would be necessary from Tank onwards.

It was therefore decided that the advance should take place *via* the Shahur, and that the Sarwekai garrison should be increased to two battalions and two guns before the withdrawal from the Gomal began. All this, however, was not possible at once, because supplies could not be transported up to the Gomal posts and to Sarwekai without a considerable weakening of the striking force.

Gomal posts rationed.—General Southey, with the 11th Rajputs, the 54th Sikhs, and the 1st Nepalese Rifles, with 4 guns of the 30th Mountain Battery, was ordered to proceed up the Gomal, *via* Khajuri Kach and Dargai Oba, and ration all posts, including Sarwekai, up to the 1st July at their strengths as they then were. The force left Khajuri Kach on the 2nd June, carrying out its mission and returning without encountering any opposition. The column then marched *via* Murtaza to Jandola, where it arrived on the 9th June. By the following day the concentration of troops which had been going on there in the meantime, was completed.

The Order of Battle of the South Waziristan Field Force will be found in Appendix B.

The heat since the middle of May had been severe, the thermometer registering 120 degrees by day in tents, with a minimum of 90 degrees by night in Tank, while at Jandola it was slightly cooler.

The Royal Air Force, which had been carrying out numerous reconnaissances, had now obtained a sufficient number of photographs to compile a map of the Shahur route.

Attitude of the Amir.—On the 29th May, the Mahsuds held a *jirga* at Kaniguram, which was attended by delegates from Khost. At this meeting Fazl Din read a letter which he had received from the Amir of Afghanistan, forbidding Mahsuds to go to Kabul for allowances as long as they were at war with the Indian Government, or to fight unless their country was invaded by troops. The *jirga* passed a resolution that they were willing to resume friendly relations with the Indian Government, and to return all stolen rifles, provided their prisoners and detenus were released and their allowances continued, but that otherwise they would fight. The Amir's letter promised to have an important bearing on the situation, for it showed the Mahsuds that they could not expect any assistance from Afghanistan and at the same time it held out some hope of a temporary settlement without an expedition. This hope was, however, of short duration and we soon found ourselves forced to adopt punitive measures. Then came the attack on Tut Narai post, an example of border-land daring which has few equals even in the annals of the Mahsuds.

Capture of Tut Narai Post, 31st May.—On the 30th May, news was received that a *lashkar* of 1,200 had collected with the object of making an attack on the Tochi. All posts were immediately warned, and a convoy, which was returning from Datta Khel, was pushed through to Miranshah without halting at Boya. About half-past ten o'clock on the following morning a party of five men and two girls was noticed approaching Tut Narai post. The party sat down in the vicinity of the post and entered into conversation with some sepoys of the militia garrison who were standing close by. Shortly afterwards three of the Mahsuds, apparently unarmed, approached the wire entanglement and persuaded a sepoy to purchase for them some sweets from the post bunniah As the sepoy approached the main gate of the post he was closely followed, but without realizing it, by the three Mahsuds. In response to a shout from the sentry on the wall of the post the sepoy turned to order the Mahsuds outside the wire entanglement. It was too late. One of the Mahsuds producing a revolver shot the sepoy while the other two dashed for the gate about five yards distant reaching it at the same time as the guard commander. Before the latter could close the wicket gate he too was killed. In an instant the three Mahsuds were attacking the remainder of the guard shooting them down before they could reach their rifles. At the first shot, the two Mahsuds who were with the girls fired at the sentry on the wall, and then ran towards the post followed by the girls who were throwing off their disguise. The latter turned out to be ex-sepoys of the Militia. In the meantime a party of about 30 Mahsuds who had been concealed in the holly-oak jungle near by entered the post and kept the remainder of the garrison whose arms were locked in the bell of arms, confined to their barrack rooms. The sentries on the wall were rushed, but the Subadar in command seizing a wounded sentry's rifle continued firing at the enemy until wounded himself in three places. The telegraph office clerk was chased from his room and murdered, but not before he had sent off the message—" Please help, raiders are plundering "—to the Political Agent at Datta Khel. This message was received at 11-6 A.M and was repeated immediately to Miranshah, whilst all local *chighas* were collected and sent to Tut Narai. The prompt assistance rendered by these *chighas*, who hurried to the scene from three directions, combined with the fire from towers which command the post on two sides, stopped the looting and resulted in the raiders being driven off. The post was occupied by the *chighas* at about 12-30 P.M. their numbers amounting to some 450. The Mahsuds, however, had succeeded in breaking open the bell of arms and decamping with 59 rifles, 120,000 rounds of ammunition, and Rs. 581 in cash. Our casualties were six killed and eight wounded, those of the enemy being estimated at about a dozen killed and many wounded. The raiders must have numbered about six hundred, of whom perhaps five hundred were Abdullai from Makin.

The success of the Mahsuds on this occasion may be attributed to the care with which their plans had been arranged, and to their knowledge of the habits of the garrison. For example, the day chosen for the attack was Thursday, the weekly holiday, when it was certain that no outdoor parade or field training would disclose the presence of large numbers of tribesmen concealed in the vicinity of the post. The time too was well selected. By that hour it could be anticipated that the inspection of rifles would have been completed, and the garrison engaged in bathing, or washing clothes at the pond below the post, or enjoying a *siesta*.

The Mahsuds too must have noticed and taken advantage of the error made shortly before, in changing the position of the sentry watching the main gate. Instead of being on the wall the sentry was posted formerly near the wicket gate, from which place he was able to watch the guard room, bell of arms and magazine.

On the receipt of the news Major G. B. Scott, D.S.O., commanding the Northern Waziristan Militia left Miranshah immediately with a small column to re-garrison the post.

On arrival at Tut Narai at 9 A.M. on the 1st June the post was found to have been but little damaged, and after reinforcing the post with militia the column returned on the following day without finding any trace of the enemy.

Distribution of troops in the Tochi.—The Tut Narai incident now raised the question of the distribution of troops in the Tochi and the policy to be pursued in that area. The Chief Commissioner of the North-West Frontier Province considered that we should either (*a*) evacuate Datta Khel, Tut Narai, and Spina Khaisora, which were, he contended, of no strategic importance and would only draw attacks, or (*b*) send a Brigade into Mashud country from the Upper Tochi. Neither of these proposals was considered desirable, and it was eventually decided that a stronger force should be located at Miranshah to deal with hostile raids in the Upper Tochi, but that the policy should remain one of active defence.

As Major-General Beynon had now assumed personal command of the force which was to advance from Jandola, it was decided to form the North and South Waziristan Field Forces, the troops in the Bannu area comprising the former and those in the Derajat area the latter, the whole coming directly under the command of General Sir Arthur Barrett, G.C.B., K.C.S.I., K.C.V.O., A.D.C., Commanding the Northern Army, whose headquarters were to remain at Murree.

Troops of the South Waziristan Field Force remained as shown in Appendix "B" while those of the Northern Force were now distributed as follows:—

At Bannu—
    31st D. C. O. Lancers (less 1 squadron).
    2nd Gwalior I. S. Lancers (less 1 squadron).
    1 section 29th Indian Mountain Battery.
    72nd Punjabis.
    2/103rd Mahratta Light Infantry.
    95th Infantry.

At Miranshah—
    1 squadron 31st D. C. O. Lancers.
    1 squadron 2nd Gwalior Lancers.
    29th Mountain Battery (less 1 section).
    1/1st Kent Battalion.
    10th Jats.
    Shere Regiment.
    Miranshah battalion (for protection of camp).
    25th Punjabis.

For work on road—
    12th Pioneers.

The whole under the command of Brigadier-General the Hon'ble G. G. Bruce, M.V.O.

The lines of communications were organised as follows:—

    (a) Administrative control from Rawalpindi to Kohat, Bannu, Tank and Darya Khan Railway stations, inclusive, under an Inspector-General of Communication with headquarters at Mari Indus, directly responsible to the Northern Army Commander.

(b) In the Derajat area, under General Beynon's orders, a defence commander and Inspector of Communications from **Darya Khan** and Tank stations.

(c) In the Bannu area, under the orders of General Bruce, an Inspector of Communications from Kohat and Bannu to Miranshah, who would also be Defence Commander cis-frontier.

As this Northern Waziristan Force was not called upon after this date to make any movement, we may now leave it and return to the Derajat area and the events that occurred there.

On the 1st June a Bhittanni *jirga* was held at Tank and it was decided to enrol one hundred of the Thatta section of the Daman Bhittannis for piqueting the two lower sections of the Jandola road, which duty they began on the 16th June.

Attack on piqueting party near Khirgi, 7th June.— Early on the 7th June a piqueting detachment of two British officers and 89 men of the 2/1st Gurkha Rifles proceeding from Zam post towards Khirgi were attacked by a party of enemy estimated at five hundred. The terrain where this took place is flat and stony, and covered with small bushes. The enemy attacked the advanced screen and attempted to surround the whole party, but were driven off after a fight lasting twenty minutes and retired in the direction of the Shuza. Our casualties were thirty-five killed, 2nd-Lieutenant Forster and seventeen other ranks wounded and three missing. 2nd-Lieutenant Forster was shot by a wounded Mahsud lying on the ground after the fight was over. The Mahsuds were reported to have lost heavily including two notorious Shingi raiders and a Manzai *malik*.

A few days later a Wazir havildar commanding Tiarza tower occupied by a mixed detachment of the Southern Waziristan Militia succeeded in deserting with twenty-five rifles, thirteen boxes of ammunition and four hand-grenades

A relation who had chanced to be passing with some laden bullocks was partaking of food inside the tower, when the havildar on the plea that the reserve was insufficient sent out the garrison except one Afridi sentry and the Adam Khel Afridi *muharrir* to collect firewood.

The Wazirs seizing their opportunity disarmed the sentry and overpowering the *muharrir* loaded their booty on the bullocks and made good their escape to Mahsud country.

On hearing this news a party of Machi Khel Mahsuds removed the kits and rations and burnt the tower, which has since not been re-built.

The Mahsuds had now become alarmed at the concentration of troops, and although certain of the *maliks* were undoubtedly in favour of a settlement, the majority of the tribesmen, encouraged by Mullah Fazl Din, were bent upon opposing our advance. The Wana and Tochi Wazirs were more or less quiet, and had so far refrained from joining the Mahsuds. On our side the concentration of troops was complete and by the 12th June all preparations for the advance were ready.

CHAPTER V.

Operations in the Shahur and Khaisara Valleys, between 12th June and 17th August 1917.

Preliminary reconnaissance from Jandola.—Frequent reports had been coming in that the Mahsuds were collecting in large numbers to oppose the advance of the striking force which they anticipated would begin operations in the valley of the Tank Zam and, as reliable information had been received that a considerable body of the enemy had arrived in the neighbourhood of the junction of the Shahur and Tank Zam, the column moved out from Jandola on 12th June to attack it. The enemy, however, did not make a stand but retired up the Tank Zam followed by a detachment of the 11th Lancers which withdrew after destroying some hamlets and stocks of fodder. Air reconnaissance showed that no large bodies of tribesmen were in the vicinity so the force returned to camp followed up by a few of the enemy who contented themselves with sniping at long range. Our casualties were three wounded.

The following day the 43rd Brigade carried out a reconnaissance to the eastern entrance of the Shahur Tangi, the Sappers and Miners and 107th Pioneers, at the same time clearing a double camel track up the river bed. Aeroplanes co-operating with the troops reported all quiet as far as Haidari Kach and information, afterwards confirmed, was received that the *lashkar* up the Tank Zam had dispersed owing to the heat and scarcity of food.

Passage of Shahur Tangi, 14th and 15th June.—It had been arranged that whenever the column moved forward it should be accompanied by a convoy carrying two days' supplies for the whole force in addition to two days' supplies in regimental and brigade supply column. In view of possible opposition at the Shahur Tangi and uncertainty regarding the state of the route through the defile, Major-General Beynon decided to advance to Haidari Kach in two echelons; the first of which would occupy the heights commanding this dangerous gorge and protect the passage of the second with the convoy. Accordingly on the 14th June the 45th Brigade moved from Jandola to Chagmalai on the right bank of the Mastang Algad at its junction with the Shahur close to the entrance of the *tangi* and there pitched camp, without encountering any opposition.

On the following day the main body of the force, the 43rd Brigade accompanied by the 21st Punjabis, 127th Baluchis, and the convoy marched from Jandola to Haidari Kach, covered by troops from the 45th Brigade who occupied the heights commanding the *tangi*, the majority of the piquets being posted on the left bank. The rapid passage of the lengthy baggage and supply trains demonstrated the value of the double camel track which had been cleared so expeditiously throughout the defile.

To assist the advance of the main force a detachment from Sarwekai made a demonstration towards Turan China. This operation was carried out successfully, three Mahsuds being killed and two taken prisoners at Kamardin village. The opposition was slight and the detachment returned without casualties to Sarwekai.

The 45th Brigade having joined the main body of the force at Haidari Kach the troops were employed in improving the double camel road through the Shahur Tangi and in destroying villages, crops, watercourses, and mills, in the area around Haidari Kach, Turan China, and the Danawat Algad, and in reconnoitring the route towards Barwand.

The Mahsuds evidently calculating on the force advancing up the Tank Zam had not removed their stores of fodder and wood, while the rice fields too had been planted recently. The thorough devastation of this area had an excellent political and military effect.

Advance to Barwand, 19th June.—From information received it was now evident that the advance of the force and the destruction done in the Shahur had roused the Mahsuds; convinced by this time that they would not be attacked from the Tochi they decided to oppose the advance up the Shahur. This it was probable they would attempt to do near Barwand, as it was reported that a large *lashkar* was to assemble at Ispana Raghza on the 19th. Mullah Hamzullah too promised the assistance of a contingent of Wazirs from Wana and Shakai. As there seemed no doubt that considerable numbers of tribesmen were collecting the 1/4th Gurkha Rifles and 1 section 30th Mountain Battery were ordered to move from Sarwekai on the 19th and join the force at Barwand.

It appeared from reports and aeroplane reconnaissances that the Shahur stream at this time of the year did not reach Barwand and that it would be necessary for the column to camp in the neighbourhood of Ispana Raghza to obtain a water supply.

On the 19th June the force moved forward from Haidari Kach, where the 21st Punjabis and 127th Baluchis had been established in a strong post. Air reconnaissances reported that no enemy had been seen ahead of the column, and the machines returned to their base at Tank. As soon however, as the advanced guard reached the heights which rise above the left bank three miles east of Barwand considerable opposition was encountered. Here and on the plateau on the right bank which is covered with small trees and bushes some 1,500 of the enemy had collected to oppose the advance. The 45th Brigade which was carrying out the piqueting duties drove back the enemy who attacked several piquets and contested fiercely each vantage point.

The 2/6th Sussex Regiment advancing steadily cleared the wooded Barwand plateau and the 55th Rifles captured the high ground on the left bank of the Shahur, both regiments having several casualties. Just after noon a storm which had been threatening all the morning broke and it rained heavily for about twenty minutes. At 4 P.M. the opposition to the advanced guard was such that further progress would necessitate a general action, and as the river was coming down in spate it was decided to camp on the plateau about one mile north of the ruins of Barwand village. The guns were in action till dark covering the construction of the piquets, which was completed in the face of considerable opposition, and also in supporting the rearguard which was hampered by casualties received close to camp.

Attack on piquet Barwand, 19th June.—Spies reported at dusk that the Mahsud *lashkar* had collected at Ispana Raghza and intended to attack the camp that night. All that occurred, however, was intermittent sniping into camp; and a determined effort to capture a piquet of the 54th Sikhs posted on a spur on the left bank of the stream. The piquet was held by Subedar Hukm Dad and thirty Punjabi Mussalmans. This party had been unable to *sangar* itself during daylight as any movement brought down an accurate fire from a near and commanding ridge, but it managed to establish itself on a ledge of rock which commanded the slope on the enemy side.

After dusk the enemy who numbered several hundred, made repeated efforts to rush the piquet, creeping up to within twenty yards and calling on the defenders—their co-religionists—to relinquish their arms, on which they would be allowed to withdraw unharmed. These attacks continued throughout the night. Assistance was rendered from camp by searchlight and gun fire directed by lamp signal from the piquet. The day dawned and the piquet was at last relieved, only one bomb and three rounds per man remaining; four men had been killed and the Indian officer and twelve sepoys wounded. The courage and determination of the defenders together with the possession of bombs and the assistance rendered by the guns undoubtedly saved the piquet from extermination.*

The success with which our troops and convoys in the Gomal had been attacked had no doubt given the Mahsuds great confidence in dealing with small bodies of our troops. The gallant defence made by this undaunted piquet of the 54th Sikhs and the casualties it inflicted did much to inspire the tribesmen with respect for, and fear, of our troops, and contributed in no small measure to the final settlement.

On the 20th the camp was moved to the western end of the Ispana Raghza plateau where there is a perennial water supply from the river, which just below this locality disappears underground. The enemy made a determined attempt to check the advance of the force and held a spur flanking the Raghza on its northern side, and dominating it. From this they were driven by the 43rd Brigade, the spur referred to above being attacked and carried with conspicuous dash by the 1/25th London Regiment and 1/4th Gurkha Rifles. The Mahsud *lashkar* withdrew to the north and the occupation of the Raghza was not further disputed except by a few snipers. Our casualties were six killed and sixteen wounded. On this day the force was joined by the 11th Rajputs from Sarwekai.

*Our total casualties for the 19th were: 9 killed and 33 wounded.

The climate was now more pleasant and the nights cool. A halt was made in order that supplies might be collected for the next advance, and the work of devastation systematically carried out in the neighbourhood.

Attack on Nanu village, 21st June.—Due north of Ispana Raghza and about two miles from it over a pass, is the village of Nanu in a valley of the same name running eastward and joining the Spli Toi. This village was the home of Kutab Khan, the chief *malik* of the Manzai section, a grandson of Umar Khan and son of Badshah Khan —names well known in the history of our relations with the tribe. Since the village was being used as a base by the *lashkar* now in the field, it was thought that its destruction would affect the moral of the Mahsuds, and Major-General Beynon decided to attack Nanu on the 21st.

On the night of the 20th-21st an alarm was raised on the north face of the camp that about forty of the enemy had been seen near the perimeter. Some wild firing broke out but it was soon checked, and it was found that no attack in force was being made. It is not unlikely that such an attack was contemplated, but finding the camp prepared the enemy abandoned the attempt. The drums of the Mahsuds in the hills to the north could be heard distinctly, and in the morning considerable numbers of the enemy were to be seen on the ridges near the Nanu Pass. The pass itself is commanded by three rocky eminences on the north-west and the whole terrain is admirably suited to defence. The Mahsuds made use of every advantage, and had constructed well sited and constructed *sangars* on the forward slopes of the hills.

Shortly after the 45th Brigade had begun its advance towards the pass air reconnaissance reported that about three hundred of the enemy had been observed in the vicinity of Nanu, and it was evident that the tribesmen had determined to make a stand on this occasion. The 2/6th Sussex Regiment moved against the pass itself while the 2/1st Gurkhas were directed on the high ground to the south of the Pass and the Mahindradal Regiment ordered to seize the rocky heights commanding the pass on the north-west, the 55th Rifles being held in reserve.

As it was soon apparent that considerable opposition would be met the 43rd Brigade was ordered to reinforce the 45th Brigade with its artillery, and to hold a battalion in readiness to assist if needed. Some difficulty was experienced by the 2/1st Gurkha Rifles and the Nepalese regiment in capturing the rocky heights dominating the pass but by 10 A.M. with the aid of steady and accurate gunfire the whole ridge had been carried, the Mahindradal Regiment in particular distinguishing itself. Major Harte, 6th Gurkha Rifles, Senior Supervising Officer of the regiment was killed at the head of his men just before the summit was reached. The pass was occupied and the Sussex Regiment pushed on to piquet the hills commanding the village, and to pursue the enemy who was being harassed in his retreat by the low-flying aeroplanes. Two guns of No. 1 British Mountain Battery now came up the pass and were of great assistance in supporting the advanced piquets, which were under heavy and accurate fire.

The work of demolition began and the village was completely destroyed by 2 P.M. In the meantime all animals except those absolutely necessary were sent down the steep and rocky track to camp. As the Lewis guns were to be man-handled the mules were also sent back to camp. All impedimenta were thus cleared away, and the withdrawal began at 2 P.M. The piquets retired quickly and skilfully and the whole brigade returned with slight molestation to camp at 4-45 P.M. Our casualties were twelve killed and forty wounded.

First overtures for peace by Mahsuds.—It appeared from information subsequently received that the Mahsuds had intended to make a bold effort to stop the advance of the force. Their defeat, however, brought home to them the futility of opposing the Government and three days later the first emissaries of peace began to come into camp.

On the 22nd June the 43rd Brigade destroyed a large village in the Waspas valley known as Shah Salim Mela. This was effected with little opposition although the enemy had made careful preparations for opposing the advance of a force attacking up the valley. The whole of the defence was turned by the troops advancing along the hill commanding the valley below. This action disconcerted the Mahsuds who retired upstream towards the Khaisara. The village was deserted. Its hundred houses and all property were effectively burned and the force withdrew followed by a few snipers. Our casualties were one killed and three wounded. A sufficiency of supplies had by this time been collected at Ispana Raghza to enable a post to be established there and a raid made into the Khaisara valley.

Situation, 22nd June.—The general situation was now reported to be as follows:—*Lashkars* numbering about four thousand in all were collected near the force, their numbers fluctuating as portions went away for rations. Small parties had been organised to harass the troops, but none had come down below the Shahur Tangi. The routes threatening Jandola-Tank line were said to be clear. According to spies the Manzai, Shaman Khel, and probably, the Bahlolzai, were quite ready to open negotiations, if given full safe-conducts. Fearing danger from Datta Khel, the Abdullai and Bahlolzai whose homes lay towards the Tochi had not joined the *lashkars* in the Khaisara. The Bhittannis were working well in piqueting the Jandola-Zam line and our own arrangements for convoys through Haidari Kach were, on the whole, satisfactory; the route through the Shahur Tangi had been blocked on the 20th by spate and delays occurred on several occasions, while there had been a good deal of sickness, mainly diarrhœa, among the troops on the Line of Communication.

Advance to Narai Raghza, 23rd June.—On the 23rd, the 11th Rajputs, Mahendradal Regiment, 1 section 30th Mountain Battery, and half a squadron 11th Lancers, were left to guard Ispana Raghza post and secure the passage of convoys, while the remainder of the force, namely, seven battalions, twelve guns, two companies Sappers and Miners and a half-squadron, moving on light scale of baggage, without tents and with three days' supplies, advanced to Narai Raghza, about seven miles, burning villages, destroying water-mills and blowing up towers on the way. The 45th Brigade furnished the advanced guard and piqueting troops and left camp at 6 A.M., being followed by a working party of the 7th and 11th Companies of Sappers and Miners to improve the route where needed. The most formidable obstacle of this stage is the Tangi below Narai Raghza, which is about forty yards long and narrows down in places to twelve feet. It is commanded by steep heights on both sides and it was expected that the Mahsuds would meet our advance here. But there were only a few of them on the hills by the Tangi which were cleared by gun fire and occupied by our piquets, the Mahsuds retiring to the hills surrounding the Narai Raghza. The advanced guard reached this plateau about 1 P.M. and was heavily attacked from the north. The road through the Tangi was now improved and all transport was through by 3 P.M.

The enemy, meanwhile, were tenaciously holding the heights on the west, north, and north-east of the plateau; the laying out of camp was done under fire; and the piquets were posted with difficulty. A piquet of the 1/25th London Regiment on a hill to the west of camp, was hard pressed for some time, but it was supported by gun fire and ultimately protected by the advance of a company of the 1/4th Gurkha Rifles who occupied the spur on the north of it. This company met with considerable opposition and made slow progress, losing two men killed and seven wounded. It was relieved by the 1st Nepalese Rifles and did not return to camp till 9-30 P.M. much hampered in the dark by casualties. After 10 P.M. the attacks ceased and the night passed quietly. A reconnoitring party of the 1/4th Gurkha Rifles which had gone out in the direction of the Shrawanai Pass returned to camp at 6-30 P.M. and reported that the heights on each side were held by the enemy. Our casualties this day were three killed and ten wounded.

Action near Shrawanai Pass, 24th June.—On the 24th June the 43rd Brigade was ordered to seize the Shrawanai Pass and hold it to enable the 45th Brigade to pass through and carry out the work of destruction in the Khaisara.

At 5-40 A.M. the guns took up a position four hundred yards north-west of the camp to cover the advance of the 43rd Brigade.

The position held by a body of the enemy on the north of the pass was indicated by aeroplanes which dropped smoke balls. As this position was seen to be some distance from the pass, the 1st Nepalese Rifles were sent to occupy a hill between it and the line of march to the pass. This was accomplished without any opposition and deceived the Mahsuds into thinking that an attack on their position was intended.

The enemy regarding the Nepalese as an advanced guard of this attack remained where they were. The

1/4th Gurkha Rifles now occupied the hills on the south of the pass which they reached without opposition at 6-45 A.M. and began to move west piqueting the route. The 54th Sikhs, at the same time, seized the pass itself and occupied the hills on the north of it with the Nepalese on their right flank. The enemy were thus cut off from the pass and found their position useless.

The piqueting of the pass was completed by 9 A.M., and the 45th Brigade then moved through the piquets to the summit and thence to the ridge, about a mile further on, overlooking the Khaisara villages. The rapid advance of this brigade enabled it to occupy the ridge before the Mahsuds could assemble in sufficient strength to resist. They were now streaming down the western slope of the hills north of the pass, but our guns posted on the *kotal* with the 43rd Brigade gave effective support to the advancing troops and to their piquets on the right which from this time to that of the retirement were incessantly attacked. A few Mahsuds gained the northern extremity of the ridge and constructed *sangars* there. During the piqueting and subsequent advance aeroplanes with Lewis guns harassed the enemy, and assisted our operations.

The destruction of villages east of the stream and north of Kundiwan was now begun. The villages of Abbas Khel, Warza, Manzai, Nana Khel, and Ghazi Kot were set on fire and destroyed, and some of the Machi Khel towers to the south were blown up. Most of the opposition came from the Mahsuds who were attacking the right flank guard. While the 2/1st Gurkha Rifles and the Royal Sussex Regiment were carrying out the destruction of Abbas Khel, which is a long and scattered village, a determined rush was made on two platoons of the 55th Rifles, who were occupying a ruined graveyard, 1,000 yards to the north of the first group of houses. The enemy came within three hundred yards before being driven off by rapid fire.

The withdrawal had been ordered for 2 P.M. but casualties among the 55th Rifles necessitated its postponement for half an hour. The retirement was followed up closely to within three hundred yards of the summit of the pass, which was reached by 3 P.M. by the rearguard of the 45th Brigade. The dangerous flank was the northern one where the ground is much broken and covered with bushes. Here two sections of the 23rd Mountain Battery, which had been covering the retirement to the pass, found themselves in some danger of being cut off, but on receiving orders to retire they limbered up smartly and went at a rapid pace up the narrow track to the pass and down to their original positions north of the camp covering two miles in three quarters of an hour.

The rearguard of the 43rd Brigade was furnished by the 54th Sikhs and one of their piquets was also in danger for a time. About thirty of the enemy had collected in dead ground three hundred yards from the piquet, and, in spite of heavy covering fire from other piquets and supports, succeeded in firing two volleys into the piquet on its retirement. The enemy did not continue the pursuit beyond the summit of the pass, and camp was reached at 6 P.M. Our casualties this day were five killed, twenty-six wounded, and one missing.

Arrival of peace emissaries.—Two emissaries from a *jirga* at Kaniguram arrived this day in camp to ask for the terms of peace and an armistice. Major-General Beynon had intended to spend a second day in the destruction of the Khaisara and had made his supply arrangements accordingly. He was, however, now assured that the damage already done in the Khaisara was sufficient for political purposes and did not, therefore, consider that the further loss of life, which a second move into that valley would have entailed was justified. A return to Ispana Raghza was, therefore, ordered.

Withdrawal to Ispana Raghza.—On the 25th, the 54th Sikhs with half a company of Sappers and Miners left camp at 5 A.M. and in conjunction with the 30th Mountain Battery destroyed a large village one mile north-east of camp, which had proved to be a nest of snipers.

The force then began to withdraw to Ispana Raghza, the 43rd Brigade moving first and piqueting the route, while the 45th Brigade followed the transport as rearguard.

A large number of Mahsuds who had collected on the Shrawanai Pass with the intention of opposing a second raid into the Khaisara, now seeing signs of a withdrawal began to advance. A piquet of the 54th Sikhs and a covering party of the 1/4th Gurkhas therefore remained in position west of the camp until the transport had passed through the *tangi*, when the 30th Mountain Battery shelled the pass effectively, information regarding the result of their fire being given them from the piquet by signal. Two other piquets on the north and one on the south of the camp also remained in their positions till the *tangi* was reported clear of transport.

The retirement down the *tangi* was necessarily slow and it was not till 9-30 A.M. that the rearguard could begin to move. During the withdrawal of the piquets a party of snipers worked their way round the right (north) flank of the first gun position near camp to within 300 yards of the guns, but the escort of the 54th Sikhs saved the section from the casualties which it was in danger of suffering by a rapid advance, before which the enemy retired. Almost immediately after this, the last piquet was withdrawn, and the rearguard and guns retired through the *tangi*. The enemy at once descended from the hills and occupied our camping ground. There they were heavily shelled by the centre section of the 30th Mountain Battery, while both the centre and left sections engaged targets of the enemy appearing on the heights north and south of the *tangi*. The intention of the Mahsuds had evidently been to envelope our rearguard, but the positions on either side of the *tangi* had been occupied by our piquets which were withdrawn under cover of the guns. The retirement was completed without a casualty, though one sepoy had been wounded in the attack on the village, and camp was reached about 3 P.M. Towns and villages which had been left standing owing to the hurried advance were now destroyed and the work of devastation in this area completed.

Value of aeroplanes.—During the operations of the striking force the B. E. 2. C aeroplanes based at Tank proved to be of the greatest assistance. Owing to the high temperature prevailing co-operation, which was requested sparingly, usually took the form of a preliminary reconnaissance carried out ahead of the column by one or two machines, which summoned others from Tank when it was observed that the force was being opposed.

Apart from co-operating with the column in this manner independent raids were carried out almost daily on parts of the country not being visited by the force. On the 22nd bombs were dropped with considerable effect in the Kaniguram valley and in a particularly successful raid on the 26th a number of direct hits were obtained on houses in Makin and Marobi, the latter being the home of Mullah Fazl Din.

The political reports now available showed that the Mahsuds were in a more reasonable state of mind; the defeat that they had suffered at Nanu, the destruction of villages and the raids of the aeroplanes on regions formerly considered safe from our attack, had disheartened them, nor could they any longer hope for help from Kabul. A letter from the Amir to the Viceroy dated June 23rd showed, indeed, that he was endeavouring to check the spread of disorder.

Terms given to Mahsuds.—On his return to Ispana Raghza on the 25th the Chief Political Officer received messages to the effect that some of the principal *maliks* were anxious to treat for peace, and also that a representative *jirga* at Kaniguram had written asking for a specification of the terms to be imposed by Government. The *jirga* appealed too for a suspension of hostilities for five days in order that the *jirga* might consider them. The terms of the Government of India which were sent them were briefly as follows :—

> (a) The settlement of Major Dodd's murder case by tribal custom as against the Abdur Rahman Khel.
> (b) All rifles captured from the military and militia since March 1st were to be returned.
> (c) The prisoners now with the Mahsuds were to be released.
> (d) The outlaws from British territory were to be surrendered or expelled.
> (e) A guarantee for future good behaviour was to be given.

Hostilities suspended, 26th June.—The military and political requirements now seemed to be identical; the operations had so far been successful, the troops required a much needed rest, and an opportunity had occurred for giving the Mahsuds that chance of coming to an agreement which it was our declared policy to offer them. Accordingly on the 26th June offensive operations including aerial raids were suspended pending the results of the Mahsuds' deliberations, the days of grace to end on the 1st July. The force remained halted at Ispana Raghza unmolested by the enemy except for the sniping of a water party on the 26th resulting in two British privates being wounded.

As it seemed probable that the force would be inactive for some time, it was necessary to find a suitable camping ground. The present site at Ispana Raghza was inconvenient and the water was rapidly receding from the west side of the plateau. The locality marked on the map as Boji Khel (or Abbas Khel) about 3 miles up stream was finally selected.

Before leaving Ispana Raghza 250 rifles of the 54th Sikhs were sent out on the 27th to destroy all the water channels near the site of the Barwand camp as this was the spring settlement of the Bahlolzai, the only section which had stood out against the rest of the Mahsuds in their desire for a settlement and had refused to send emissaries with them on the 26th. They were, therefore, considered as being outside the terms of the armistice. On the 29th and 30th June the force transferred its camp to Boji Khel the situation of which but for the steep ascent to the camping ground from the river bed was excellent and the water supply ample and good.

Mahsud hostages and surrender of rifles.—Events now turn on the peace negotiations which were being conducted by the Political officers of the force. The *maliks* agreed to the terms imposed and as a token of good faith 9 of them, three from each of the main sections of the tribe remained as hostages in camp. On the 9th a first instalment of 124 rifles was surrendered, and the *maliks* arranged to send out parties to the various sections of the tribe to collect the balance.

Withdrawal to Manzal.—In view of the satisfactory attitude of the tribe the force moved back without incident on the 11th and 12th July to a camp at Manzal at the junction of the Shahur and Danawat valleys thereby enabling cultivation to be commenced and villages restored in the Upper Shahur valley. Rifles and prisoners were now being surrendered in batches to the Political Officers at Sarwekai and finally on the 10th August a full ceremonial *jirga* was held at Sarwekai attended by the Force Commander, General Beynon, Sir John Donald, Resident in Waziristan, and some 3,000 Mahsuds. 208 Government and 83 militia rifles, valued at nearly three lakhs of rupees, had been surrendered and all prisoners and kidnapped Hindus returned. About 95 rifles were still outstanding, but of these 19 had been taken to Afghanistan and were irrecoverable by the tribe, 40 had been sold to Wazirs in Birmal, and the rest could not be traced. The Mahsuds, however, handed over rifles of their own as security for the return of all recoverable rifles, and hostages were also appointed for this purpose.

<small>Full *jirga* interviewed at Sarwekai, 10th August. Terms complied with.</small>

Peace announced.—In connection with the murder of Major Dodd both men suspected of connivance in the outrage were duly tried according to tribal custom and acquitted. The formal written agreement with the tribe was carefully explained and attested, and a duplicate copy was handed to the leading *maliks*. Peace with the tribe was then announced and British territory opened to them for trading purposes. The *jirga* led by the *maliks* having repeated the solemn prayer on enduring peace was dismissed to their homes by the Force Commander.

Force returns to Jandola.—The force returned to Jandola, the 43rd Brigade with force headquarters on the 11th, and the 45th Brigade on the following day. The demobilization of the force and return of troops to India was then begun in accordance with a programme drawn up by Army Headquarters.

Climatic conditions. Health of troops.—The force had thus fully accomplished its task, and, although the operations had lasted only a short time, they were carried out during the hottest and most enervating season of the year in one of the most unhealthy areas in the Trans-Frontier Provinces where dysentery, diarrhœa, malaria and sand-fly fever are rife. Of all frontier expeditions there was none in which the troops had undergone more adverse climatic conditions, or in which they had undertaken more continuous hardship and fatigue. During the operations the troops were marching at dawn, piqueting heights and fighting all day in a broiling sun, and reaching camp late in the evening to construct the defences of their bivouacs. The diurnal variations of temperature too which averaged from 20 to 43 degrees and were sometimes even in excess of this, were remarkable and added considerably to the hardships of troops on a reduced scale of baggage. The British troops and Gurkhas and a good proportion of the Indian troops were young and unseasoned, and it is therefore not surprising that the arduous campaign affected the health of the force, and that a high sick rate prevailed. Statistics show that in the South Waziristan Force the general admission rate was 33·22 per cent. The admission rate for the British ranks was 55·39 per cent. and for the Indian ranks 41·59 per cent. On the other hand the death-rate was remarkably low.

A statement showing the casualties from 10th May to 15th July will be found in Appendix ' C.'

Another unique feature of the campaign was that it was the first occasion on which the Royal Flying Corps, British Territorial battalions, and regiments of the Nepalese army had participated in operations against the tribesmen of the North-West Frontier. The last-named troops were accompanied in the field by their General, Sir Baber Shamshere Jang Bahadur Rana, K.C.I.E.

CHAPTER VI.

EVENTS LEADING UP TO THE CAMPAIGN OF 1919-20.

Plan of campaign in Waziristan during Afghan War, 1919.—During the period from August 1917 to the outbreak of the third Afghan War on the 6th May 1919, the situation in Waziristan remained normal. The beginning of hostilities with Afghanistan found the troops in Waziristan distributed as shown in Appendix D, and the Bannu and the Derajat Brigades with the Northern and Southern Waziristan Militias were brought under the command of Major-General Woodyatt, C.B., C.I.E., and constituted the Waziristan Force, under the orders of the General Officer Commanding, the North-West Frontier Force.

The plan of campaign allotted an active defensive role to the Waziristan Force, and it was decided that if necessary, the areas which lay between the administrative and political borders and held by militia garrisons should be evacuated temporarily; for their retention would have involved us in a series of sieges demanding measures for their relief and consequent dissipation of transport from the principal theatre of operations.

About the 21st May information was received of a concentration in Khost, and of the movement of Afghan troops towards the Upper Tochi and in the direction of Wana. Major-General Woodyatt was instructed, therefore, not to despatch troops up the Gomal valley to Wana or to operate beyond Miranshah, as it was considered that the troops at his disposal were not sufficient for any widely extended operations.

As it seemed probable that the presence of Afghan regular troops on the borders of Waziristan would result in a general rising of the Mahsuds and Wazirs, and since it was impossible to despatch troops to support the militia posts in the Gomal it was decided, in view of the uncertain behaviour of the Khyber Rifles even when closely supported by regular troops, that it would not be possible to trust the Waziristan Militias when left unsupported. Orders were issued, therefore, that should Afghan regular troops advance to the vicinity of Wana and be joined by the tribes Wana and the Gomal posts were to be evacuated, the British officers withdrawing to India with such men as remained loyal. Similar orders applied to the garrison in the Upper Tochi, and to those at Spinwam and Shewa.

Situation in Northern Waziristan, May 1919.—On the 24th May Brigadier-General F. G. Lucas, C.B., D.S.O., commanding the 67th (Bannu) Brigade, desiring to reassure the Militia garrisons and the tribes in the Upper Tochi, despatched the moveable column, which is held permanently in readiness at Dardoni, the new cantonment near Miranshah, to Muhammad Khel. In consequence, however, of information received that General Nadir Khan in Khost was preparing to move either towards Thal or Miranshah, the General Officer Commanding the North-West Frontier Force ordered the immediate return of the column to Dardoni where it would be more suitably placed to meet the threatened attack. On receipt of this order, Brigadier-General Lucas decided to order the evacuation of the Upper Tochi posts as he considered the withdrawal of the moveable column would be followed inevitably by the wholesale defection of the garrisons with their rifles and ammunition.

Evacuation of Upper Tochi posts.—The evacuation of the militia posts began on the 25th May, small columns of the regular troops visiting Datta Khel, Tut Narai, and Spina Khaisora. As transport was insufficient only the more valuable stores were removed, the remainder being destroyed. The garrisons returned with the troops to Muhammad Khel. Boya post was also evacuated and handed over for safe custody to Khan Muhammad Khan, a Daur *malik* who was considered to be trustworthy.

The news of the evacuation of the Upper posts and the destruction of the stores quickly spread among the tribesmen, and by dusk large numbers of Wazirs had collected in the vicinity of Muhammad Khel and Boya.

Troops had been out since 6 A.M. and it was necessary to give them a rest, so the return march to Dardoni was ordered to begin at 8 P.M., but by this time the Wazirs having overawed the adherents of Khan Muhammad Khan seized the post at Boya and began to sack it. Consequently the march of the column was interrupted by a treacherous attack as the transport was fording the river.

E 2

Owing to the darkness there was considerable confusion, and several transport camels carrying ammunition broke away. After a short halt to drive off the attackers and to re-organize the transport the column proceeded unmolested, except for occasional shots at the rearguard, and reached Dardoni at 5 A.M. on the 26th May. Here it was discovered that about 150 of the Militia taking advantage of the darkness had deserted during the march.

Withdrawal of garrisons of Spinwam and Shewa.—The problem of evacuating the militia posts of Spinwam (Kaitu River) and Shewa presented great difficulties as these were situated 21 and 29 miles respectively from Idak, the post to which the garrisons were to withdraw. Owing to the absence of water on the route there were no intermediate posts, which might have afforded a sanctuary for the militia if hotly pursued from Spinwam. It had been reported too by the political authorities that the tribesmen of this area were very uneasy regarding the situation in Khost and the Tochi, and that comment was rife on the absence of reinforcements for these outlying garrisons.

Lieutenant Poulton, Northern Waziristan Militia, commanding the posts at Spinwam and Shewa who had been made aware of the intention to evacuate these posts in the event of Afghan regular troops crossing the frontier and being joined by *lashkars* of local tribesmen, was keeping in close touch with the situation. To assist the withdrawal of the garrisons arrangements were made also for three squadrons under the command of Lieutenant-Colonel B. P. Ellwood, 31st Lancers, to move from Khajuri towards the Kaitu in support of the militia when the necessity for their retirement arose.

On the 24th news reached the officer commanding at Spinwam that General Nadir Khan with his force including artillery had left Spinkai Lashti, a village on the Kaitu, had crossed the frontier and was expected at Spinwam on the 25th. Consequently orders were issued that the garrison of Shewa should withdraw on Spinwam and preparations were put in hand for the further retirement to the Tochi.

As was anticipated the invasion by the Afghan forces was the signal for raising the standard of revolt and the tribesmen of the Upper Kaitu flocked to join Nadir Khan or collected to assist his enterprise. The withdrawal of the Shewa garrison was harassed by Wazirs from Datta Khel (Kaitu River) and a Mohmand subedar and 15 of his men were taken prisoners. It was at first thought that these militia men had deserted but the outcome of subsequent enquiries regarding their escape from the Afghan forces before Thal, removed all suspicion regarding their conduct on this occasion.

The retirement from Spinwam was carried out with skill. The small militia force had scarcely crossed to the right bank of the river when it was seen that Afghan regular troops and armed tribesmen were within three hundred yards of the burning post. Supported by the squadrons from Khajuri the militia withdrew across the open Sheratulla plain and by the afternoon of the 25th had reached Idak, and the cavalry had returned to Khajuri. The militia marched the following day to their headquarters at Miranshah.

The timely decision made by the General Officer Commanding the 67th (Bannu) Brigade to evacuate the Upper Tochi posts was more than justified by the subsequent events. Had the withdrawal not taken place when it did, the majority of the garrisons thinking they had been abandoned would have deserted, and the Wazirs having risen and being supported by the Afghans, no troops could have been spared from Dardoni to assist the retirement of the loyal portions of the militia.

Consequent on the evacuation of the Upper Tochi posts and the withdrawal of the moveable column to Dardoni the Upper Tochi Wazirs consisting of the Madda Khel, Manzar Khel, and Khiddar Khel streamed down after the column, carrying with them the Upper Daurs; a large number of Mahsuds also joined the *lashkars* which collected rapidly near Miranshah.

Situation in Miranshah—Attitude of Northern Waziristan Militia.—A most serious situation had now arisen in Miranshah post garrisoned solely by the Northern Waziristan Militia. Letters had been received previously from Afghan officials in Khost calling on the Wazir officers of the militia to desert with their companies, and to take part in the expulsion of the British from Waziristan. The recipients brought these communications to the notice of their British officers, and this action was taken at first as evidence that the local elements of the corps intended to adhere to their allegiance. The incidents of the last few days, however, and the fact that their sections of the tribe were now in open revolt had excited the Wazirs still in the post.

On the 26th, therefore, a detachment of two hundred rifles of the 1/41st Dogras was added to the garrison with the object of steadying the Wazirs and supporting the loyal members of the militia. During the following afternoon, however, instigated by Jemadar Adjutant Tarin, a Tori Khel Wazir, and Subedar Pat, a Madda Khel Wazir, who had frequently distinguished himself in the field and had been awarded the Indian Order of Merit, the Indian Distinguished Service Medal and the Croix-de-Guerre, about six hundred Wazirs of the militia mutinied and openly declared their intention of leaving the post with their rifles and joining the *jihad*. The Khattaks remained staunch, but it was by no means certain what attitude the trans-frontier portions of the corps would adopt. At the request of the Political Agent a further detachment of one hundred Dogras and one gun reinforced the troops in the post.

Owing to the situation of the barrack rooms and the scattered positions held by the loyal Khattaks, the doubtful and much excited Afridis, and the hostile Wazirs, it was quite impossible to isolate the rebels or to adopt any vigorous and concerted measures against them, as any movement inside the post led the Wazirs to indulge in much indiscriminate firing. The Dogras had been disposed in commanding positions along the parapet wall and over the gateways, but under cover of darkness the Wazirs dug holes through the outer walls of the post and made good their escape with their rifles, but suffered casualties in so doing. With the departure of the rebels the situation was much improved and discipline and order soon restored.

Communication with Bannu except by wireless had now been interrupted by the hostile tribesmen and the reported advance of Afghan troops to the frontier above Dardoni pointed to an impending attack on Dardoni itself. The defences were improved, and a covered way protected by wire was constructed from the camp to the water supply some six hundred yards north of the camp.

Attacks on Tochi posts.—The tribal *lashkars*, who had been led to believe that our military weakness would also necessitate the evacuation of Dardoni and Miranshah, maintained their positions on the neighbouring hills awaiting their opportunity to fall on the retiring troops and sack the posts, looting the treasure the latter were believed to contain. The bolder spirits sniped the posts and burnt the deserted *sarai*, but any further enterprises were driven off by the troops with loss.

On the night of 26-27th May all the Lower Tochi posts except Saidgi were attacked and it was further reported that the Militia garrisons of Tal, Surkamar, Isha, Khajuri, and Shinki had deserted with their rifles and ammunition. It is only right to mention that the Khattaks of these garrisons in nearly every case succeeded in reaching either Idak or Saidgi with their equipment.

Such then was the grave situation caused by a policy, which had demanded hurried retrograde movements of our troops, accompanied by the destruction of much valuable stores, without a single shot being exchanged with an Afghan tribesman or regular, thus violating with lamentable results a well-known principle in warfare against an uncivilized enemy.

This was the state of affairs in Northern Waziristan which faced Major-General S. H. Climo, C.B., D.S.O., who had assumed command of the Waziristan Force, with full political powers, on May 27th in relief of Major-General Woodyatt who had been transferred to the command of 4th (Quetta) Division.

Situation in Southern Waziristan—Attitude of Southern Waziristan Militia.—The situation in Southern Waziristan was not a whit less serious. During the first fortnight in May the situation at Wana and in the Gomal had given no cause for alarm. The Southern Waziristan Militia with its headquarters at Wana was holding twelve outposts. The corps consisted of 8 British officers, 37 Pathan officers and about 1,800 rifles, composed as under—

Wazirs	06
Khattaks	230
Yusafzais	350
Bhittannis	90
Afridis	40
Orakzais	780
Gaduns	130
Shiranis	90

About May 21st reports had been received of the movement of Afghan regular troops towards Musa Nika with the object of advancing on Wana. Major G. H. Russell, the Commandant of the Southern Waziristan Militia, was at headquarters, and was in constant communication with the Political Agent, Major C. G. Crosthwaite, O.B.E., who was paying the Mahsuds their allowances at Sarwekai. On May 22nd Major Russell received from the Political Agent the instructions issued by the Hon'ble the Chief Commissioner regarding the policy to be adopted in the event of Afghan regular troops crossing the frontier and being supported by the local tribes. The former began his preparations by despatching officers to certain important outposts to await orders.

The evacuation of the Wana Agency.—On May 25th the report of the evacuation of the Upper Tochi posts arrived at Wana like a bolt from the blue. The Political Agent on learning the news conferred by telegraph with the Commandant and Extra Assistant Commissioner who were both at Wana, and as senior officer in the Agency decided that the evacuation of the Southern Waziristan Militia posts should begin before the situation in the Tochi became generally known and the Mahsuds had time to rise. The evacuation was therefore fixed for 6 P.M. on the 26th May. The withdrawal of these Militia garrisons was an operation of extreme difficulty and danger. It had been arranged previously that the garrisons of the posts west of, and including, Khajuri Kach would withdraw into the Zhob; those of the remainder concentrating on Murtaza.

Captain H. R. Traill with Lieutenants R. E. Hunt and A. R. Barker left Wana at 6 P.M. on May 26th with sixty infantry and ten sowars, and proceeded *via* the Tora Tizha route to Karab Kot. There Captain Traill and Lieutenant Hunt were to evacuate the garrison and move on to Tanai. Lieutenant Barker in the meantime went to Khajuri Kach with the object of withdrawing the garrison to Moghal Kot in the Zhob.

At 7-30 P.M. Major Russell assembled the Pathan officers at Wana and informed them of the orders he had received and of his intention to move at once. The officers, though somewhat surprised, appeared to understand the necessity of the withdrawal and dispersed to make the necessary arrangements for their companies, as transport was sufficient only for the light baggage of the officers, and some treasure.

Everything appeared to be going well when several shots were heard, and it was found that the Wazirs and some Afridis with their officers had seized the Keep, containing the treasure, ammunition (about six hundred thousand rounds), records, etc., and the transport for the same. Efforts were made to quieten the men in the Keep, but without success.

Great disorder now prevailed inside the fort and all that remained of the transport were eight riding camels. As the withdrawal to the Zhob was to consist of forced marches, and there was a probability of the camels being required for the transport of casualties no baggage was taken. Those of the men who remained loyal numbering about three hundred paraded at 9-45 P.M. and shortly afterwards set out on their perilous journey, accompanied by the following officers :—

- Major G. H. Russell . . . ⎫
- Captain C. T. Burn-Murdock . ⎬ Southern Waziristan Militia.
- Lieutenant C. S. Leese . . ⎭
- Major Owen . . . . Medical Officer.
- Lieutenant E. J. MacCorstie . . Garrison Engineer.

A circuitous route towards the Pir Gwazha Pass was taken with the object of proceeding *viâ* Toi Khula post. On reaching the pass the party was re-organised and it was found that there was no Afridi officer present and only four or five sepoys of that class. There were no Wazirs present. The remainder consisted of sepoys and recruits and about one hundred unarmed followers, natives of India.

The column marched all night and at 7 A.M. on 27th May arrived within 1,400 yards of Toi Khula post. Attempts to gain communication with the garrison were greeted by rifle fire from the east followed immediately by several ragged volleys from the post. As it was apparent that the garrison had been evacuated and that the local Wazirs had already seized the post, Major Russell decided to continue the march to Moghal Kot, a distance of fourteen miles.

The day was exceedingly hot, the ascent to the Tesh plain steep, all were worn out after a night march of over twenty miles and no water was procurable *en route*. Progress was consequently very slow, and it was only with the greatest difficulty that the column was kept together. Parties of Wazirs continued unceasingly to harass the rearguard.

The Tesh plain having been reached, the going became easier and it was here that a junction was effected with Captain Traill's party consisting of the loyal elements of the garrisons of Karab Kot, Tanai, and Toi Khula. The tribesmen appearing in considerable numbers became bolder in their attacks, and it was almost impossible to get the piquets into position. Fortunately for the weary column the Zhob Militia from Moghal Kot assisted in piqueting the last two miles of the route. Mughal Kot was reached at nightfall but stragglers continued to come in during the night and a great many did not arrive until the next day. Here Lieutenant Barker with seven sowars, all that remained of the Khajuri Kach party, joined the column.

The situation was reported to the Political Agent in the Zhob, who suggested that the post should be evacuated the following day and the march continued to Mir Ali Khel. This was, however, out of the question as the men were exhausted, footsore, and incapable of marching. The total number of rifles with the column was three hundred, but about one hundred of the men were recruits and at least half of the remainder were trans-frontier men and therefore of doubtful reliability in the crisis which had arisen. During the night of 28th-29th May the tribesmen sniped the crowded post and inflicted several casualties.

On the morning of the 29th the only supplies available in the post were flour for one and half days and gram sufficient for three days' animal rations. During this day heavy sniping wounded eight men and killed the water bullocks. This made it more difficult than ever to obtain water, and several casualties occurred during the attempts made to fetch it.

The evacuation of the post was now imperative and arrangements were made for the withdrawal to begin at 6-30 A.M. on 30th May. One hundred and thirty rifles of the Zhob Militia accompanied by one hundred mounted infantry of the same corps were to leave Mir Ali Khel at

3 A.M. and piquet half way to Moghal Kot. From this point the mounted troops were to push through towards Moghal Kot, where it was estimated they should arrive at 6-30 A.M. On the following day as there was no sign of the mounted infantry at 8-30 A.M. Major Russell ordered the evacuation to begin; heavy enemy fire was opened immediately by the tribesmen. Unfortunately the first piquet to be posted went too far and, failing to return when signalled to do so, moved in the direction of Mir Ali Khel. This movement became infectious and soon numbers of the militia were to be seen fleeing in the direction of Mir Ali Khel, many abandoning their arms *en route*. The officers attempted to stem the route but in no case with success, for when an officer turned away from those he had collected, the men immediately disappeared. After four or five miles had been thus traversed the mounted infantry of the Zhob Militia appeared in sight holding piquets to cover the progress of the column. Efforts were again made to rally and reorganise the Southern Waziristan Militia party in the rear of the Zhob cavalry. These were partly successful but the men were quite out of hand; the Pathan officers and non-commissioned officers no longer had authority, and there were very few men who were at that time in possession of their rifles.

The appearance and action of the Zhob Militia stopped the onrush of the Wazirs who had hitherto been carrying out a vigorous pursuit; and the survivors of the Waziristan Militia made their way to Mir Ali Khel.

The officer casualties during the withdrawal from Moghal Kot were :—

Killed.

Captain C. T. Burn-Hurdock	S. W. Militia.
Captain H. R. Traill	S. W. Militia.
Captain A. F. Reilly	Zhob Militia.
Lieutenant C. S. Leese	S. W. Militia.
Lieutenant E. J. MacCrostie	1-25th London Regiment Garrison Engineer, Wana.

Wounded.

Major G. H. Russell	S. W. Militia.
Lieutenant R. E. Hunt	S. W. Militia.

The above casualties with the exception of Captain Reilly occurred at the beginning of the action and within one mile of Moghal Kot when the officers were attempting to stem the route. The Extra Assistant Commissioner Khan Bahadur Muhammad Yar Khan was also killed. The casualties among the other ranks are not known accurately but are believed to have been about forty killed and wounded. Some of the column made their escape *via* Mani Khwa and the Sherani country, and reached the Derajat some days later.

Regarded merely as a feat of endurance at this period of the year, the withdrawal of this party was, of itself, a fine achievement; but taking into consideration the almost insurmountable difficulties which beset it on the road and the dangers through which it emerged, the exploit stands out as one of the finest recorded in the history of the Indian frontier. The success of the operation was due in large measure to the personality of Major G. H. Russell, 126th Baluchistan Infantry, who conducted the withdrawal with remarkable skill, courage, and endurance, and set a fine example to those under him. The steadfast fortitude of these men in circumstances before which most would have quailed, is a stirring example of the height to which the devotion of the British officer can rise.

The evacuation of the other Southern Waziristan Militia posts was carried out without any further incident except that large numbers of Afridis and all the Wazirs deserted during the night of the withdrawal to Murtaza.

Of the original strength of the Southern Waziristan Militia less than six hundred finally reported themselves at Tank where the corps was reorganised. The number of desertions was estimated as more than 1,100 and among the losses were about 1,190 rifles, 50 muskets and about 700,000 rounds of ·303 ammunition. The Wazirs and Mahsuds busied themselves looting the evacuated posts, and as was anticipated, this had deferred their incursions into British territory.

Situation in the Tochi at the end of May.—To return to the events in the Tochi where the posts at Dardoni, Miranshah, Idak, and Saidgi were in a state of siege.

On May 27th an aeroplane on reconnaissance from Kohat over Spinwam arrived at Dardoni and landed. Although it crashed when taking off the effect of its appearance on the *lashkars* investing Dardoni and Miranshah was considerable, and large numbers of the tribesmen were reported to have returned to their homes.

A local mullah created a mild sensation at this time by claiming to be able to bring to destruction any aeroplane by casting a spell on it.

His boast was short-lived however, as an effective bombing air raid was carried out in the Tochi on June 2nd.

On the 28th May reports, afterwards confirmed, were received that the Afghan force with its attendant *lashkars* at Spinwam had moved from that place towards Thal. The moveable column from Bannu however, remained at Kurram Garhi, as it was possible that there might be a repetition of an Afghan concentration at Spinwam or in the Lower Tochi.

On this date the troops available in Bannu were three squadrons of cavalry, one section of Sappers and Miners, two mountain guns, two battalions of infantry and details from the 2-2nd Gurkha Rifles and 112th Infantry; of these one squadron of cavalry, 2 guns and portions of both infantry battalions were on moveable column duty at Kurram Garhi.

In view of the possibility of an incursion of Mahsuds into British Territory from the Khaisora and Shaktu direction, and the probability of encountering strong opposition in the Shinki defile in an advance into the Tochi valley General Climo decided to postpone any attempt to reopen communication with Dardoni and to relieve Idak which was reported to be closely invested, until the arrival of the Headquarters 43rd Infantry Brigade and one mountain battery and two battalions which were then *en route*. The Militia garrison at Saidgi, however, was reinforced by forty regulars from Bannu.

Attitude of Mahsuds.—In the meantime Jandola post garrisoned by regular troops was being besieged by a large Mahsud *lashkar* headed by Mullah Fazl Din.

Consequent on the evacuation of the Southern Waziristan Militia posts and the considerable quantity of booty which had fallen into the hands of the Wazirs, the Mahsuds had become very restless, and thinking probably that it was the intention to evacuate Jandola had assembled in large numbers around that place. A force under Brigadier-General P. J. Miles, C.B., had begun to assemble at Khirgi on the 29th May when it became known that communication with Jandola was interrupted. Other posts had also been threatened by Mahsud and Sherani *lashkars*, notably Murtaza, Gomal, Manjhi, and Zarkani, and many urgent demands for military assistance for posts held by the Frontier Constabulary were received from the civil authorities.

These problems demanded immediate solution and Major-General Climo decided to deal with the Tochi first, as with the troops at his disposal both operations could not be carried out simultaneously. The garrison of Jandola had nothing to fear so long as water lasted, and the post was not subjected to effective artillery fire.

On the 1st June the Waziristan Force was withdrawn from the command of the General Officer Commanding the North-West Frontier Force and came directly under the orders of the Commander-in-Chief.

Formation of Tochi Relief Column.—The Headquarters of the 43rd Infantry Brigade having arrived in Bannu on the 30th May, the formation of the Tochi Relief Column began.

Reports had been very persistent at Miranshah of an impending advance of Afghan troops by the Upper Tochi and Kanibogh, but these were discounted later by a reliable report that these forces were short of transport and supplies, and were adopting a defensive role.

Their leader however, continued to incite the Wazirs to continue their attacks, and by the 31st May large numbers of tribesmen were reported to have re-assembled in the villages on both banks of the Tochi in the vicinity of Darpa Khel. The General Officer Commanding the 67th (Bannu) Brigade at Dardoni decided to disperse these *lashkars* and to destroy certain villages whose inhabitants were known to have committed offences, and to have participated in attacks on the posts.

The following day the Dardoni Moveable Column with 250 rifles of the Northern Waziristan Militia moved out and fought a very successful action. The enemy was put to flight with a loss of about 90 and the towers from which he had been sniping Miranshah post were destroyed. Our casualties were:—

2nd-Lieutenant P. H. B. Furley, 1/41st Dogras, and two Indian ranks killed, and five Indian ranks wounded.

Tochi posts relieved.—The results of this action had a marked effect not only on our own troops and the Militia, but also on the tribesmen who were now convinced that our forces could and would operate against them, and also that no further evacuation of the Tochi was contemplated. To this fact must be ascribed the almost unmolested march of the Relief Column which left Bannu on the 2nd June on which day Saidgi was reached without incident. The following day the column was able to traverse the Shinki defile without opposition and re-occupy Khajuri, from which place a squadron of the 31st Lancers was sent on ahead. The latter on reaching the vicinity of Idak village sighted parties of hostile Daurs. The cavalry got to close quarters and charged a party of fifty men killing 8 of them with the lance. The remainder got into a *nala* with precipitous banks where the cavalry could not follow but several were seen to fall wounded or killed.

The main body of the column arrived at Idak at noon, but the rear guard did not reach camp until 5-30 P.M. The march was extremely hot and trying to the troops, and there were sixty-four cases of heatstroke or heat exhaustion.

On the 4th June the column opened up communication with the Dardoni force, which was now reinforced by the 1-103rd Mahratta Light Infantry from the Relief Column.

Punitive measures against lower Daurs.—Punitive measures against the lower Daurs were now undertaken by columns operating from Dardoni under the orders of Brigadier-General F. G. Lucas, C.B., D.S.O. These operations, which were carried out in very hot weather, had an excellent political effect but were to some extent limited by the necessity of keeping the troops ready to concentrate rapidly for co-operation with the Kohat-Kurram Force, but the villages of Spalga, Anghar, and Tughri were burnt, and fines were inflicted on others which had not been so deeply implicated in the attacks on Idak and Miranshah.

Had there been any immediate military object in doing so, it would have been possible at this stage to have re-occupied the Upper Tochi posts with little opposition, as the tribes were thoroughly cowed.

Situation in the Derajat.—Meanwhile the situation in the Derajat had not improved. Large *lashkars* of Wazirs and Sheranis were reported to have assembled in the district with the object of attacking posts and villages.

Mahsud raiding parties were operating also in the Murtaza area. One such party consisting of about fifty men was observed on the morning of the 30th May returning to the hills north of Murtaza post. This gang, pursued immediately by a squadron of 27th Light Cavalry under the command of Captain S. Dudley, was overtaken and lost about twenty killed and many more wounded. The remainder sought safety in flight. The losses of the cavalry were two Indian officers killed and four Indian other ranks wounded.

This exploit, full of a fine cavalry spirit, did much to restore the situation in the area, and to calm the excited inhabitants.

A force despatched to the relief of the Gomal police post succeeded in evacuating the garrison, and Draband and Kulachi were occupied by mixed detachments on the night, 1st-2nd June. On the following day a Wazir *lashkar* of about four hundred was driven into the hills with a loss of thirty men, and Manjhi post was reinforced by a column from Tank after some fighting. On the 4th a *lashkar* of five hundred Mahsuds which was threatening Girni post was driven off and the garrison reinforced. Jandola, though the water supply had been cut and the post surrounded by Mahsuds and Bhittannis, had not been seriously assaulted. The garrison had supplies up to the 24th June, and water storage for 15 days from the 20th May. Wholesale desertions had occurred from the Frontier Constabulary at Domandi, Moghal Kot, Drazinda, and Luni. Chaudhwan was attacked on the night, 4-5th June, and partially looted by about two hundred Sheranis.

Relief of Jandola, 9th June.—With the arrival of three Indian infantry battalions from the Tochi, Major-General Climo was enabled to arrange for the relief of Jandola. Consequently a force under the command of Brigadier-General P. J. Miles. C.B., left Khirgi for Jandola on the 9th June. An aerial reconnaissance the previous day had reported the route between Khirgi and Jandola practically deserted and very little movement in the village of

Jandola. The latter fact was due to the Bhittanni inhabitants having learnt of the assembly of a relief column at Khirgi, and fearing punishment for their misdeeds had removed their families and cattle to the hills. Little opposition was anticipated, and, in fact, Jandola was reached without a shot being fired.

The post of Jandola was under the command of Captain R. C. Anderson, 76th Punjabis, and had a garrison of—

British officers	2
Indian officers	4
Indian other ranks	170
Sub-Assistant Surgeon	1
Followers	15

There were also in the post a few members of the Postal Department and two Supply Agents. The garrison was found to be in excellent spirits despite their experiences since the post was cut off on May 28th. The water ration had been limited to two-and-a-half water bottles daily for drinking, cooking and washing. The discomfort and privation entailed by such a limited water-supply at a time of the year when the thermometer stood sometimes at 115° Fahrenheit can well be imagined. To conserve the water-supply all animals were turned out of the post at the beginning of the siege.

A gallant detachment of ten rifles under Havildar Bari Sher, 1-76th Punjabis, in the isolated tower about eight hundred yards from the post, proved itself equal to the occasion and in spite of an uncertain water-supply defended the tower for fourteen days against frequent attacks.

During the siege a havildar of the local Bhittanni Levies succeeded occasionally in eluding the enemy at night and conveying water to the tower in three or four water bottles at a time. For his gallantry this havildar was promoted and was awarded the Indian Distinguished Service Medal.

The post having been re-victualled and the garrison relieved, the column returned to Khirgi without incident on the 11th June.

Afghans in Wana.—About the 9th June reports were received and were subsequently confirmed that, in spite of the terms of the armistice between the Indian and

Afghan governments, an Afghan force of about three hundred men with two six-pounder mountain guns had reached Wana and occupied the deserted post. This detachment appeared to have been given a purely passive role and to have confined its activities mainly to anti-British propaganda among the tribes.

Raid on Drazinda.—On the 11th June, on receipt of reliable information that the village of Drazinda in Sherani country was serving the purpose of a supply depôt for the various Sherani and Wazir gangs in the vicinity, an air raid was carried out against it and a number of bombs dropped. This raid was followed by another carried out by four squadrons of cavalry and a section of mountain artillery with two aeroplanes co-operating. The large village was destroyed and over five hundred head of cattle captured. The effects of these raids was considerable and for a time the activities of the tribesmen showed a marked decrease.

Towards the end of the month active operations except when forced on us ceased on account of the great heat that was prevailing, and of a severe outbreak of cholera, which originating at Kohat spread to Bannu and the Tochi valley and finally to the Derajat. This epidemic accounted for 169 deaths out of a total from all causes up to this date of 319.

Preparations for advance into Khost.—Early in July a small force of all arms was concentrated at Dardoni with the object of co-operating with the Kohat-Kurram Force in an advance into Khost should the peace negotiations then being conducted between the Indian and Afghan governments fall through.

Attack on Bannu aerodrome.—The assembly of this column was interpreted by the tribes as preparatory to an advance into the Upper Tochi, and on the 7th July the Political Agent reported that a large *lashkar* of Wazirs and Mahsuds were taking up a position near Boya. Next day a half-hearted attack was made on the North Waziristan Militia piquets as they moved out from Isha. The militia casualties were four killed, and on the 14th a cleverly organised night attack on the aeroplane shed at Bannu was carried out by a band of about seventy Wazirs and Mahsuds.

The aerodrome, which is situated about five miles out of Bannu on the Tochi road, was guarded by a platoon of 2/27th Punjabis. Reports had been received that such an attack was contemplated and in consequence a barbed wire entanglement surrounding the hangar was in process of construction. At about 1-30 A.M. the tribesmen rushing through a gap in the wire made a determined attempt to break in the doors of the hangar, but were counter-attacked with bayonet and bomb and driven off with loss. No damage was done to the aeroplanes. Our casualties were two Indian other ranks killed and five Indian other ranks wounded.

On the 24th July consequent upon the capture by Wazirs of a convoy at Kapip in Zhob, and subsequent reports that large Wazir *lashkars* were harrying that district, Major-General Climo concentrated at Murtaza a force of one squadron of cavalry, one section of mountain artillery and one and a half battalions of Indian infantry, as well as a large amount of supplies, his intention being to give the impression that preparations were on foot for an advance up the Gomal and thereby to draw the Wazir *lashkars* back to oppose this force. The stratagem was completely successful.

Attacks on road piquets in the Tochi.—Several minor enterprises were carried out by the tribesmen against our road piquets in the Tochi between the 28th July and the middle of August. On the 29th July a Northern Waziristan Militia piquet was ambushed near Khajuri losing three killed and seven wounded and nine rifles; on the 3rd August piquets south of the road between Isha and Miranshah were engaged all day with tribal *lashkars* and suffered some casualties; on the 8th August a detachment of the 82nd Punjabis moving out to piquet the road between Saidgi and Shinki was cleverly ambushed by about two hundred Abdullai Mahsuds under their well-known leader Musa Khan, and suffered heavily losing one Indian officer and nineteen Indian other ranks killed and four other ranks wounded. The enemy's casualties were estimated at about twenty including a prisoner who died of his wounds.

The situation in the Tochi was unchanged, and on the morning of the 23rd the piqueting troops from Saidgi were attacked by about two hundred and fifty Wazirs who finding their line of retreat threatened withdrew with their casualties estimated at thirty-five killed and wounded. Armoured cars from Bannu co-operated in this action with considerable effect.

These incidents and notably the last-mentioned can be attributed to a lack of experience in observing the principles of frontier warfare, and a failure to recognize the necessity for careful scouting and scrutiny of the ground to be traversed and for constant vigilance when dealing with enemies like the Mahsuds and Wazirs, who are experts in the art of ambuscade.

During this period Mahsud and Wazir gangs, varying in strength from seventy to two hundred showed increased activity in the Derajat and troops were constantly on the move endeavouring to intercept them. Several of these bands were encountered but they invariably retired to the hills as soon as they observed any sign of converging movement against them.

The climatic conditions were bad and although the cholera epidemic had been stamped out, the troops were subjected to a great strain owing to the daily piqueting of routes for the passage of convoys, and to minor operations during the intense heat. A noticeable and reassuring consequence of the keenness and good moral of the troops was the vigorous co-operation of the police and village pursuit parties during this period.

Raids by Mahsuds in August.—About the middle of August Mahsud raiding gangs became especially active and Tank City was attacked on the nights of the 14th and 15th. On the first occasion the raiders succeeded in carrying off cloth and other articles valued at Rs. 15,000 but on the following night the thieves were driven off with a loss of six killed, several wounded, and one man taken prisoner.

By employing the ancient ruse of demonstrating at one side of the post to induce the garrison to concentrate there while another party dug a hole through the opposite wall, a gang of about fifty Mahsuds effected an entrance into Girni post during the night of the 27th. The Mahsuds were finally ejected at a cost to the garrison of two killed and four wounded and two rifles. This incident was followed by an outrage typical of the wanton cruelty so frequently displayed by Mahsuds.

A gang consisting principally of Shaman Khel Mahsuds returning from a raid at Isa Khel in the Mianwali district where it had secured sixteen rifles from the local police attacked a Labour Corps camp near Gambila on the night of the 29th August. Of the Labour Corps fifteen were killed and fourteen wounded, but on the arrival of troops and police the raiders retired towards the border. During the running fight that ensued fresh parties of Frontier Constabulary took up the pursuit and the Mahsuds finally reached their hills having lost 15 killed, several wounded, and two prisoners.

From reports subsequently received it was estimated that at least thirty Mahsuds died of thirst, heat exhaustion, or wounds.

The first half of September was marked by a comparative freedom from raids, and on the whole that month was considerably quieter than the previous one. Climatic conditions began to show improvement though the heat by day was still severe.

Action at Zarkani, 19th September.—The chief event of the month was an action which occurred near Zarkani on the 19th. On receipt of a report that a party two hundred strong, consisting of Mahsuds, Zalli Khel Wazirs, some militia deserters, and a few Sheranis had collected near the Sheikh Haidar pass Major W. G. W. Durham, 27th Light Cavalry, with one squadron and a Stokes mortar left Draband and arrived at Zarkani at dawn. Major Durham accompanied by ten sowars and twenty rifles of the Southern Waziristan Militia proceeded to reconnoitre the approach to the Sheikh Haidar pass. While traversing some broken country covered closely with tamarisk bushes the party was attacked. Major Durham was killed, some of the militia captured, and the cavalry detachment fell back. Part of the troops at Zarkani advanced to the scene of the occurrence and gained touch with the enemy but in the face of superior numbers were compelled to retire to Zarkani with slight loss. Our casualties in this action were one British officer, one Indian officer, and four Indian other ranks killed and five wounded. Nine rifles and a Hotchkiss gun were also lost.

Actions near Manjhi, October 1919.—During October the tribesmen showed a tendency to collect in large numbers and on four separate occasions actions of more than minor importance were fought.

The beginning of the month was marked by serious reverses to our arms. On the 5th three troops of the Bhopal Imperial Service Lancers and a platoon 1/150th Infantry under Captain C. E. Broughton started from Manjhi post at 8-20 A.M. as an escort to a telephone construction party. On arriving some 5 or 6 miles from Manjhi the telephone wire was repaired and the post informed that the party would begin its withdrawal at 2-30 P.M. An hour later the Manjhi post commander heard heavy firing, and at 4-45 P.M. a survivor reached the post and reported that Captain Broughton had been killed and his party exterminated. The actual facts of what occurred are difficult to obtain, but what appears to have happened is that when about four miles from Manjhi the party was attacked suddenly in difficult country covered with high standing grass, by about two hundred tribesmen some of whom opened fire at a range of twenty yards. Captain Broughton was killed immediately and the enemy charging overwhelmed the remainder of the party, causing casualties numbering twenty-eight killed and ten wounded. During the night some stragglers made their way to Manjhi post.

On the following day a force of one squadron of the Bhopal Imperial Service Lancers and two companies of infantry under the command of Major J. M. L. Bostock, Special Service Officer with the Lancers, left Kaur Bridge to bring in the wounded and dead of the previous day's action. Manjhi was reached at 12-45 P.M., and at 1-30 P.M. when preparing to continue the advance to the scene of the fight of the 5th the troops were fired on by some tribesmen who, however, quickly disappeared.

The column proceeded without further investigation and with an inadequate flank guard. At 3-50 P.M. while moving across country much broken and intersected by *nalas* containing clumps of high standing grass the rearguard was suddenly attacked and the rear platoon of the 109th Infantry taking up a position on a sand dune was overpowered and annihilated. The supporting platoon also suffered heavy casualties, and was reinforced by a platoon of the 3rd Guides. Meanwhile the cavalry was ordered to cover the withdrawal of the remainder of the company of the Guides which had been instructed to push on into more open country. Unfortunately the cavalry failed to perform its mission and left the infantry isolated. The tribesmen numbering about three hundred now closed in. Sharp fighting ensued in which Captain Ferguson commanding the company of the Guides was killed, but in spite of many gallant stands the infantry was forced to withdraw, each man fighting for his life, until the open country was reached.*

The reverses suffered on these days are attributable to a great extent to the inexperience of the officers in command and the consequent relaxation of precautions while there was even a remote possibility of encountering the enemy. The protective detachments too failed to perform their duties efficiently.

Air raid on Wana plain.—As a reprisal for the attacks of the 5th and 6th the 52nd Wing, now 1st (Indian) Wing, Royal Air Force, carried out on the 9th a bombing raid with sixteen aeroplanes on villages near Wana to which the *lashkars* belonged.

As the small villages on the Wana plain do not offer favourable targets, the moral effect of the air raid was considerably greater than the material, while the fact that the aeroplanes used incendiary bombs created a considerable sensation among the tribesmen.

Emboldened by their successes, a further large *lashkar* collected in the vicinity of Murtaza post on the 17th and cut the water channel which provides the water-supply of that place, Jatta, and Kaur Bridge. This necessitated the dispersal of part of the moveable column of the Line of Communication Defences which was then assembling at the last-named place.

After suffering at least twenty casualties at the hands of the garrison of Murtaza Post which itself suffered none, this gang moved to the vicinity of Girni on the night of the 20th October.

Attacks on convoys near Girni and Khajuri, 21st October.—On the following day a column of three companies

---

*In this action we lost three officers, Captains Ferguson, Guides and Mottram, 109th Infantry, and Lieutenant Bhagavan, I.M.S., and eighty Indian other ranks.

with a section of mountain artillery proceeded to Girni from Manzai to withdraw one hundred men of the Labour Corps from the post. On the column beginning its retirement about two hundred and fifty tribesmen left the hills and pressed closely on the column. A well-timed counter-attack put the enemy completely to rout and they fled to the hills with a loss of about seventy casualties. Our losses on this occasion were six Indian other ranks killed and sixteen wounded. As a result of this action the *lashkar* withdrew from Girni and dispersed.

On the same day a convoy was attacked near Khajuri by a body of about three hundred Wazirs who had also piqueted Shinki in such a way as to prevent the garrison of that post from rendering any assistance. The situation was undoubtedly critical until the arrival by motor vans of reinforcements of the 43rd Brigade from Idak, when our superiority was established and the convoy proceeded.*

The conclusion of the peace negotiations with Afghanistan on the 8th August did not affect the situation in Waziristan. In fact, at this time the hostility of the Wazirs and Mahsuds towards us was increased by a widespread belief that the British Government had agreed to transfer Waziristan to the Amir six months after the peace had been signed.

The tribesmen who had depended on General Nadir Khan's oft-repeated promises that the peace terms would include a general amnesty for those tribes that had supported the Afghan arms, now called on that official to redeem his pledge, or at least to occupy parts of Waziristan with detachments similar to that at Wana.

Maliks visit Kabul.—Consequently at the beginning of October General Nadir Khan summoned the leading Wazirs and Mahsuds to Matun, where the more important headmen were selected to accompany him to Kabul to be presented to the Amir.

On their arrival at the capital the *maliks* were received by the Amir in person with every mark of honour and

---

* Our casualties in this action were (a) Captain Andrews, I.M.S., and two Indian other ranks killed and one British officer, one British other rank, 10 Indian other ranks and six followers wounded.

The enemy losses were estimated at about fifty.

(a) Captain Andrews was awarded a posthumous Victoria Cross for exceptional gallantry and devotion to duty in attending wounded under heavy fire in an exposed position until he himself was killed.

conducted to a *sarai* which had been reserved especially for their use.

Later at a durbar the Amir announced that peace had been concluded with the British and thanked the *maliks* for their services in his cause and that of Islam. He flattered the Wazirs on their success in driving the militias from Wana, the Gomal, and from the Upper Tochi. He also twitted the Mahsuds on their failure to make the most of their opportunities. Subsequently the Amir issued rewards and presented medals to the *maliks*. The latter were similar to those issued to his own troops for the recent operations against the British. Of the officers who had deserted from the militias each received a special award of Rs. 300 and the sepoys Rs. 100. He concluded his speech by advising the tribesmen to come to an agreement with the British. Subsequently the *maliks* were interviewed by General Nadir Khan and other officials, and the *maliks* returned to Waziristan at the beginning of November, convinced that hostilities between the Amir and the British would soon be resumed.

The tribesmen though deprived of their main hope of assistance still maintained their contumacious attitude and continued committing outrages.

Summary of offences by Wazirs and Mahsuds, May to November 1919.—A brief summary of offences committed by the Mahsuds and Wazirs from the beginning of the third Afghan War to the beginning of November 1919 is given below, many of which are described in detail in this and the preceding chapters.

Tochi Wazirs.—Fifty raids and offences of various natures, resulting in our losing approximately thirty-five killed, sixty wounded and five missing, and in the carrying off of an enormous amount of loot in the way of cattle, stores, and money.

Mahsuds.—Over a hundred raids and offences of various natures, in which we lost approximately one hundred and thirty-five killed, one hundred and ten wounded, and thirty-eight missing. Some four hundred and forty-eight camels, one thousand six hundred and seventy-four cattle and property valued at about Rs. 35,000 were looted.

Wana Wazirs.—Thirty-two raids and offences of various natures, resulting in our losing fifty-five killed, one hundred and six wounded, and eighty-three missing. A very large amount of property was looted including a number of camels and cattle.

The casualties sustained by the Waziristan Force during the period from the conclusion of the Afghan War to 2nd November 1919 were—

Killed	139
Wounded	159

The proportion of killed to wounded is very remarkable and is attributable to the close fighting and to the possession by the tribesmen of high-velocity rifles.

Necessity for punitive operations.—The recapitulation of this list of wanton outrages emphasises the conclusion that punitive measures could not be avoided.

The defection of the Mahsuds and Wazirs was not due to any particular grievance; they were merely acting under the stimulus of a feeling, deeply rooted in the psychology of the borderland, that every true Muhammadan must rise and fight for Islam whenever there is an opportunity of striking a blow at the unbeliever, and this feeling was turned to full account by Afghan adventurers in Waziristan. It must be remembered that these tribesmen are fanatical in the extreme, and easily excited to hostility against us at the mere whim of their religious leaders.

The defection of the tribal Militias had also had a disturbing effect on the tribesmen. It led to some two thousand six hundred modern rifles and at least eight hundred thousand rounds of ammunition falling into their hands, and this measure of success tended greatly to embolden them.

Factors governing policy to be adopted.—The question of our attitude towards Waziristan and of the punishment to be meted out to the tribesmen had now to be taken up. There seemed to be two courses open, which may be conveniently described as the maximum and the minimum policy. The former was to take over and administer the whole country up to the Durand Line, and to crush and disarm the tribesmen. This drastic measure, which of course, involved the complete and permanent occupation of Waziristan, was that generally favoured by the Government of India, but it presented certain serious difficulties.

From a military point of view, the troops were everywhere in need of leave which had been denied them for five years; demobilisation of British troops was in rapid progress, units were being relieved by young troops from England who were not acclimatised; the Indian Army was furnishing large garrisons overseas as well as troops for internal security in India, with the result that many units with frontier experience were not available and lastly preparations had to be made to meet the possibility of further operations against Afghanistan. From a financial point of view the adoption of the maximum policy of total occupation would involve large additional expenditure.

In spite of these obvious drawbacks the political effects of inaction on our part had to be borne in mind, coupled with the fact that Afghan adventurers were still intriguing among the tribesmen and sparing no effort to misrepresent our intentions and lower our prestige. Moreover, the measure of success which the tribesmen had secured tended to embolden them, and compelled us to win security for our harassed border population and convince the whole frontier of our strength. After such flagrant offences immunity of the tribesmen would make our position very difficult, particularly, in the event of further trouble with Afghanistan.

Policy decided on.—In the light of recent events it seemed possible that the Government would be forced shortly to re-examine the whole basis of its policy towards Waziristan, and to consider whether in the long run permanent occupation and administration of the country up to the Durand Line would not be advisable. But as this would necessitate much discussion and extended operations, it was decided to adopt the minimum policy and to summon and communicate the following terms to the Wazirs and Mahsuds.

Terms to Wazirs and Mahsuds.—*First.*—There was no foundation for the report of the Amir having secured an amnesty for the tribesmen, and that there was no question of their country being made over to the Amir.

Second.—Such reparation and compensation as might be fixed for damage done would be demanded.

Third.—The tribesmen were to be informed of our intention to make roads and locate troops in any part of the so-called "protected areas" which we might consider necessary.

Regarding the third term the proposal was to locate mixed brigades in Northern and Southern Waziristan, respectively, probably in Miranshah and Sarwekai, and to undertake if finances permitted the construction of the following roads for mechanical transport :—

(1) Thal to Idak,
(2) Khirgi to Sarwekai,
(3) Sarwekai to Tanai and Khajuri Kach,
(4) Murtaza to Khajuri Kach,

with extensions in the early future to link Tanai with Wana and Khajuri Kach with the Zhob.

Measures taken on sanction of punitive operations.— Punitive operations against the tribesmen in Waziristan having been sanctioned, the following measures were taken :—

(a) *Tochi Wazirs.*—A *jirga* was summoned to be held at Miranshah on the 9th November to hear Government's terms. The troops would advance to Datta Khel and the tribe's reply be received there on 17th November. Should the terms be refused, intensive aerial bombardment and punitive measures by troops would take place to enforce acceptance of our terms.

(b) *Mahsuds.*—A *jirga* was summoned to attend at Khirgi on 3rd November, when our terms would be announced, and the Mahsuds' reply was to be given by the 11th November. If the answer was unfavourable the whole of Mahsud country would be subjected to intensive aerial bombardment followed by punitive measures by land.

(c) *Wana Wazirs.*—Terms were to be announced as it was thought that, in case of an unfavourable reply being received, a lengthy period should not intervene before condign punishment could be meted out.

The terms announced at the Durbars held at Miranshah and Khirgi will be found in Appendix " E."

In the event of the terms not being accepted the plan was first to deal with the Tochi Wazirs and then with the Mahsuds.

CHAPTER VII.

Operations of the Tochi Column.

The operations of the Waziristan Force from 3rd November 1919 fall under two heads,—namely, the advance to Datta Khel in the Tochi Wazir country, and the operations of the Derajat Column against the Mahsuds.

Distribution of troops, November 1919.—In the advance, two infantry brigades, the 43rd Brigade under Brigadier-General Gwyn-Thomas, C.M.G., D.S.O., and the 67th Brigade under Brigadier-General Lucas, C.B., D.S.O., with attached troops were under the command of Major-General A. Skeen, C.M.G., and formed the striking force, which was designated the Tochi Column. See Appendix " F."

The remainder of the Waziristan Force was employed in guarding the Lines of Communication. Railheads were at Bannu in the north and Darya Khan and Tank in the south. From Darya Khan supplies and stores were taken across the Indus to Dera Ismail Khan and thence by Decauville railway to Tank. The value of this line which was laid along the side of the main road was again clearly demonstrated. Besides removing wear and tear of the road by transport carts, its carrying capacity was 200 tons of stores daily, or the equivalent of one thousand camel loads.

The Force was not only responsible for the defence of communications west of the Bannu and Tank, but also for the whole area between these places and the Indus as far as Kalabagh on the north, some sixty miles east of Bannu, and the borders of the Dera Ghazi Khan district on the south. This necessitated the protection of about 350 miles of communications.

As regards the 52nd Wing, now 1st (Indian) Wing, Royal Air Force the total machines available were:—At Mianwali east of the Indus, a detachment of 3 D. H. 10's and a flight of 9 D. H. 9A's and at Bannu and Tank a squadron of 18 Bristol Fighters.

Concentration of Tochi Column, 8th November.—The Tochi Column was concentrated at Miranshah by the 8th November, with a strength of—

Officers and other ranks	8,444
Followers	6,464
Horses and equipment animals	1,382

The transport consisted of 2,288 mules and 5,087 camels. Tents were carried.

Advance to Datta Khel, 12th November.—On the 12th November the Column began the advance to Datta Khel in three echelons.

The first echelon, which comprised the bulk of the force, formed the main column. The second echelon composed of two battalions, including Pioneers, a field company Sappers and Miners, and an armoured motor battery, was formed for the purpose of improving the unmetalled road during the advance for the use of Ford van convoys. The third echelon, which consisted of an infantry brigade with attached troops, was detailed to guard the road and expedite the collection of supplies at Datta Khel.

The advance encountered no opposition. On the 14th November the first echelon reached Datta Khel, the second Degan and third Boya. Permanent piquets for the protection of the road between Miranshah and Datta Khel were established without incident. A ten days' reserve of supplies, ammunition, and stores for the whole column was moved from Dardoni to Datta Khel, in readiness to carry out punitive operations if our terms were refused.

In the meantime notices had been dropped from aeroplanes in Tochi Wazir country warning all the tribesmen that non-acceptance of our terms would be followed by immediate air operations. They were also warned that if they declined to accept our terms, their women and children should be moved to places of safety.

Tochi Wazirs accept our terms, 17th November.—Major-General Climo reached Datta Khel on the 17th November, and met the *jirga* on the same day. The *jirga* which was fully representative except for the Madda Khel and two minor sub-tribes in the Kaitu valley accepted our terms. The Kazha Madda Khel inhabit a valley north-west of Datta Khel, and as these in a false sense of their security had not submitted by the 18th they were bombed the next day by seventeen aeroplanes. This had the desired result. All their representatives made complete submission the same evening.

The two minor sub-tribes—the Titti Madda Khel and the Hassan Khel—live in the Kaitu valley 20 miles north-east of Miranshah.

They were not dealt with until the middle of December when they were effectively bombed from the air, and in consequence made a verbal submission.

Mahsuds reject terms, 11th November.—In view of the decision not to re-occupy the Upper Tochi posts it had been proposed in event of the tribesmen accepting our terms that the column should make a march by way of a demonstration through the Madda Khel country which had not been visited by regular troops since 1897. Besides teaching the Wazirs that their country was not inaccessible it was anticipated that the young and inexperienced troops of which the column was composed would gain valuable training in mountain warfare and be well fitted to encounter the Mahsuds whose *jirga* on the 11th November had assembled at Khirgi and rejected our terms *in toto*.

Withdrawal of Tochi Column to Dardoni, 26th November.—The political authorities, however, deprecated the march as likely to excite the tribesmen to acts of hostility, and to delay the fulfilment of our terms. It was also urged that the recalcitrant Mahsuds should be dealt with as soon as possible in order that the operations against the Wana Wazirs should not be delayed until the late spring. Orders were therefore issued for the withdrawal of the column to Dardoni. This was carried out in echelons similar to those formed for the advance, and the whole column was back at Dardoni by the evening of the 26th November.

Troops transferred to Derajat and Derajat Column formed.—On the morning of the 27th November the Tochi Column was broken up and re-named the Derajat Column on the same date and began its march from Dardoni to the Derajat *viâ* Bannu and thence by road *viâ* Pezu to Tank. The march of 140 miles was carried out in nine groups each of approximately two battalions with additional transport. The concentration of the Derajat Column on the line Tank-Jandola was completed by the 13th December, its composition and location on that date being as shown in Appendix " G."

CHAPTER VIII.

OPERATIONS OF THE DERAJAT COLUMN—FIRST PHASE.

Factors governing choice of Takki Zam route.— Although Kaniguram is only thirty miles in a direct line south of Datta Khel, there were several reasons against undertaking an advance into Mahsud country from that direction. It would have entailed the crossing of the Razmak Narai—fifteen miles south-east of Datta Khel—which in winter is a snow-covered pass, some 7,000 feet above sea-level,—and the construction of a camel road over difficult country. Besides, there were no suitable intermediate camping grounds for a force of the size of the striking column, and there was a great scarcity of water. It would also have entailed the protection of about 95 miles of Lines of Communication from the railhead at Bannu. Further, it was hoped that the concentration of our striking force in the vicinity of Jandola following on very intensive air operations, would cause the Mahsuds to accept our terms and so make an advance into the heart of their country unnecessary and admit of the operations against the Wana Wazirs beginning forthwith.

The methods adopted in 1901-02 of employing small converging columns moving on bivouac scale had to be rejected for several reasons, the chief of which was the possession by the tribesmen of large numbers of high velocity rifles thus endangering the safety of a small column temporarily isolated, also the vast amount of transport for the carriage of the winter scale of baggage and the impedimenta which public opinion now demands shall accompany our unseasoned troops in the field. Owing to the conditions which obtained on other parts of the frontier, the available transport was just sufficient for the needs of the Derajat Column and the Lines of Communication beyond railhead.

An advance on a single line is economical from every standpoint, since one line of communication demands fewer defence troops, a smaller number of administrative establishments, and consequently a lessened demand on transport and supplies.

From the point of view of operations the single line fully justified its adoption, and produced the situations and opportunities it was intended to bring about.

Namely, it left the tribesmen in no doubt as to which line to defend and consequently they were encouraged to collect in the greatest available strength and to stand their ground more stoutly than they would have done had they been looking over their shoulder anxious as to how the defenders of other approaches into their country were faring: the latter is the effect produced by converging columns and generally results in manœuvring the tribesmen out of their positions without inflicting punishment

The casualties sustained by the Mahsuds and Wazirs (when the latter joined the former in the field) have never been approached in any previous campaign, and never before have the dead of any tribe been left on the ground in such numbers; it is justifiable therefore to assume that a single line of advance by encouraging a vast display of tribal force and inducing a sense of security from other points, enables our forces to bring the tribesmen to battle and to inflict casualties which in every action of importance were considerably heavier than our own.

Rinderpest and foot-and-mouth disease greatly reduced the amount of transport and it was only the arrival of six Ford Van Companies and the construction of the Decauville railway from Dera Ismail Khan to Tank which enabled the Lines of Communication to keep the Force in advance of Tank fully supplied with all requirements.

Measures adopted to secure L. of C. west of Khirgi.— In order that the narrative of subsequent operations may be understood it is necessary to explain shortly the measures which were adopted to secure the Lines of Communication west of Khirgi.

Under normal conditions, to maintain a column of the size of the striking force, daily convoys of pack animals had to be despatched along the Lines of Communication, and their protection was rendered more difficult owing to the abundance of modern rifles in the hands of the tribesmen. The large number of troops required to ensure adequate protection by means of escorts prohibited their use. A system was therefore introduced of establishing permanent piquets at fairly close intervals on the most commanding ground on each side of the route used. These sangared posts were strongly built for all round defence, provided with traverses and protected with thick barbed wire entanglements. Their construction led to the majority of the actions which took place during these operations. The full strength of the Derajat Column had on occasions, to be employed to drive the enemy off the ground selected for the various piquets and then to cover and support the working parties whilst the defensive works were being constructed. Several days were often required to make the locality selected thoroughly strong against attack and, until its defences were completed, all the troops had to withdraw to camp each afternoon.

As convoys sometimes amounted to over 4,000 pack animals, it was necessary to improve and provide several tracks in the river bed along which the advance was to take place, in order that the animals could march on a broad front. Otherwise, they had to move in single file, which so increased the length of the column, that it would have made the completion of a stage during daylight impossible.

Preliminary preparations for advance over Spinkai Raghza, 11th-13th December.—For this reason, on the 11th December, to prepare for the advance, a force of two battalions and one section of mountain guns made good the Spinkai Raghza, 1½ miles north of Jandola camp and work on the road and of its defence was begun. During the day the enemy snipers were busy and when the troops withdrew on the same afternoon the rearguard became actively engaged with bodies of tribesmen estimated at one hundred. These advanced down the deep *nalas* which intersected the Spinkai Raghza and attacked fiercely any small parties crossing these depressions.

Our casualties during the day were Second-Lieutenant Douglas of the 3rd Guides, one Indian officer, and two Indian other ranks killed, and one Indian officer and eighteen Indian other ranks wounded. The enemy casualties are not known but were probably not heavy. On the 12th and 13th December the work was continued. During these three days we sustained 46 casualties, chiefly from enemy snipers.

Air operations.—During the past month all available aeroplanes had been carrying out a programme of intensive air activity including night raids, against the Mahsud villages until it was ascertained that these had been vacated. Damage was done to material and personnel, and throughout the country the greater proportion of the inhabitants left their homes and took to caves and to the hills. To enable the harassing of the tribesmen to be methodically carried out the Mahsud country was divided into three sub-areas, each of which was allotted to one squadron, at least one machine being over each area all day. This proved effective, and much damage was done to flocks and personnel.

An interesting outcome of this programme was that cattle and sheep were distributed in small herds to minimise targets. This entailed a large increase in shepherds and watchers, hindering the assembly of any *lashkar* or large raiding parties.

Between the 25th-29th November three more Bristol Fighter aeroplanes were lent to the Force and a specially intensive programme of aerial bombardment was made, a daily average of over 10,000 lbs. of bombs was dropped but in spite of these endeavours at no time did it appear possible that the Mahsuds would submit from the effect of air operations alone.

As the employment of aeroplanes on the frontier had not been carried out on a large scale prior to these operations, the experiences gained are of much interest. It is not intended to go fully into the technical side of the question here; let it suffice to record the fact that aeroplanes had dealt successfully with the recalcitrant tribes in the Tochi, and that although considerable moral effect and a certain amount of damage to personnel and property had been obtained against the Mahsuds it had not been sufficient to bring them to terms, and it was therefore necessary for the land forces to take the field to bring them to submission.

A noticeable feature of the air operations was the readiness of the inhabitants sheltering in the vicinity to re-enter their villages after a raid. This applied to the smaller villages as the bigger ones having received so many visitations were practically deserted. A possible solution for this is the provision of bombs with delay action fuzes of various lengths.

Judging from the results seen later at Kaniguram and Marobi which were frequently bombed, it would appear that the heaviest bombs only are effective against these frontier villages, and that the effect is not really worth the explosive used. Even the damage done by the biggest bombs is very little as the mud roofs and walls localize explosions to a great extent. Some form of incendiary bomb would therefore probably be more effective than those employed during these operations which have done little harm except to dry fodder and similar inflammable materials. The total weight of bombs dropped on Kaniguram, a perfect target for aerial bombardment, was about 16 tons, which was out of all proportion to the material damage done.

The ability to fly at low altitudes depends greatly on the employment of sufficient machines, the dispersion of targets and consequently of fire. The rate of flight of low flying machines at close quarters and the feeling of danger induced by the noise they make militate against accurate fire on the part of the tribesmen. These points were exemplified in a marked degree during the air raids in the Kazha valley on 19th November 1919 where our machines were handled with a singular boldness and escaped unscathed.

Equipment of Derajat Column.—Before beginning the narrative of the operations against the Mahsuds, a few points regarding the equipment of the Derajat Column will be of interest.

The Column marched on winter scale with tents and in addition were carried :—

    one extra blanket per man,

    one extra pair boots,

    one extra pair socks,

    two sandbags on the man.

Each battalion was supplied with sixteen Lewis guns and sixteen rifle grenade discharge cups.

A large amount of barbed wire, stakes, and explosives accompanied the Column, also of ammunition and supplies.

The Striking Column normally consisted of :—

    two mountain batteries,

    one company Sappers and Miners,

    one Signal company,

> one battalion of Pioneers,
> six battalions Infantry,

accompanied by

> one Indian Field Ambulance,
> one combined Field Ambulance,
> one Bearer Unit,

with a supply column carrying four days' supplies.

Although camels carried six maunds each, the transport for the striking force alone aggregated 2,800 camels and 1,400 mules.

Strength and armament of opposing forces.—At the beginning of December it was estimated that the enemy forces available to oppose the Derajat Column were:—

	Fighting men.	Modern rifles.
Mahsuds (including Urmars of Kaniguram)	16,000	8,000
Wana Wazirs	7,000	3,000

but that no *lashkar* of more than 3,500 tribesmen was likely to take the field, owing to difficulties of obtaining supplies locally.

At no time in their history had the Mahsuds and Wazirs been so well armed as at this juncture, since in addition to their normal armament considerable quantities of government rifles and ammunition had fallen recently into their hands. To supplement their stocks the tribesmen had received large supplies of ammunition through the agency of anti-British officials in Khost. These tribesmen have long been remarkable for their courage, activity, and hardihood, and when the mountainous and difficult nature of their country is considered, together with the fact that their numbers included about 1,800 deserters and others highly trained in our tactics and methods of fighting, it will be realized that they constituted a formidable enemy.

It is interesting to note that although the Mahsuds and Wazirs were in possession of large numbers (approximately 10,000) of Martini and other large bore breech loading rifles, their use was forbidden in the field except at night; General Skeen, who was present in every engagement in the Takki Zam, states he saw only two black powder discharges by day during the four months campaign. The number of small bore rifles owned by the Mahsuds did not exceed 3,500, and this, together with supply difficulties, made this number (*viz.*, 3,500) the usual strength of the *lashkar* opposed to us. Large contingents armed otherwise were usually in close attendance to replace casualties and bring up food and water. It is estimated that not less than 8,000 Mahsuds and Wazirs collected in the neighbourhood of Marobi on the 7th February 1920 to dispute our advance on that village. This was the largest number assembled by them up to date and was encouraged by the presence of Shah Daula's guns. High hopes were built on the results these guns were to achieve. Their abject failure accounts for the melting away of the tribesmen and the feeble resistance made to our advance.

The moral of the Mahsuds at this time stood at a high level. This was due to the failure of aircraft to force their submission, to their successes in several encounters with our troops during the summer, to their still fervent hope that the Amir would compel Government to discontinue punitive measures, and to the belief that, as in the past they would succeed in gaining a reduction if not an abrogation of Government's terms by adopting a threatening attitude. Added to this was their belief that the Great War had reduced our army so greatly both in numbers and training that the Mahsuds could defeat any force which we could bring against them.

The Wana Wazirs, who had not yet received the terms that Government intended to impose, were hand in glove with the Mahsuds and ready to assist them in opposing our advance. The Tochi Wazirs had accepted our terms, but were unable to prevent the hot-heads of their sections, of whom there were a considerable number, from joining the Mahsuds.

Headquarters of Derajat Column moves to Jandola.— On the 17th December the Headquarters of the Derajat Column with the 67th Brigade and attached troops marched without incident from Khirgi to Jandola along the bed of the Tank Zam which had been secured by the establishment of seven permanent piquets.

On the same day, as several representatives of the tribesmen professed to be desirous of submitting, Major-General Skeen interviewed them and ascertained that their only object appeared to be to secure immunity for their own property. While these men were still in camp, numbers of Mahsuds were observed on the northern portion of the Spinkai Raghza, and on the Sarkai ridge whence they were moving eastward. At this time the construction of the camp protection piquets on the left bank of the Tank Zam opposite Jandola post was being pushed on as rapidly as possible.

Attack on piquets at Jandola, 17th December.—Suddenly at 3-30 P.M. a determined attack was made on these piquets and their covering parties. The easternmost piquet was overwhelmed, after the covering party had been driven in. Although the attack was made in the face of the close fire of mountain and machine guns from the vicinity of the post and of the fire of the covering troops, it was pressed home with the utmost gallantry, the leaders shouting and waving their swords high in the air, and dashing in among the troops. After some hand-to-hand fighting the Mahsuds withdrew with a loss of eight killed and twelve wounded.*

There can be little doubt that this incident was due to the ignorance of the troops of the psychology of Pathans and to the false sense of security into which they had been lulled by the presence in camp of Mahsuds ostensibly sueing for peace, and for a similar reason the significance of the Mahsuds' movement across the Spinkai Raghza to gain a covered line of approach for their attack was not appreciated at its correct value.

Information was received on the night of the 17th December and confirmed the following morning, that a Mahsud *lashkar* about 2,000 strong was at Mandanna Kach and that about 1,000 Wana Wazirs were in the Shahur on their way to join in opposing the advance of the Derajat Column.

The presence of these tribal gatherings in strength so near Jandola both on the Shahur and the Tank Zam gave some hope that a decision might be forced at our very doors, if the tribesmen stood their ground.

At the time the Mahsuds were under the impression that we only required the Shahur for the passage of troops to Sarwekai and Wana, and to this reason was ascribed

---

* Our casualties were thirty-four killed and wounded.

the assembly of the *lashkars* at Do Tak at the junction of the Shahur with the Tank Zam.

Advance to Palosina, 18th December.—Major-General Skeen decided to advance across the Spinkai Raghza, but detailed the 68th Brigade (less 1½ battalions) with two sections of guns, under Brigadier-General J. L. R. Gordon, C.B., to make good the river route to Do Tak in case it should be required by the transport. This was accomplished without difficulty and the brigade returned to Jandola that afternoon.

The main column which consisted of—
Column headquarters,
1 squadron (less 1 troop) 21st Cavalry,
No. 6 British and No. 27 Indian Mountain Batteries,
55th Field Company Sappers and Miners,
67th Infantry Brigade,
2/19th Punjabis (from 68th Brigade),
3/34th Sikh Pioneers with attached troops

advanced at 8 A.M. to clear the Sarkai Ridge and then to secure the Spinkai Ghash in order to cover the occupation of a camp on the Palosina Plain, three miles north-northwest of Jandola camp.

The 1/103rd Mahratta Light Infantry advancing steadily cleared the north-eastern portion of the Sarkai Ridge and the broken ground where the Sagar Algad trends south from Sandar-band. Here the smoke of fires had disclosed already the presence of parties of the enemy, and the contact aeroplanes were informed accordingly.

See Panorama No. 1

On the left the 1/55th Rifles having secured the dominating point of the ridge continued their advance against the steep Spinkai Ghash with the 2/112th Infantry on their right moving against the ridge to the east of the Spinkai Ghash, which by 1-30 P.M. was in our possession. The Mahsuds retired mainly up the Tank Zam pursued by our aeroplanes. By 4-30 P.M. the transport which consisted of 2,330 mules and 2,750 camels had reached the camp without incident. During the day our casualties amounted to 78, including 7 killed. Those of the enemy were reported to have been thirteen killed and wounded but this was probably an under-estimate.

There seems no doubt that up to the actual moment of an advance the Mahsuds expected us to advance by the Shahur. The discovery of their mistake probably accounted for the slight resistance which they put up.

Description of country round Palosina.—As the column was obliged to remain in camp at Palosina for some time, and several minor engagements took place in the immediate vicinity, a short description of the ground will be of interest and will enable the difficulties of the operations of the ensuing days to be followed and understood.

See sketch map No 1 at page 106.

The right bank of the Tank Zam, opposite the Palosina camp rises in steep cliffs to a small plateau, some 200 feet above the river bed. The north end of this plateau terminates in a rocky bluff, called Mandanna Hill overlooking Mandanna Kach and the river to the north. The plateau, which is about 300 yards broad, is bounded on the west by a steep-sided ravine. This ravine starts from a tangled mass of broken ground known as "Broken Hill," 600 yards south-west of Mandanna Hill, and runs for about 2,000 yards in a south-easterly direction until it joins the Tank Zam.

On the west of the ravine is a ridge which forms the main feature in the vicinity. The southern end of this ridge consists of two features known as "Black and White Hill" and "Black and White Breasts." Going north along the ridge there are four decided features; a group of rocks which runs east and west and was known as "Red Rocks"; "Sandbag Hill" a rough and commanding point some 700 yards west of "Red Rocks"; and "Comb Rocks" 200 yards north of "Sandbag Hill." The intervening space between "Sandbag Hill" and "Comb Rocks" comprises a steep drop of 150 feet, then an exposed strip of flat ground up to the foot of the latter. The fourth feature on the ridge is known as "Broken Hill," and covers Mandanna Hill from the south-west.

North of "Broken Hill" the ridge ends in an abrupt drop to "Pink Bowl" on the right bank of the Tank Zam. The slopes of Tsappar Ghar, 3 to 4 miles west of Mandanna Kach overlook the whole neighbourhood.

Action near Mandanna Hill, 19th December.—On the 19th December a permanent piquet was established on Sarkai Ridge without opposition. The same day a force, which consisted of two battalions of the 67th Brigade, crossed the Tank Zam from Palosina Camp with the object of establishing a permanent piquet on Mandanna Hill to cover the advance up the Tank Zam. The ravine immediately west of the plateau was cleared by shell fire from three sections in action on the camp perimeter, and the 1/103rd Mahratta Light Infantry rapidly seized "Red Rocks" and "Sandbag Hill," and at the same time a company of the 1/55th Rifles occupied the lower slopes of "Sandbag Hill" and "Broken Boulders." The remaining three companies of the 1/55th Rifles were in position on the left of the 1/103rd Mahratta Light Infantry.

Although a certain amount of movement down the Tank Zam and in the vicinity of "Broken Boulders" and "Sandbag Hill" had been seen there was nothing to indicate that any large numbers of the enemy were holding "Comb Rocks." The original plan was to rush the ridge from "Sandbag Hill" and "Broken Boulders" but it was discovered that the broken nature of the ground made this impossible. The Mahsuds in force were now in position on "Comb Rocks" and "Broken Hill" from which they were bringing a heavy and effective fire to bear on the attacking troops. For nearly an hour the 1/103rd Mahratta Light Infantry reinforced from Red Rocks made several gallant but unsuccessful attempts to resume their advance on "Comb Rocks" despite the intense and accurate gun and howitzer fire which was directed on the objective. The battalion had now suffered heavy casualties including the commanding officer and two British officers killed and two wounded. Under cover of the deadly fire from "Comb Rocks" some Mahsuds moving up the depression between "Sandbag Hill" and "Comb Rocks" delivered a most determined attack on the troops holding the former eminence. The battalion was forced to withdraw. In a few moments considerable numbers of Mahsuds emerging from "Comb Rocks" seized "Sandbag Hill," and poured in a heavy fire on the retiring troops. As the 1/103rd Mahratta Light Infantry had exhausted its supports in reinforcing the attacks on "Comb Rocks" there was no definite line on which the battalion could fall back. The companies on the right and left being outflanked were compelled also to withdraw Parties attempted in vain to seize " Red Rocks " and the vicinity to cover the general retirement which was now in progress. Meanwhile the enemy who had developed great strength estimated at 900 riflemen, pressed the whole line back to the river, and forced our troops to re-cross to the east bank. Our casualties were heavy and included 95 killed and 140 wounded while our loss in material totalled 131 rifles and 10 Lewis guns. The Mahsuds admitted a loss of 13 killed and 40 wounded which is probably a fair estimate.

The reverse was due to several causes the chief of which was the neglect to observe the principle of distribution in depth. There was no reserve of troops and the small local supports were insufficient to restore the situation when the retirement became general. The behaviour of the troops showed that the men were not masters of their weapons, and they did not know what to do when their officers had become casualties.

Operations to establish piquet on Mandanna Hill, 20th December.—It was now necessary to re-establish confidence by repeating the day's operation and by using every available means to ensure success. Accordingly on the 20th December the attack was resumed by the following troops under Brigadier-General Lucas :—

2/19th Punjabis,
1/55th Rifles,
109th Infantry,
2/112th Infantry,
2 sections 55th Company Sappers and Miners and two companies of the 3/34th Sikh Pioneers.

The line of advance was practically the same as that taken on the previous day.

Shortly after the attack began, the 2/112th Infantry secured the outlying features known as " Black and White " hill. By 10 A.M. the troops were in possession of " Red Rocks " and the northern end of the plateau and half an hour later the 1/55th Rifles had established themselves on the eastern end of " Comb Rocks " and in the vicinity of " Broken Hill."

The success of the operation was largely due to the precision and thoroughness with which the Royal Air Force co-operated with the attacking infantry. The accurate bombing and machine gunning of the reverse slopes of "Comb Rocks" combined with the fire of the guns and howitzers on "Sandbag Hill" and Mandanna Hill, greatly lightened the task of the infantry and must have saved many casualties. Indeed up to this point our casualties were only 3 killed and 15 wounded while the enemy's were believed to have been heavier than on the previous day.

Considerable numbers of Mahsuds could be seen retiring up the Tank Zam and many more were observed advancing from Kotkai. These latter, however, halted on seeing the heavy bombardment that was taking place. Work to put Mandanna Hill into a state of defence for the permanent piquet was begun at once. By the afternoon it was decided that the defences, though incomplete, were sufficiently far advanced to establish a piquet there for the night, and 100 rifles under a British officer were accordingly posted. The piquet was exposed to enfilade fire from "Comb Rocks" and "Broken Hill" at ranges from three to six hundred yards but no suitable traverses had been built.

The troops which had covered the construction of the piquet were then withdrawn covered by the fire of guns and aeroplane co-operation, and by 4-30 P.M. they were back in camp without having sustained a single casualty.

At 4-45 P.M. Captain Cuthbert, 2/19th Punjabis, commanding Mandanna Piquet reported tribesmen collecting at a distance north and west of his position, and at the same time about thirty tribesmen some of whom were unarmed, were seen from Spinkai Ghash running across the Tank Zam to the foot of Mandanna bluff.

Attempts were made immediately to warn the piquet commander of the presence of this party but without success, as the telephone suddenly failed.

It appears that at this time the majority of the garrison having deposited their rifles and equipment in the piquet were employed in carrying up their blankets. water, and reserve ammunition which had been dumped some distance from the piquet. Suddenly fire from enemy snipers on "Comb Rocks" and "Broken Hill" forced this working party to seek shelter among the rocks. Under cover of this accurate fire the above-mentioned party of

Mahsuds swarmed up the hillside and reached some dead ground within a few yards of the northern end of the piquet; at the same time another small party delivered a determined attack on the piquet from the west. Captain Cuthbert and some of his men charged these tribesmen but he and his party were all killed. On seeing this the remainder of the garrison became disorganised and, leaving the piquet, retired across the river into camp many of them having their arms and equipment wrenched from them by the Mahsuds who showed great boldness in the pursuit. Heavy gun and rifle fire was at once brought to bear on the tribesmen looting the piquet.

It is difficult to arrive at the true story of this incident, but it appears from subsequent reports that the Mahsud attack on the piquet was not pre-arranged, and that the tribesmen who approached the position from the river thinking that the troops here had delayed their withdrawal to camp too long, hoped only to achieve some small success.*

Operations to establish piquet on Black Hill, 21st December.—It was now more than ever necessary that the confidence of the troops in themselves should be restored, so an operation was arranged for the following day to establish a permanent piquet on the feature known as "Black Hill" or Tarakai, a tumbled mass of ridges running west of Sagarzai peak and commanding the camp at a range of 1,700 yards.

The area surrounding Black Hill is difficult and rocky affording excellent cover for an advance from Sagarzai, but about 120 yards to the north of the piquet is a low ridge which commands most of the ground in which bodies of the enemy could collect and over which they must debouch. The steep rise to the piquet and the flanking ridge and the formation thence towards camp, made it easy to cover a withdrawal or organise and cover an attack. The distance of the ridge from camp, *i.e.*, 2,100 yards from the river bank, made support by gunfire an easy matter.

See Panorama No. 2.

By 10-30 A.M. "Black Hill" and the neighbouring ridges were occupied without opposition by the 82nd

---

* Our casualties for the 19th and 20th December amounted to 113 killed including 5 British officers, and 200 wounded.

Punjabis and 109th Infantry with the co-operation of aeroplanes, and work on the piquet was begun in spite of some long range sniping fire. When the construction of the post was half finished and the wire entanglement almost completed, some enemy were seen massing at a point half-way between " Black Hill " and the Sagarzai peak. Prior to this considerable numbers of tribesmen had been observed crossing the Tank Zam from the direction of " Pink Bowl." These concentrated at Ibrahim Gul and subsequently advanced against Tarakai Hill. Shortly after 1-30 P.M. sniping from close range increased and was followed almost at once by a rush of tribesmen from three directions which caused the troops covering the right of the piquet to recoil, uncovering those in the centre who withdrew followed at once by those on the left. Meanwhile the officer in command of the working party of the 3/34th Sikh Pioneers took all his men into the half-finished post where they were immediately attacked fiercely at close range by the Mahsuds in front and on both flanks. Four attacks were beaten off and the fifth had developed when the officer in command finding that ammunition and grenades were running short, withdrew down the hill towards camp. At this time it was estimated that the Mahsuds on the ridge were about 800 strong. These were now engaged by the fire of guns and howitzers, that of the latter being especially effective, and being responsible for the heavy losses suffered by the enemy.

The covering troops, who had been reorganised and reinforced on the ridge half-way to camp, launched a counter-attack which reached the foot of the steep rise to the piquet, but failed to make further progress owing to the fire of well-concealed riflemen, and, accordingly, at 4 P.M. our troops were withdrawn under orders, to the camp on Palosina plain.

The redeeming feature of this engagement was the behaviour of the working party of the 3/34th Sikh Pioneers and 1st Sappers and Miners and of the stretcher-bearers of the Field Ambulances and Bearer Unit. The gallant staunchness of the former showed that the old fighting spirit of the Indian soldier still existed, and a splendid example was set by the devotion of the latter who traversed the bullet-swept slopes with cool courage and recovered many a wounded man who had been left behind.

The inability of our troops on this occasion to repel the advance of the tribesmen and the failure in the counter-attack to recover the lost ground must be ascribed once again to the inadequate individual training of the soldier especially in the effective use of his rifle. A tour of the ground on the following day disclosed the fact that the position occupied by the covering troops in the vicinity of the piquet did not afford a good field of fire or view.

The sangars constructed by these troops were of the most perfunctory nature, and besides being ill-suited as firing rests they were not proof against the modern bullet. Had our troops been able to recapture and hold their position it is possible that the Mahsuds would have sustained a reverse which would have much accelerated the end of the campaign. Their losses were severe, and were reported later at 250 killed and 300 seriously wounded. These were much in excess to our own, which amounted to **66** killed or missing and **256** wounded, but undoubtedly the moral victory remained with the enemy.

The Mahsud attack on Black Hill is one of the best examples of combination of fire and shock action. The organization of their fire power was perfect. At ranges up to 1,500 yards, and from positions on which our artillery fire could be brought to bear, their riflemen developed a volume of aimed fire under which their swordsmen scaled the hill unseen and unscathed.

By this date, the 21st December, five battalions had been heavily engaged with the enemy, and although severe losses had been inflicted on the Mahsuds, three of these battalions were badly in need of rest. It was therefore decided that they should be replaced in the column by other troops. Accordingly the 2/19th Punjabis, the 82nd Punjabis, and 2/112th Infantry were withdrawn into the Lines of Communication, and the 4/39th Garhwal Rifles, 2/76th Punjabis and the 2/152nd Punjabis from the 43rd Brigade took their place.

Permanent piquet established on Black Hill, 22nd December.—On the following day " Black Hill " was re-occupied without much opposition and from that date was held permanently by a piquet. Fifty dead Mahsuds and many rifles were found on the hill and in its vicinity, and during the day many burials were seen to take place near Kotkai four miles away, and reports were received that many dead and wounded had been carried off by their relatives to their homes.

Negotiations for settlement.—No operations were undertaken on the two following days as owing to low clouds and rain close co-operation with aeroplanes was impossible. Intimation was now received from the Mahsuds *maliks* that they were prepared to visit Jandola with the object of effecting a settlement and they asked that the operations might be suspended pending the result of the *jirga*.

The real object of the *maliks* seemed obvious. The *lashkars* which had been in the field since the middle of the month were now dispersing owing to casualties and lack of supplies, while the inhabitants of the Kotkai area were hurriedly removing their families and cattle to distant valleys. The *maliks* with a view to recovering their standing among the tribesmen and with Government hoped to effect a settlement which would ensure at least the immediate withdrawal of the troops to Jandola. This sanguine expectation was probably based on a similar concession gained by the Mahsuds during the operations in 1917.

Jirga at Jandola, 29th December.—In spite, however, of being told that advance would not be stopped pending the outcome of the meeting, the *maliks* arrived at Jandola during the 28th and on the 29th December Major-General Climo held a *jirga*. Representative *maliks* were present from nearly all the tribes and sub-tribes; the only notable exception were the Abdullai, who inhabit the country in the neighbourhood of Makin.

Original terms enhanced.—In view of the opposition that had been encountered the severity of our original terms was increased. These additional terms demanded the surrender of one hundred more rifles which would be confiscated permanently. In addition the representatives were told that our advance would continue until the sincerity of their submission was proved by the payment of the fine and the surrender of the tribal rifles. In spite of these terms complete submission of the Mahsuds was made, and was signed and sealed by those present.

Submission of *maliks*.

In the meantime the work on Mandanna Hill was continued on the 25th. Numbers of tribesmen were seen near

Kotkai and on the slopes of Tsappar Ghar. These were continuously harassed by aeroplanes and probably for that reason did not interfere in any way with the operations. In the evening all the troops returned to camp. The following day the work was completed without opposition and the piquet occupied.

The period from the 17th to 28th December formed the first phase in the operations against the Mahsuds.

End of first phase.—The losses which they had sustained on the 21st December caused most of the *lashkars* to disperse to their homes, and without doubt their heavy casualties made them for a time at least, desist from pursuing the rushing tactics which had up to this time proved so successful in their encounters with our troops. This breathing space enabled our troops not only to establish several important permanent piquets without opposition, but also made them realize that the losses of the tribesmen had been heavier than our own.

It must be emphasised that the tribesmen had fought in a way they had never done before, and this was due to their high state of moral and knowledge that our battalions were composed of inexperienced soldiers. Their attacks were well organized, and their combination of fire and shock tactics, the latter carried out with remarkable recklessness, was excellent. This undoubtedly was due to the presence in their ranks of many ex-militia and retired regular soldiers.

CHAPTER IX.

Operations of the Derajat Column—Second Phase.

Advance to Kotkai, 29th December.—In accordance with the decision communicated to the jirga on the 29th December at Jandola a column consisting of Column Headquarters with the 43rd Brigade and attached troops left Palosina camp and advanced with little opposition to Kotkai, a distance of four miles, a third of which was covered by permanent piquets established during the operations round Mandanna Kach. The remainder of the striking force halted at Palosina to admit of supplies being accumulated at Kotkai camp.

Action near Kotkai, 2nd January.—The column remained at Kotkai till the 7th January. During this period permanent piquets were established at various points between the latter place and Jandola, in order to complete the defence of the road and give adequate protection to the convoys. Permanent piquets were also occupied north of Kotkai in preparation for the next advance. These operations were carried out with little opposition from the tribesmen except on the 2nd January, during the construction of a permanent piquet on Scrub Hill about 2,500 yards north-west of Kotkai camp situated on the Kalwa Raghza.

The 4/39th Garhwal Rifles who were detailed to form the covering troops reached their positions on Spin Ghara ridge without much opposition. But between 11 A.M. and 3 P.M. sniping was continuous and three determined attacks were made on their right company. Each of these attacks was pushed home in a most resolute manner and the enemy who had got to within stone throwing distance were only driven off after severe fighting. Difficulties in the removal of the wounded down a very steep slope necessitated some delay in the withdrawal to camp, which began at 3-15 P.M. Under a heavy covering fire from the peaks to the north and west, a body of Mahsuds succeeded in establishing itself immediately below the forward crest of the position held by the covering troops. The latter made several attempts with bombs and stones to dislodge this party, but without success

See Panorama No. 2.

owing to the accuracy of the Mahsud covering fire which had already caused several casualties. When the rearmost party of the Garhwal Rifles began its withdrawal, the above mentioned body of Mahsuds rushed forward in close pursuit. Seeing this Lieutenant Kenny* with about ten men turned and counter-attacked the tribesmen with the object of gaining sufficient time for the remainder of the Covering Party to get away. This gallant party fighting to the last was annihilated, but its object was achieved, for the Mahsuds fell back and being subsequently shelled effectively by the supporting guns were prevented from following up the withdrawal. The enemy casualties were estimated at 77 killed and wounded whilst the 4/39th Garhwal Rifles lost 35 killed (including two British officers) and 43 wounded. The battalion displayed in this action great endurance and gallantry and taught the tribesmen a wholesome lesson.

It was now reported that a fresh *lashkar* had collected in the vicinity of the Ahnai Tangi, and that the Jalal Khel and Haibat Khel whose homesteads were within striking distance of the column had decided to co-operate from the direction of the Shuza valley where their families had taken refuge. On the 5th the 43rd Brigade moved out to cover the re-construction of Scrub Hill and Whitechapel piquets, the walls of which had been demolished by the tribesmen. These piquets had not been occupied on the day of their construction as Whitechapel was uncompleted and it was not intended to hold Scrub Hill.

These mistakes, which were too frequent at the outset of the operations, were due to the inexperience of the junior officers, British and Indian, and their inability to recognise the important part that time plays in mountain warfare. Operations such as these must be carried out with the utmost despatch and according to a pre-arranged programme in order that the advantages gained by surprise should not be lost. The piquets were occupied and the troops returned to camp, the rearguard on the Whitechapel side being followed up closely. Our casualties were eight killed and forty wounded, attributable to the fact that the enemy was prepared this day for the repetition of the operation. On the 6th January the 67th Brigade reached Kotkai camp from Palosina camp.

---

*This officer was awarded a posthumous Victoria Cross for his extreme gallantry and devotion on this occasion.

Preliminary operations for capture of the Ahnai Tangi.
—The next task before the Column was the capture of the Ahnai Tangi. The latter is about four miles from Kotkai Camp. The actual gorge is about eighty yards in length and only thirty yards wide. The sides are precipitous and rise to a height of 150 feet above the river bed.

A description of the country traversed in approaching the Tangi will enable the progress of the fighting to be more easily followed. The Spin Ghara range, a series of prominent hills rising to a height of 700 feet above the river, runs in a south-westerly direction from the Tangi and commands all the approaches from the south and south-west. Between the range and the river, the Tangi consists of a plateau intersected by numerous deep ravines which can only be crossed at a few points by troops moving in single file. Opposite the plateau, on the left bank of the Tank Zam, the Konr range, a mass of crags rising to a height of 1,200 feet above the bed of the river, commands all approaches from the east.

See Panorama No. 3.

*It was decided to make the main attack across the plateau and seize the west flank of the Ahnai Tangi protecting the right of the attack by occupying the country on the east bank of the river with another body of troops. Accordingly on the 7th January, the 43rd Brigade made good the east bank for a distance of some three miles from the camp thereby protecting the advance of the 67th Brigade, which at dawn moved across the plateau and by 11 A.M. was in a position to attack the west flank of the Tangi. By this time, however, the enemy had massed on the lower slopes of the Konr range, south of the Tangi, where the conformation of the ground gave him every advantage and where his line of retreat up the Tank Zam or the Shuza was secure. It then became evident that, before the Tangi could be secured and a camp formed forward of Ghurlama Kach, it would be necessary to occupy the heights on the left bank. The short period of daylight now left made it impossible to carry out this operation so the troops were ordered at 1 P.M. to withdraw to Kotkai camp. During the withdrawal a party of the enemy rushed a small covering party of our troops but coming themselves under crossfire lost about thirty killed.

Except for this incident there was no serious action by the enemy. Our casualties on the left bank of the river were eight killed and eighteen wounded, and the remainder two killed and sixteen wounded.

Unsuccessful attempts to establish strong point S. E. of Zeriwam, 9th and 10th January.—Although the enemy's tactics of massing on the left bank made it appear desirable to launch the main attack on that side of the river, yet the ground was so difficult and so suitable for defence by a few well-posted men that any idea of attack in that direction had to be abandoned. Accordingly, it was decided to adhere to the original plan and to make a turning movement against the western flank of the Ahnai Tangi. But to ensure success, orders were issued to establish as a preparatory operation, a strong point south-east of Zeriwam in order to protect the flank of the subsequent main movement, and at the same time to establish the 67th Brigade in a camp to the north of Kotkai in order to make the approach march towards the Tangi as short as possible.

With this object in view, the 67th Brigade left Kotkai Camp at 8 A.M. on the 9th January and formed a camp two miles upstream. Meanwhile the 43rd Brigade began the construction of the permanent piquet south-east of Zeriwam. The work proceeded rapidly and the garrison with its stores moved up towards it by 11 A.M. Hostile rifle fire, which had been desultory all the morning against the covering troops in position on the main ridge of the Konr range, about this time became intense, and the troops on the right flank were attacked and driven back with loss. Assistance was sent up by the 67th Brigade from Ghurlama Kach but as the defences of the piquet had not been completed the 43rd Brigade was withdrawn at 3 P.M. The tribesmen, who immediately rushed into the half finished work in search of loot were shelled with great effect by our artillery from Kotkai plateau, they also suffered heavily in some close fighting with the 4/39th Garhwal Rifles on the northern slopes of Kafir Luta.*

Another attempt to establish the piquet was made on the following day but was again unsuccessful. The enemy advancing again from the direction of the Shuza attacked the covering troops on the main ridge with great deter-

---

* Our casualties in the action were eighteen killed, including one British officer and forty-two wounded, including four British Officers.

mination, and eventually overbore their resistance by heavy and accurate sniping. The advanced troops having fallen back on the piquet, and as there was no time to organise an attack on the rocky ridge from which the covering troops had been driven, the Brigade was ordered to withdraw to camp which was reached at 5 P.M. Our losses on this day were twenty-five killed and eighty-four wounded. The enemy casualties were estimated at forty-seven killed and wounded. The 2/9th Gurkha Rifles arrived at Kotkai from Jandola on this day, and two companies of the battalion were employed to cover the withdrawal of the 43rd Brigade to camp.

Capture of Ahnai Tangi, 11th January.—Although the establishment of the permanent piquet south-east of Zeriwam had not been achieved, Major-General Skeen decided that it was not advisable to delay any longer the capture of the Ahnai Tangi. Without the necessary protection on the right flank the advance of the column to the Tangi would be a difficult and hazardous operation. The moon, however, was in her last quarter and as this favoured a night march General Skeen decided to make use of this advantage to surprise the enemy and secure the difficult ground before the tribesmen had time to organise an attack.

The 43rd Brigade under Brigadier-General Gwyn-Thomas which consisted of—

    4/39th Garhwal Rifles,
    109th Infantry,
    2 Companies 2/150th Infantry (joined the Column on 29th December),
    2/152nd Punjabis,

was therefore ordered to move from Kotkai at 5 A.M. on the 11th January so as to be in position at dawn, about 7-15 A.M. ready to develop an attack against two prominent features of the Konr Range overlooking the eastern flank of the Ahnai gorge but at some distance from it.

The 67th Brigade, under Brigadier-General Lucas, composed of—

    1/55th Coke's Rifles,
    57th Wilde's Rifles,
    2/76th Punjabis,
    2/5th Gurkha Rifles (joined the Column on 4th January)

was at the same time ordered to occupy during the night the Spin Ghara range and to be ready to attack at dawn the western side of the Ahnai Tangi in conjunction with the attack of the 43rd Brigade.

The 67th Brigade was clear of its camp by 3 A.M. The operation proved entirely successful, and the enemy, being completely surprised, sought safety in flight. By 10 A.M. the west bank of the Ahnai Tangi was in our possession and by 11-15 A.M. the occupation of the east bank was successfully accomplished. Piquets were quickly established to hold the Tangi. Rain had begun to fall at 1 P.M. and visibility became very bad, but the withdrawal of the covering troops including that of the 43rd Brigade to Kotkai Camp was carried out without a casualty. The 67th Brigade formed a new camp west of Zeriwam afterwards known as Ahnai Camp. Our casualties on this day amounted to five killed and twenty-eight wounded. Bearing in mind the great difficulties of the terrain over which our troops had to operate the success of this important operation at so small a cost reflects great credit on both leaders and troops, and also on the Royal Air Force whose-co-operation with the troops by means of D. H. 9 A.'s and Bristol Fighters was excellent.

Reports were now received to the effect that the determined opposition shown by the Mahsuds on the 9th and 10th was due to a rumour that had reached the tribesmen that the Derajat Column was about to raid the Shuza valley. The *lashkar* which during the week had been joined by Wazirs from Wana and Tochi had now split up, some being at Shilmanzai Kach and in its vicinity and others in the Shuza.

The 12th January was occupied in the construction of several roads to the river bed and the relief of piquet garrisons so as to allow the 67th Brigade to move forward complete in the next advance. On the following day Column headquarters and Column troops joined the 67th Brigade at Ahnai Camp where final preparations had been made for the advance through the Ahnai Tangi. During the afternoon a hostile attack which cost us three killed and three wounded, was made on an observation post detached from the Ahnai left bank piquet.

See sketch map No. 2, at page 118.

Advance through Ahnai Tangi, 14th January.—
See Panorama No. 3.
The advance through the Ahnai Tangi took place on the 14th January, and a short description of the country will help to make clear the account of the next day's fighting. Running north from the Tangi, on the east bank of the Tank Zam is a long narrow spur culminating in a flat topped hill, some 150 yards in length called " Flathead Left." The latter over 900 feet above the Tank Zam completely dominates the bed and the right bank of the river. Any further advance upstream from " Flathead Left " is threatened from a mass of cliffs known as " Marble Arch " and, more to the east, by a hill which is separated from " Flathead Left " by a steep and precipitous nala. This second hill was known as " Flathead Right."

A reconnaissance from the high ground in the vicinity of the Tangi showed that the country beyond was very difficult, and that the most important tactical feature in the area was the ridge on the left bank culminating in " Flathead Left " and that it was necessary to hold this point to secure the passage of the Column towards Sorarogha.

Operations at Asa Khan, 14th January.—In accordance with orders, a strong advanced guard consisting of 1/55th Rifles, two companies of 2/5th Gurkha Rifles and two guns of No. 27 Mountain Battery advanced up the bed of the river on the morning of the 14th January. Meanwhile the remainder of the 2/5th Gurkha Rifles under Lt.-Colonel Crowdy, D.S.O., starting from Ahnai Left Bank at 7-30 A.M. moved along the spur to secure " Flathead Left " where it was proposed to establish a permanent piquet.

The main body was under Major-General Skeen and consisted of—

1 troop of cavalry,

4 guns,

3 battalions,

1 Field Company Sappers and Miners,

and attached troops.

Brigadier-General Lucas with four guns and two battalions was detailed to protect the route from the camp to Ahnai Tangi and to escort the transport which numbered 1,480 mules and 2,800 camels. The detail of troops engaged is shown in Appendix "H."

The advanced guard under Lieutenant-Colonel Herdon, 1/55th Rifles, met with opposition on reaching the cultivation near Asa Khan and shortly afterwards its progress was retarded by accurate rifle fire from the "Marble Arch" cliffs and "Flathead Right." On the special flanking detachment reaching "Flathead Left" at about 8-30 A.M. it encountered considerable opposition from the direction of "Flathead Right." At the same time the advanced guard pushed forward to establish a piquet on a steep spur running down from "Marble Arch." Immediately afterward some forty tribesmen emerging from a nala on the left bank rushed this piqueting detachment and threw the vanguard, moving in the river bed, into some confusion. Hand-to-hand fighting ensued but eventually the enemy was driven off with heavy loss and, thanks to the guns with the advanced guard, gave little more trouble in this part of the field. It was now seen that to ensure the safe passage of the column it was imperative to hold "Flathead Right" and orders were therefore issued to the flanking detachment to occupy this dominating feature. But this detachment had for some time been heavily engaged, and was now calling for reinforcements and ammunition.

A company of the 2/76th Punjabis was consequently sent up but before its arrival the Gurkha detachment having run out of ammunition had driven back the enemy with the bayonet, but in doing so had lost their Commanding Officer, Lt.-Colonel Crowdy, D.S.O., who was killed. On the situation being known the remainder of the 2/76th Punjabis was sent up from the river bed at 11-30 A.M. under Lieutenant-Colonel Chamberlayne under orders to restore the situation and make good "Flathead Right" so as to facilitate the capture of "Marble Arch," which menaced the whole of the area in which the Force was now concentrating. In addition to the above troops a company of the 2/9th Gurkha Rifles had also been sent to "Flathead Left" by Brigadier-General Lucas from Ahnai Tangi. The steep ascent of over 900 feet was scaled rapidly and the reinforcements arrived in time to ensure the retention of "Flathead Left." The attack on "Flathead Right" was resumed but the hostile fire proved too heavy and accurate. Several gallant efforts were made to advance but these were of no avail, and orders were therefore issued to consolidate the ground gained.

As it was then 1-30 P.M. and as the transport was through the Tangi and well closed up in the river bed it was too late to return to Ahnai Camp. A further advance was impossible as "Marble Arch" had not been captured. Major-General Skeen too was reluctant to surrender important ground gained at the price of severe casualties and decided to form a camp where the force then lay, although the locality was most unsuitable. The camp, afterwards known as Asa Khan Camp, was in the bed of the Tank Zam and was not only closely surrounded by hills, the loss of any of which might have created a critical situation, but was also cramped and confined.

During the afternoon the enemy was reported massing in a ravine to the west of the camp. On Dazzle Hill, an important height about a mile from camp two Companies of the 109th Infantry, the only troops in hand, were sent to drive them off. Too weak to carry out their mission, they sustained heavy losses but held to ground gained, and by so doing enabled the camp defences in that direction to be completed, and secured the camp from attack from the west.

Meanwhile the position on "Flathead Left" had become more critical. The tribesman made four more determined attacks supported by powerful and accurate covering fire, and it was only with difficulty that our troops maintained their hold on this vital point. Another company of the 2/9th Gurkha Rifles originally destined for picquet garrison had just arrived at "Flathead Left" in time to turn the tide in our favour and helped to beat off a last determined assault in which bayonets, stones, knives, and grenades were freely used. After this the enemy pressure died down and no further attacks were made. Our troops on the ridge spent the whole night in consolidating their positions.

This action proved to be the most stubbornly fought of the whole campaign. Our casualties amounted to nine British officers killed and six wounded two Indian officers. and three hundred and sixty-five Indian other ranks killed or wounded.

Owing to the necessity of escorting the transport and securing the road only a few units were available for the actual fighting, but the heavy casualties that those units suffered, especially in British officers, in no way shook their moral. The enemy's losses were reported later at about four hundred killed or seriously wounded. Forty to fifty enemy dead were found in front of our lines, and a large number of our own and tribal rifles were recovered as late as two days after the action.

The Mahsuds fought with their usual reckless gallantry. They took full advantage of the difficulties of the ground and by accurate fire covered the concentration and assault of their braver spirits. Many of these assaults were pushed home, but in the hand-to-hand fighting that ensued our troops proved themselves superior to the enemy.

Co-operation of Royal Air Force.—The co-operation of the Royal Air Force was most effective and rendered material assistance towards the success of the day's action. The offensive spirit of the pilots who recognised the fierce nature of the fighting had a remarkable effect on the enemy as is exemplified by the following episode. Two aeroplanes, finding good targets finished their bombs and ammunition some time before reliefs were due to arrive. The enemy was then harassing our troops and the aviators knew that the departure of the aeroplanes would be the signal for the renewal of the attack. They therefore remained and by continually diving low at the enemy succeeded in pinning him to the ground thus preventing the development of any offensive movement against our hard pressed troops. Unfortunately two of our aeroplanes were shot down by the enemy but the occupants, though slightly wounded, succeeded in reaching our lines. On this day too a machine had to make a forced landing in the Shuza, within Bhittanni limits. The occupants were taken in safety to Khirgi by three Mahsuds, who were in our employ as intelligence agents.

During the next three days Column Headquarters, with column troops and the 67th Brigade remained at Asa Khan Camp, whilst the wounded were evacuated, supplies collected and preparations made for a further advance.

Importance of training as shewn by Asa Khan operations.—The action of the Ahnai Tangi is a good example of the desperate nature of the fighting that had taken place up to this stage of the operations, and which would have tried highly trained units, even the pre-war Frontier Force or similar regiments with long experience and training on the frontier. It is very essential for us, even those who fought on the frontier as late as 1917 and 1918, to realise to what extent conditions have been altered with the great improvement in the armament of the tribesmen. Their tactical knowledge and training have greatly improved. The presence of a large body of Militia deserters forms a strong nucleus of well trained men on which to build their tribal gatherings. We must appreciate the standard of individual training that is required for infantry in the conditions that prevail on the frontier to-day. The standard of training that we had perforce to be content with in France in the later years of the Great War, although it enabled us to gain a final victory, does not suffice on the frontier to-day, nor are the tactical methods that we adopted suitable in many respects, though the principles underlying these tactics apply equally. Tactical methods and training are interdependent, and where large bodies of men can be employed the actual numbers alone give the more timorous a sense of safety and power. In an action such as has been described however, masses cannot be used and a man's fighting value and his own safety depend on his own efforts and on his ability to use his weapons. The paramount importance of sound musketry training and all that pertains to it is well exemplified in this particular action.

From reports received later it appeared that the very large numbers of tribesmen, (said to have been at least 4,000), sheltering in the numerous caves near Sarwekunda and in the Shilmanzai Kach area had appreciated the tactical value of " Flathead Left " and anticipating that a permanent piquet would be established on it, they made their preparations accordingly to dispute the possession of this important feature. Consequently on the 14th when shortly after 7-30 A.M the Mahsuds heard the continuous " precautionary " fire of the Lewis guns and rifles of the 2/5th Gurkhas clearing the spur for the advance of the special flanking detachment, considerable numbers of tribesmen hurried to their selected positions and prepared to put up a stout resistance. Within an hour in the desperate fighting that ensued the detachment had run out of ammunition, and but for the bayonet charge carried out under the personal leadership of their gallant commanding officer the whole detachment must have been overwhelmed.

Disposal of *lashkar*.—As is usual after an important action such as that of the Ahnai Tangi the *lashkars* of both Wana Wazirs and Mahsuds began to return to their homes with their dead and wounded, and the former too expressed an intention of not returning. At this time too peace overtures were made to the Force Commander through the Political Officer who was then at Jandola. The genuineness of these offers was suspected at the time, and later intelligence proved that the overtures were insincere, and that their object was to stay our advance. The period of the halt at Asa Khan Camp was employed in establishing permanent piquets in advance of camp, including one on "Marble Arch," which on this occasion was not held by the enemy. Except for a few minor brushes with the enemy, little real opposition was encountered as most of the *lashkars* had dispersed, but our daily casualties averaged about four killed and ten wounded.

Advance to Sorarogha, 18th January.—On the 18th January the Striking Force, with the addition of the 3rd Guides, who had joined the Column from the 68th Brigade, left Asa Khan Camp and moved forward some four miles to the Sorarogha plateau. The enemy offered but little resistance to the advance. Several good camel tracks leading from the Sagar Algad to the plateau having been rapidly constructed by the Pioneers, 1,500 mules and 2,800 camels were soon passed through to camp. Later in the evening the enemy attacked the two most advanced camp piquets, interfering seriously with their construction and, in the case of the piquet on the left bank of the Tank Zam preventing its occupation that evening. The work was completed during the night and the piquet occupied. Our casualties this day were eight killed and fourteen wounded.

Aerodrome formed at Sorarogha.—The Sorarogha plateau, some three hundred feet above the river, formed an excellent open camping ground. The disadvantage of having to bring up water to the plateau was more than compensated for by the ease of protection, the ample space and the good surface of the whole area. The space was sufficient to include an aerodrome which was of the greatest value in the subsequent operations, especially as it permitted pilots who had flown from Bannu or Tank to learn before beginning operations the position of our troops and the state of the situation. The striking force halted at Sorarogha Camp until the 27th January.

This long halt was necessary to collect ten days' reserve of supplies, ammunition, and stores for the striking force. It had originally been decided to advance by stages of from ten to twelve miles and not to embark on a new stage until ten days' maintenance for the striking force had been accumulated at the head of the old stage. This was a necessary precaution to take, as, although every possible arrangement had been made to ensure the protection of the Lines of Communication, they were always liable to temporary interruption by weather or the enemy. But, fortunately for us, the latter's strategical knowledge had not increased with his improvement in tactics and no serious attacks on the Lines of Communication took place.

End of second phase.—The period, 29th December 1919 to 20th January 1920, formed the second phase of the operations against the Mahsuds. It was a phase of steady progress and hard fighting which broke down the resistance of the enemy.

During these thirty days there had been twenty actions in nearly all of which more than one Brigade had been employed. Although this had naturally imposed a great strain on battalions already depleted in numbers, it was a period of practical training for all ranks and many lessons were learnt. The initial phases of five of the larger operations had been successfully carried out in the dark, during the early hours of the morning and over difficult country. This alone was a high test of discipline and efficiency.

These numerous and successful actions inspired the troops with confidence and made the Column a really formidable force, ready to undertake with determination the most difficult operation.

CHAPTER X.

OPERATIONS OF THE DERAJAT COLUMN—THE ADVANCE TO PIAZHA RAGHZA.

Afghan intrigues.—In spite of repeated appeals, sometimes accompanied with threats from the Wazirs and Mahsuds, Shah Daula the commander of the Afghan irregular force at Wana had steadfastly declined to lend his guns to the tribesmen for use against the Derajat Column. He had occasionally distributed small amounts of rifle ammunition to the Wazirs but up to this period that was all the material help he was able to give the tribesmen and all they now expected of him. As a result of the severe reverses they had suffered, the Mahsuds sent several messengers to Khost to report their plight and to ascertain what hope there was of help or intervention from that quarter, but these men returned with empty messages of sympathy and good-will from the officials of that district. Finding, however, that the Mahsuds were weakening several prominent individuals with anti-British leanings now appeared in Mahsud country from Khost with large amounts of rifle ammunition and promises of reinforcements in the form of *lashkars* accompanied by artillery. Among these emissaries were the fanatical Mullah Lala Pir and Haji Abdur Razak, once Court Mullah at Kabul but now a prominent agitator. Letters from Khost also reached Shah Daula who immediately busied himself with the collection of a Wana Wazir *lashkar*, which he promised to supply with ammunition and to accompany with his two mountain guns.

Description of Barari Tangi.—About one and a quarter miles north of Sorarogha Camp, the Tank Zam cuts through the Sarkai Ghar ridge forming a gorge called the Barari Tangi. The latter is some three hundred yards in length and sixty yards wide, with sides which rise precipitously to an average height of 100 feet. The bed of the river here turns almost due west and is joined by the Barari Algad from a north-easterly direction. After passing through the Tangi there are three important features which command any advance up the Tank Zam. These are " Barari Centre " and " The Barrier " between the Barari Algad and the Tank Zam and " Gibraltar " opposite the latter

See sketch map No. 3 at page 130.

on the right bank of the river. The last-named feature is a rocky and bushy bluff, whose existence was not discovered during the preliminary reconnaissances from Sorarogha Camp. Before attacking "Barari Centre " it was necessary to secure the Sarkai Ghar ridge on both sides of the river. The part of the ridge on the right bank, though the most formidable, was higher and less exposed to dangers than the part on the left bank and gave observation over the latter and its intricate surroundings.

Preparations for the advance through Barari Tangi, 23rd and 25th January.—On the 20th the Mahsud *lashkars* which had retired to Ahmadwam and Sarwek numbered about two hundred in each place, but since that date these had been reinforced by small parties of tribesmen including some Wazirs from Shakai. Active operations preparative to the further advance began on the 23rd January when Brigadier-General Lucas with the—

1/55th Rifles,
2/5th Gurkha Rifles,
2/9th Gurkha Rifles,

moving out at 5-30 A.M. traversed the intricate nalas and bush that lay north of the Sorarogha plateau and, ascending the precipitous slopes of Sarkai in the dark, established himself without loss in positions covering the site selected for the construction of a permanent piquet which was named subsequently the "Bluff Piquet." Meanwhile two companies of the 3rd Guides were disposed to protect the left flank against the small *lashkar* previously reported in the Sarwek valley. Shortly after daybreak the 2/9th Gurkha Rifles, who were covering from above the construction of the piquet, became engaged with the enemy who had appeared from the direction of Ahmadwam. Compelled to occupy a ridge to the north-west of the Bluff Piquet to cover the ridges in rear, the advanced company of this battalion soon began to sustain losses from hostile fire from the northern slopes of Sarkai Ghar. These casualties continued until the piquet was finished, equipped, and occupied. The withdrawal began at 1-45 P.M. The Mahsuds then attacked the advanced company with determination undeterred by shell fire, bombs, or Lewis gun fire from the aeroplanes. The company,

See panorama No. 5 at end of book.

however, was skilfully handled and completed its withdrawal with the loss of its British officer and seven Gurkha other ranks killed. The remainder of the withdrawal was carried out over the most precipitous and broken ground, but the fire of the supporting artillery especially that of the 2·75 guns was most effective in keeping the tribesmen under cover. Our losses on this day were ten killed and twenty-one wounded. During the operation the assistance rendered by the aeroplanes was of the greatest value and was undoubtedly responsible for the comparatively small losses sustained. They used the new aerodrome at Sorarogha for the first time, and the pilots were thus enabled to maintain the closest touch with the troops with whom they were co-operating Heavy rain accompanied by snow on the night of the 23rd January precluded operations on the following day as low clouds and bad visibility prevented co-operation from the air.

On the following day a permanent piquet on the Karkanai ridge was established at a cost of five killed and fifteen wounded. The majority of these casualties were incurred during an attack at 11-30 A.M. by about two hundred Mahsuds from the Shuza who drove in the advanced troops of the 57th Rifles, but with the assistance of the artillery the situation was restored, and the covering troops re-occupied their position. The enemy who had apparently suffered casualties failed to follow up the withdrawal inspite of the nature of the *terrain* which was admirably suited to his tactics.

A hold on both flanks of the Barari Tangi having thus been secured the construction of three camel tracks to the river bed in preparation for the next advance was undertaken This was completed on the 26th January without opposition. On the same day the 43rd Brigade arrived at Sorarogha from Kotkai having been relieved by the 67th Brigade from Jandola, the latter forming No. 2 Section, Tank Line of Communication Defences.

During the stay of our troops at Sorarogha several attempts were made by the Mahsud *maliks* to open negotiations with a view to effecting a cessation of hostilities. The *maliks* also hoped that the presence of Afghan emissaries in their country might induce Government to forego or modify its terms to the Mahsuds. These overtures, however, met with no response as it was evident that the tribesmen were entirely out of control of their *maliks* and had no intentions of fulfilling the conditions to which the *maliks* had already agreed at Jandola. Major-General Climo, therefore, ordered that punitive measures involving the destruction of property should be carried out when the force advanced from Sorarogha. This decision had been delayed as long as reasonable hope of a settlement had remained.

In consequence of the propaganda of the Afghan adventurers, and the energies of the Mahsud leaders, Mullah Fazl Din and Musa Khan, a *lashkar* composed chiefly of Shabi Khel and Abdullai and amounting to about 1,200 rifles was concentrated at this time in the vicinity of the Barari Tangi. The hope was therefore entertained that the *lashkar* would make a stand and give the column an opportunity of inflicting on these recalcitrant sections the punishment they so richly deserved.

The possession of the Sarkai ridges paved the way for a further advance and covered the approaches to "Barari Centre." The capture of the latter feature was an essential prelude to an attack on "The Barrier" which threatened to be a formidable obstacle and a likely position for the enemy to hold. The crest of the ridge was nowhere more than a few feet wide with natural cover in the rocks and an easy slope falling away on the far side providing easy lines of retreat. The southern approach to the crest of "The Barrier" was difficult especially the last part which involved a precipitous climb. It was estimated that an attack on this position would cost at least one hundred casualties so Major-General Skeen decided to seize "Barari Centre" at daybreak and push the attack against "The Barrier" before the enemy could concentrate for its defence.

Capture of Barari Tangi, 28th January.—Accordingly Brigadier-General Lucas with the following troops who had become accustomed to night operations in this area moved from Sorarogha Camp at 5-30 A.M. on the 28th January—

    1/55th Rifles,
    2/5th Gurkha Rifles,
    109th Infantry,
    2 companies 3rd Guides.

By daybreak "Barari Centre" was in our possession, and Brigadier-General Lucas was in a position to cover the attack on "The Barrier." At daybreak, about 7 A.M., the advance guard of the main column, consisting of the 57th Rifles and 2/150th Infantry under Brigadier-General Gwyn-Thomas, entered the Tangi and pushed on towards "The Barrier" and "Gibraltar."

Immediately behind the advanced guard came the special flanking detachment composed of the 4/39th Garhwal Rifles and two companies of the 2/9th Gurkha Rifles detailed for the capture of "The Barrier." As the advanced guard cleared the Tangi the special detachment swung to the right on to its objective. The former met with opposition in the Tangi, but, after dispersing about fifty tribesmen composing an enemy's piquet, pushed forward as directed. The tribesmen had been taken by surprise, and by 10 A.M., with practically no opposition, "The Barrier" was in our possession, and our position there was rapidly consolidated. Meanwhile the vanguard had got well past "Gibraltar" and was approaching Bangiwala, when a detachment from the 57th Rifles despatched to piquet the former feature was held up by accurate sniping from a network of nalas and wooded plateaux some 600—1,000 yards to the south and north-west. Reinforcements were sent up without avail, and finally two companies of the 2/9th Gurkha Rifles were employed. Skilfully handled these two weak companies passing through under close artillery support, drove back the enemy and at 1 P.M. captured "Gibraltar." Owing to persistent hostile rifle fire consolidation was not completed until after dark. The column camped at Ahmadwam, just north of Barari Tangi,

<small>Camp at Ahmadwam.</small> except the bulk of the transport which, owing to the limited extent of the camp, had to return to Sorarogha Camp. Our losses were seven killed and sixty-two wounded, and the enemy's casualties were reported as twenty killed and sixteen wounded. In the meantime the 67th Brigade having established the permanent piquet on "Barari Centre" returned to Sorarogha Camp.

Enemy guns in action against our troops.—During the 29th January the construction of posts on the localities selected for permanent piquets was completed. Considerable numbers of the enemy were seen during the day up the Tank Zam and confirmation was obtained of the reports previously received that a Wana Wazir *lashkar* accompanied by the local Afghan commander Shah Daula with his two mountain guns had joined the Mahsud *lashkar*. These two six-pounder guns firing fixed ammunition came into action at Shin Konr against us for the first time, but did no harm to our troops. They had a range of about 2,000 yards and the majority of the shells did not burst. Heavy rain during the night of the 29th made the camp a morass and impassable for the transport and operations had to be postponed until the 1st February, the intervening period being utilized for reconnaissances and the construction of causeways through the camp to enable the transport to move at the earliest opportunity.

On the 31st January all preparations for the advance were complete, the 109th Infantry having taken over all the permanent piquets in this area.

Advance to Aka Khel, 1st February.—Orders were issued for the advance to continue on the following day. Considerable opposition was expected, as hearing of the arrival of Haji Abdur Razaq, Lala Pir, and Shah Daula with his guns and a Wazir *lashkar* estimated at 1,600, Mahsuds from every quarter began to rally and by the 30th a *lashkar* as large as any that had previously collected, amounting to some 4,500 armed and unarmed men, was distributed between Dwa Toi and Bangiwala.

The character of the country north of the Barari Tangi changes, the hills are thickly covered with scrub and bush which afford good concealment for hostile snipers and prevent accurate observation from aeroplanes. The area too is much intersected by deep, precipitous ravines affording covered ways for any enemy movement against the flank of an advancing column. Further it appeared that the main body of the *lashkar* was at Shin Konr, and that the villages between that place and Ahmadwam were occupied by small bodies of the enemy. For these reasons and to avoid severe casualties Major-General Skeen decided to carry out the first stage of the advance under cover of darkness.

On the 1st February an advanced force of three battalions with a proportion of Pioneers and Sappers and Miners under Brigadier-General Gwyn-Thomas moved out from camp at 3-15 A.M. just after the moon had set, and advancing in column of route up the river bed under close cover of the right bank occupied the difficult country overlooking the latter. Thus two miles of ground had been secured without the enemy suspecting the presence of troops, and by daylight the piquets on this side were practically completed. Another force of one-and-a-half battalions and one section of No. 27 Mountain Battery moved out at 4-15 A.M. to piquet the left bank of the river from Bangiwala past "Slug Hill" to the ground covering Aka Khel from the north and west. Just before dawn a small party of the enemy occupying Aka Khel village discovered this force and opening a wild and ineffective fire fled upstream. The troops pushed on rapidly and gained their positions without casualties. By daybreak all objectives had been secured and were being rapidly strengthened, thus affording especially on the right bank, a series of successive strong points against which it was hoped the enemy would concentrate and offer good targets. This, unfortunately, did not happen, the enemy being apparently discouraged by the loss of the strongest tactical features in the area and by the obvious failure of Shah Daula's guns, which opening shortly after daybreak from a position in front of a cave at Shin Konr were silenced by a couple of shells from a section of 2·75 guns in action on the Aka Khel plateau.

The Royal Air Force during the day reported the presence of large bodies of tribesmen close to our advanced troops and these were dealt with by the Howitzers and the 2·75 guns, the latter using half charges with good results. The Royal Air Force too played an important part in harassing these hostile parties and preventing their concerted action, though snipers continued to prove troublesome throughout the day.

This action was an excellent example of a successful surprise and of the great demoralizing effect it has on unorganized tribesmen. The approaches to the piquet positions which were traversed in the dark were most difficult and the success which attended the night movements shows the high standard of discipline and moral to which the troops had now attained.*

---

* The enemy's casualties in the day's operations were subsequently reported as seventy chiefly due to fire from the aeroplanes. Our casualties were ten killed including a British officer and nineteen wounded including an Observer officer of the Royal Air Force.

During the following day six permanent piquets were constructed and occupied preparatory to the renewal of the advance on the 3rd February. The country was even more difficult than that already traversed and Major-General Skeen was obliged to decide on another night operation of a more hazardous and intricate nature than the former; the performance of his troops, however, on the 1st February making him confident of success.

Reports received showed that the tribesmen who had retired towards Dwa Toi were dispersing to their homes. The considerable number of Mahsuds who had collected at Shin Konr only to witness the complete failure of the Afghan guns and their inability to stay the advance of the Derajat Column, were much disheartened and realised that their hopes had been buoyed up with the false promises made them by their prominent *mullahs* and by the minor officials in the neighbouring Afghan districts. It appeared that the majority of the Mahsuds had been led to believe too that Haji Abdur Raziq was an accredited agent of the Amir and that he had come empowered to effect a settlement for them with the British, also that it was in order to give the Haji an official status that the Afghan guns had been brought from Wana.

Advance to Janjal, 3rd and 5th February.—It was evident from reconnaissances and intelligence reports that although the main body of the tribesmen had withdrawn bodies of them were still in the vicinity of Shin Konr village. At midnight of the 2nd/3rd February the 3rd Guides occupied Cliff End village and tower, followed by the 2/5th Gurkha Rifles who left camp at 1 A.M. to secure Cloud End over a mile distant. These battalions were to be supported later by a force leaving camp at 5 A.M. Shortly after 1 A.M. sleet began to fall. This was accompanied by a biting wind. By 4-30 A.M. it was apparent that, apart from the cold, visibility and movement would be so affected by the weather conditions as to make operations impracticable. The Guides were ordered to consolidate their positions but the 2/5th Gurkha Rifles were recalled as they were undesirably far from camp although the battalion had reached its objective with only one casualty. These two battalions suffered considerably from the severity of the cold, and all the troops underwent much discomfort during the day from the snow and mud. Bad weather continued to prevent operations from being resumed until the 5th February. On that day the advanced troops moved out at 1 A.M. the main column leaving camp at 5-30 A.M. The heavy rain and snow had ceased but the cold was very severe and the night march ranks as a very fine feat of endurance on the part of all ranks. Not only was the temperature 25 degrees below freezing point but a strong bitter wind added to their discomfort. The Tank Zam had to be forded many times, and each time the troops emerged from the river their boots and putties were encased immediately in ice. Icicles formed on the cables where they crossed and were struck by the stream, and all channels of the Tank Zam, except for a very narrow strip of the main stream, were thickly crusted with ice. The men working in the dark on the construction of defences on the high ground had first to wrench up the stones which were frozen fast to the ground and then handle this icy material without respite or means of warming themselves. In spite of the hardships so bravely endured by the troops the operation proved a most signal success and so thoroughly disheartened the enemy that he offered no combined opposition.

Prominent features dominating the route were promptly secured by the advanced troops and the column proceeded rapidly, concentrating at Janjal by 5 P.M. with the loss of only one casualty during the day. On the following day a camp was formed on a good site, on a plateau west of the Piazha Algad and on the 7th daily staging between the latter place and Sorarogha, a distance of nine miles, began.

Camp at Piazha Raghza.—The column remained at Piazha Raghza Camp until the 14th February, in order to collect a reserve of supplies and improve the roads to the river bed. Permanent piquets were established with a loss of seven casualties up to Dwa Toi where the Dara Toi and Baddar Toi streams join. Considerable punitive destruction was carried out especially in the villages of the Shabi Khel, much firewood being collected from the villages as they were destroyed. The weather continued very cold with much snow and rain and the accumulation of the reserve of supplies was only completed with considerable difficulty.

Punitive operations and preparations for advance to Makin.

Sniping into this camp occurred almost nightly, and occasionally into the permanent piquets but for short periods only and with little effect. Up to this period there had been very little sniping by night into camp and this was attributed to the fact that the tribesmen realised that unaimed fire is a waste of ammunition, and that what had been suitable and comparatively effective with inferior weapons is unsuitable with modern weapons when a much better result with equal safety to the firer can be obtained by aimed sniping. Day sniping in consequence had increased and was responsible for many casualties, especially during the first two days' halt at Palosina Camp.

On the 13th February news reached the Column of the collapse at Kotkai of a village tower occupied by a piquet, which lost fifteen killed and seven injured.* On the following day the 67th Brigade moved from Sorarogha to Piazha leaving a battalion of the 43rd Brigade at Sorarogha. Preparations for the advance on Makin were now complete.

---

* The accident was due to excess of sandbags on a roof already weakened by rain.

CHAPTER XI.

The Advance to Makin and Kaniguram.

While the column was at Piazha the tribesmen were informed that, as their attitude continued to be unsatisfactory, the original terms handed to them and all amendments thereto were now null and void, and that negotiations for peace would not be re-opened until the stipulated number of tribal rifles had been handed in and all fines paid in full. Further, that Makin and Kaniguram would be destroyed unless a specified number of government rifles were surrendered in addition before our arrival in those areas. This was fixed at two hundred for Makin and two hundred for Kaniguram. During our advance every possible facility had been given to the Mahsuds to comply with our terms, but nothing we could do, and no steps we could take, would convince the tribesmen of the reality of our intentions.

Advance to Marobi, 16th February.—The intense cold still continued and the troops were issued with leather jerkins which greatly added to their comfort. Leaving the 43rd Brigade, with its base at Piazha Raghza to become No. 3 Section, Lines of Communication Defences, the column consisting of:—

Column Headquarters.

Headquarters 67th Brigade.

2/5th Gurkha Rifles.

2/9th Gurkha Rifles.

4/3rd Gurkha Rifles (joined the column on 12th February).

1/55th Coke's Rifles.

3rd Guides.

3/34th Sikh Pioneers.

No. 6 Mountain Battery.

No. 27 Indian Mountain Battery.

55th Field Company Sappers and Miners.

Medical and Supply and Transport Units.

commenced its advance towards Makin on the 15th February. In order to combine the protection of the left flank during this movement with the establishment of permanent piquets protecting the route were most exposed to attack from Maidan. Brigadier-General Gwyn-Thomas with a force of two-and-a-half battalions and some Sappers and Miners moved out at 5 A.M. and prepared and occupied permanent piquets on the ridges, known as "Dwa Toi East" and "Oxford Circus," without opposition.

The main column moved off at 6 A.M. the advanced guard under Lieutenant-Colonel D. M. Watt, D.S.O., 2/5th Gurkha Rifles, moving into the narrow Dwa Toi defile at 7-30 A.M. Opposition from the snipers commenced at once. These though quickly driven back, continued to harass the advance until Marobi was reached and piquets had been established well ahead of that place. The piqueting troops having been used up about a mile from Dwa Toi, the main body under Brigadier-General Lucas, took up the task of making good the route, and camp was formed on the Marobi spur and in two *kach* areas south-east of it, all troops and transport reaching camp before 4 P.M. though the operation of establishing camp piquets was not complete till 6 P.M.*

Advance to Tauda China, 16th February.—Seven permanent road piquets had been established on the 15th instant; these were completed, garrisoned, and fully equipped under cover of the rearguard of the main column on the following day during the advance to Tauda China, a distance of one and three quarter miles. The movement commenced at 8 A.M. and was completed by 5 P.M.

The 3/11th Gurkha Rifles from India joined the column at 9-30 A.M. and were sent forward to assist in securing camp. Opposition to the advance and to the establishment of camp piquets was encountered, which resulted in casualties amounting to one killed and twelve wounded. The enemy were reported to have lost three killed and eight wounded. The force encamped on a *Raghza* a few hundred yards east of the Tauda China stream, and about two miles from Makin town and less than that distance from the other villages in the area and the cultivation which occupied most of the extensive valley.

On the 17th February additional permanent piquets were established and empty transport animals returned to Piazha Raghza. At 2 P.M. about 50 Mahsuds attacked a detachment of the 4/3rd Gurkha Rifles covering parties

---

* Our casualties for this action were three killed, and twenty wounded. Enemy casualties are stated to have been eight killed and wounded.

collecting firewood from a demolished village to the south-west of camp. The enemy was driven off but a dozen of them took refuge in a village where they put up a stout resistance—necessitating the employment of the whole battalion. The village was carried without many casualties but these could not be removed owing to the accurate fire of snipers ensconced in the vicinity. Eventually it was found necessary to await dusk before carrying out the withdrawal which was effected without further incident, our casualties totalling ten killed and thirty-seven wounded.

Punitive measures in Makin area, 19th-28th February.—As the recalcitrant tribesmen of this area had made no attempt to hand in the number of rifles demanded by Government to be surrendered at Makin, punitive measures began on the 19th February. Makin is the name given to the whole of this valley area up-stream of the camp a distance of about two-and-a-half miles. This area contains extensive cultivation consisting of well-terraced fields above which lie the town of Makin and the large villages of Umar Khel, Band Khel, and Manzakai.

As a prelude to the major operations it was necessary to occupy the prominent features of " Tree Hill " and " Split Hill " north-west and south-west of camp respectively and this was done under cover of darkness. The success of the operation effecting the occupation of " Tree Hill " was delayed for a while by the failure of a detachment of the 4/3rd Gurkha Rifles to secure its objective and begin the construction of its piquet before daylight. Dawn found this detachment on a feature several hundred yards to the east of its objective.

This was the first and last occasion during these operations on which a unit taking part in night movements missed its objective, and the mistake on this occasion is attributed to the fact that there had been no opportunity to reconnoitre the difficult ravines which lay between camp and the objective.

The remainder of the force left camp at 6 A.M. while it was still dark and under cover of " Tree Hill " piquet aimed at penetrating Makin, trusting to the enemy being unable to concentrate in sufficient force to take advantage of the confined nature of the country. By 7-15 A.M. the advanced troops were approaching the vicinity of " Tree

Hill," but the ground in advance of this hill proved much more difficult than had been anticipated. To the north-west in a valley lay fallow fields flanked on both sides by wooded spurs which were dominated by three villages and several towers which were occupied by the tribesmen.

To clear the spurs of the enemy took time, but by 10 A.M. the 3/11th Gurkha Rifles were in possession of the most important position and were preparing for an attack on the easterly end of Makin. Shortly after this the enemy attacked the Gurkhas but were driven off with loss. As the 3/11th Gurkha Rifles were concentrating to resume the attack their front line came under the fire of our howitzers which were in action in camp. This unfortunate accident caused casualties and obliged the leading companies to recoil. The evacuated positions were seized promptly by the enemy who by heavy fire also compelled the 2/9th Gurkha Rifles on the right to fall back. A considerable time elapsed in removing our casualties, and it was decided that no further operations should be undertaken. Four towers were demolished, several hamlets burnt, and " Hill Tree " piquet established, and the troops were withdrawn to camp, which was reached at about 3 P.M.* During the following night a party of Mahsuds bombed " Tree Hill " piquet causing four casualties but they themselves lost heavily from the fire of the piquet.

The operations for the 20th were intended to deal with the villages south-west of the Dara Toi and west of the Makin gorge, and to cover the construction of a permanent piquet on " Split Hill." A force consisting of the 1/55th Rifles and a company of Pioneers with a section of Sappers and Miners left camp at 2-30 A.M. and occupied without opposition " Split Hill " and a number of points covering the southern flank of the projected operations. Work on the " Split Hill " piquet was progressing well when at 6-45 A.M., while it was still dark, the Mahsuds attacked the covering troops. The enemy, however, was driven off, and the piquet was established without further incident.

Losses from snipers.—The main column under Brigadier-General Lucas gained its objective by 9-40 A.M.

---

* Our casualties for this action were thirty-four killed and twenty-eight wounded. Several parties of the enemy came under our shell fire during the day and the tribesmen eventually acknowledged a total loss of sixteen killed and thirty-eight wounded.

and the work of destruction continued until 12-30 P.M. The advanced troops again experienced considerable hostile rifle fire from the cover of houses and cultivation walls which caused several casualties. The withdrawal however, was completed by 3-30 P.M. The destructive work on this day included seventeen towers, one hundred and sixty houses and a large number of retaining walls in the fields.* The heavy losses suffered by our troops during these two days showed clearly that the destruction of a frontier village is a much more dangerous operation than it used to be in frontier expeditions. A very much larger number of troops must be employed to keep the tribesmen at a distance from the scene of destruction. The villages are generally situated in open spaces surrounded by high rocky hills thickly covered with undergrowth affording ideal cover for snipers whose accurate fire at known ranges is concentrated on the troops working in the villages and takes a steady toll.

Time therefore is a most important factor in this type of operation. Towers should be demolished as soon as prepared and any attempt to obtain a spectacular effect should be repressed, but no house should be fired without express orders as the dense smoke emitted is liable to interrupt communication and mutual support of bodies of troops, and also to hinder the essential artillery support during the withdrawal. Should it appear likely that the retirement will be pressed, signals by Verey lights denoting permission to begin firing the village can be employed with good effect.

Settlement by Umar Khel section to save their property. —On the 21st February the Umar Khel section of the Bahlolzai living on the right bank of the Dara Toi sent in a deputation which offered to surrender immediately twelve Government rifles on condition their property was spared from further destruction. The deputation also promised that no sniping would take place from their area. This offer was accepted by Major-General Climo who was visiting the column.

Description of Marobi, 21st February.—Partly to test the value of the Umar Khel undertaking, and partly to

---

* Our casualties were twenty-seven killed and sixty-three wounded. The enemy losses were acknowledged as six killed and ten severely wounded.

cover the re-victualling of the piquets, two-and-a-half battalions and two howitzers proceeded on the 21st to "Split Hill" to destroy some prominent towers in the Makin gorge by shell fire. At the same time a small party covered the re-victualling of "Tree Hill" piquet. There were no casualties and the Umar Khel fulfilled their agreement. On this day Marobi, the village of the recalcitrant Mullah Fazl Din and of his notorious father Mullah Powindah was razed to the ground, the mosque only being spared. This was the village in which so many plots involving the murder of British officials had been hatched, and it was hoped that the destruction of the place would break permanently the temporal power of a relentless enemy to Government.

On the 23rd February operations were resumed against the Makin villages on the left bank of the Dara Toi. The Umar Khel villages and fields held no snipers, and within two hours all preparation for the withdrawal having been made the villages were set on fire. The withdrawal was carried out without untoward incident, . our casualties amounting to five killed and seven wounded. The two following days were also employed in carrying on the work of destruction with small loss to ourselves.

On the 27th an imposing tower known as "Eddystone" standing on a prominent and imposing bluff at the very junction of the Upper Dara Toi and the Dashkai Algad, was destroyed by howitzer fire at a range of 4,700 yards with an expenditure of ten shells only.

On the following day all remaining towers in sight except those belonging to the Umar Khel were levelled to the ground by gunfire, thus bringing the total destruction in this area up to 51 towers and about 450 important houses. The villages in the Makin gorge were not visited by the column. The steep crags and slopes in the gorge overlook every move in the advance to this area, and the troops operating in the villages would have been exposed to snipers at ranges of from three hundred yards upwards, and judging by previous experiences it was decided that the results to be obtained would not justify the heavy losses the operation would entail. During the first few days our troops sustained over two hundred casualties but after that opposition decreased to such an extent that we only had some twenty casualties during the last two days.

It was decided to evacuate Makin area on the 1st March and to advance on Kaniguram, which we had told the tribesmen we intended to do in the event of their not complying with our terms. On the 29th February the preliminary arrangements for the withdrawals from the Makin area were set in motion.

The 3/11th Gurkha Rifles,
3/34th Sikh Pioneers,
1 section 27th Mountain Battery,

proceeded to Marobi to pass up camel transport required for the column, to return the surplus stores in Piazha, and to arrange for the reduction of the stores in permanent piquets near Marobi. Similar steps were taken at Tauda China camp.

Evacuation of Makin.—Several permanent piquets had been established well forward to facilitate the daily operations against Makin and the withdrawal of these piquets, especially "Tree Hill" and "Split Hill" was a difficult problem. It was undesirable to disclose our intention to withdraw by removing the piquets previously, and a withdrawal by daylight on the 1st March would have added two miles to a withdrawal which it was anticipated, would be followed up closely by an exasperated enemy. Major-General Skeen decided that these forward piquets should withdraw after the moon had set, about 2 A.M., trusting to darkness for immunity. Shortly before nightfall on the 29th February the "Tree Hill" piquet reported one man killed and another wounded by snipers between the piquet and the camp, and later signalled that it expected difficulty in withdrawing to camp. It was too late to despatch a party to evacuate the casualties. "Split Hill" piquet also reported enemy in the vicinity of its proposed line of retreat. Fortunately the piquet commanders had studied the ground carefully and were able to effect the withdrawal of their piquets at the appointed hour and without casualty. These young British officers in command and their men showed great courage and skill in carrying out a movement fraught with grave risk and in a situation in which every condition was against them. In the meantime at 5-50 A.M. two detachments of one battalion each, moved off to take up positions covering the flanks of the route to Dwa Toi, the advanced guard following at 6-15 A.M. with artillery to take up successive positions to cover the withdrawal from the camp. All transport was loaded in the dark and using all roads was clear of camp by daylight. The infantry had by this time occupied a series of positions and the withdrawal of the camp piquets began. Some Mahsuds were seen to enter " Split Hill " piquet, where a " booby " trap was reported later to have accounted for four.

The withdrawal which had proved a great surprise to the tribesmen was not pressed except during the evacuation of a camp piquet on the right bank of the stream. where the enemy succeeded in working down the river bed and firing at close range on the piquet during its withdrawal. The troops supporting the withdrawal of this piquet were too far out of range to afford this party any useful assistance. The piquet lost two killed and six prisoners; the latter, Punjabi Mussalmans were released eventually by the Mahsuds and rejoined their unit at Dwa Toi.*

The enemy followed up the withdrawal to within a mile of Marobi frequently coming under the fire of guns and aeroplanes.

The Column encamped in the afternoon on cultivation at Dwa Toi and the empty animals of the second line transport were sent to Piazha.

Our casualties on this day were four killed and one wounded. The enemy losses were reported subsequently as twenty-eight killed and a number severely wounded. chiefly due to gun and aeroplane fire while searching for food and loot on the deserted camping ground.

This action by the enemy had been anticipated, and several " booby " traps were arranged, the principal being a sham grave containing a charge of fifty pounds of guncotton. This trap caused eight casualties of whom seven were blown to pieces.

Preparations for advance on Kaniguram.—To support the withdrawal of the column from Makin the 43rd Bri-

---

* These men were court-martialled and sentenced to death for cowardice, but the sentences were commuted to one of three years' imprisonment.

gade under Brigadier-General Gwyn-Thomas had moved out from Piazha and constructed and occupied two permanent piquets on the right and left bank of the Baddar Toi, upstream of Dwa Toi camp. The next few days were employed in the construction of piquets up the valley of the Baddar Toi as a preliminary step to the advance of the column to Kaniguram. These piquets were not completed without casualties from enemy snipers concealed on the hillsides, which are comparatively thickly covered with small trees affording excellent opportunities, as the cover is sufficient to protect the snipers from view, while insufficient to limit their range of vision. The most effectual method of dealing with enemy snipers was to detail especially intelligent men to stalk or fire at likely places. Although enemy snipers may not have been killed in this manner they were certainly driven off. The use of rifle grenades too proved very useful in clearing wooded country of snipers.

Surrender of rifles to save Kaniguram.—On the 29th February while the column was at Tauda China camp, some Mahsud representatives signified their intention of surrendering the rifles demanded to ensure the immunity of Kaniguram from destruction. The total handed in, however, amounted to 103 Government rifles, 113 tribal rifles and about Rs. 2,400. Some fifty of the Government rifles were without bolts, and many without magazines. As the numbers were below the specified number, the *maliks* were informed they might withdraw the rifles and that the march to Kaniguram would begin. The headmen, however, preferred to leave them in our possession and promised to renew their efforts to collect the balance. On the 2nd information was received that the Mahsuds had given up hope of effecting the surrender of the necessary rifles and had dispersed to their homes.

Difficulties of Maliks in collecting rifles.—The difficulties that beset the *maliks* in their efforts to collect the rifles were—

> (a) In many cases an individual was in possession of 3 or 4 Government rifles and although willing to surrender one wished to keep the remainder or be paid compensation for them;

(b) in many cases a rifle was held conjointly by some ten men, some of these belonging to the peace and others to the war party;

(c) many rifles had been buried and their possession concealed. In addition to this there was the fear of the tribesman that the full numbers not being forthcoming his individual sacrifice might be in vain.

Advance to Ladha, 3rd March.—The advance towards Kaniguram began at 5-30 A.M. on the 3rd March, the advanced guard consisting of two battalions and a section of guns with a proportion of Pioneers and Sappers and Miners. These technical troops were to assist in the construction of the five permanent piquets which reconnaissance had shown to be necessary.

Shortly before dawn the enemy hidden in the rocky and bush-covered slopes on the right bank opened a heavy fire on the leading troops, who however steadily pushed on up the *nala* bed and secured "The Dam", a spur from the Maidan plateau projecting between the Baddar Toi and the Maidan Algad.

See panorama No. 6.

The able handling of the advanced guard secured for the column the series of rocky bluffs commanding the route at short range which on account of their ruggedness and steep bush-covered slopes made this portion of the route the most difficult of the whole series of the *tangis* traversed by the column since leaving Jandola.

Heavy hostile fire from the right bank continued to enfilade the troops occupying "The Dam" to which position a section of guns had been ordered. Fortunately at this time the howitzers came into action in the river under cover, and searched the wooded hills very thoroughly with their fire. Under cover of this fire the section was enabled to get into action without a casualty, and as soon as the detachments were established behind their shields in action the hillsides were sprayed with shrapnel. The enemy having been thus driven off the advance was resumed. The column encamped on the cultivation below Ladha, and nearly all the camel transport was passed back to Piazha to bring up supplies the next day.*

---

* Our casualties on this day were, one killed and nine wounded.

It was evident that the heart had gone out of the Mahsuds and that it was now most unlikely that any large *lashkar* would again take the field. Haji Abdur Raziq and Shah Daula had moved to Shakai and had taken with them the Afghan guns. All that could be anticipated from the tribesmen was occasional sniping in the defence of particular villages or localities.

As a precaution against interruption by the weather or the enemy, and to control the upper exit of the defiles near the Dam, a strong point was constructed on the site of the present Ladha Camp. On the 4th and 5th March the troops were employed in constructing two camel tracks to avoid the impassable *tangi* near Paiozar village, three-quarters of a mile upstream. The permanent piquets named " Prospect " and " Clubhouse " were also established.

Column arrives Kaniguram, 6th March.—The 3rd Guides having taken over the Ladha Strong point and the permanent piquets in this area the column resumed the advance to Kaniguram on the 6th March. Permanent piquets were established *en route* and the column encamped about 800 yards east of Kaniguram. Little opposition was encountered but accurate sniping caused us a loss of thirteen men while establishing piquets in the area north-west of the town.

Kaniguram is, properly speaking, the only town in Mahsud country. Although the inhabitants are principally Urmars it is regarded as the capital of the country. The town is built in terraces on the south side of a steep spur about a mile in length flanking the left bank of the Baddar Toi, and consists of about one thousand houses and five towers. It is the chief commercial centre of the country and contains a fairly large bazaar, several rifle and knife factories. Here all important Mahsud national assemblies take place at the expense of the Urmars who, tradition demands, should provide free entertainment for their hungry guests.

Attitude of Mahsuds.—On the following day a deputation of prominent Urmars visited the camp and announced that the Mahsuds had failed to collect the rifles necessary to save Kaniguram and that they did not intend to take any further action in the matter. This obduracy of the tribesmen is at first sight difficult to explain. Our demands were not excessive and the Mahsuds had had ample time to collect double the numbers demanded, if they had wished to do so. It can only be concluded therefore, that the situation was due to the results of former policies when terms were a matter of mutual concessions and anything in the nature of insistence or full compliance with original terms was unknown. The childish subterfuges of trying to pass unserviceable rifles or parts of rifles and of producing half the numbers demanded showed that the tribe had been educated for so long in the art of mutual concessions that it was unable to realize the fact that Government was determined on this occasion to obtain a complete submission.

The Mahsuds had suffered heavy casualties and much destruction of their property had taken place, but these punishments failed to coerce the tribe into accepting our terms, and no destruction could compensate adequately for this failure. It appeared, therefore, that this coercion could not be attained without a prolonged stay in the country as it was impossible to force this tribe of unruly and obdurate individuals, recognizing no responsible leaders and no form of organized government, to make any engagements, or to keep such promises if made, once the troops had left the country. Under these new conditions the destruction of the amenities or of the resources of the country seemed inadvisable as they might be required for ourselves. The opportunity was therefore taken to give the tribesmen a further extension of time in which to comply with our demands.

During the stay of the Column at Kaniguram the Mahsuds gave little trouble, and much useful survey work was completed. The weather however, was most unsettled and heavy snow falling on the 12th and the 13th caused interruption to convoys and great discomfort to the troops and animals. On the 18th during a terrific thunderstorm two sentries were struck by lightning, and severely injured. Most of the tribes now began to make genuine efforts to collect and pay in their shares of the fine and their proportion of tribal and Government rifles, but certain sections especially those further removed from our line of advance, made little or no effort. The worst offenders were the inhabitants of the upper valleys of the Baddar Toi who believed themselves out of reach of our troops.

Punitive operations up Baddar Toi, 6th-8th April.—These people were well known recalcitrants and, as no troops had penetrated into their country for many years it was decided to punish them. Accordingly a force composed of detachments from all units numbering 6 guns and 2,620 rifles with 2,000 transport animals moved from the new camp near Karon on the 6th April and advanced up the Baddar Toi. No opposition was encountered during the march but on forming camp at Sine Tizha about 4 P.M. sniping began, causing two casualties. The day's operations included the destruction of two towers at Mano Tsilai and the villages and towers of Sine Tizha.

On the following day the Column continued its advance to Giga Khel with the object of carrying out punitive measures against the villages and property of the Abdur Rahman Khel in that area. The towers were demolished in spite of opposition and the troops began to withdraw. The retirement was followed up by some three hundred tribesmen who met with little success except against a small party of the 4/3rd Gurkha Rifles which descending into a ravine, found itself delayed by a waterfall, and was overwhelmed. This incident besides showing a lack of previous reconnaissance and the danger of using a *nala* as a line of retirement demonstrates the fact that ravines are more dangerous than ever since the tribesman possibly to avoid gunfire, uses them to cover his pursuit of a retiring piquet. The troops were all in camp by 4 P.M. our casualties during the day being ten killed and twenty-nine wounded. The enemy principally Wazirs from Shakai lost approximately the same number.

See panorama Nos. 7 and 8 at end of book.

The withdrawal to Kaniguram began at 6-45 A.M. on the 8th April and was followed up by about one hundred of the enemy. These at first contented themselves with long range sniping but later a determined attack was pressed down the Baddar Toi and caused a few casualties to the rear parties. The Column was back in Kaniguram at 5 P.M. losing this day five killed and fourteen wounded.

Active operations cease, 7th May.—The operations in the Baddar Toi valley closed the active work of the Derajat Column. After a sixteen-foot road graded to suit Mechanical Transport had been constructed from Kaniguram to

Ladha, the whole column concentrated at the latter place and began then the construction of a permanent camp.

As all resistance had practically ceased and our troops were unmolested, it was decided to reduce the garrison at Ladha to one Infantry Brigade with a battery of artillery, a field company of Sappers and Miners and a Pioneer battalion. Similarly a reduction was effected in the garrisons of permanent piquets; thus affording opportunities of better training and permitting the larger posts to send out strong patrols, and assume the spirit of aggression. The ambushes and offensive measures adopted by the posts on the Lines of Communication were meeting with success, and there was a general feeling of apprehension and uneasiness among the tribesmen. Alarms, generally ill-founded were constantly raised among them of projected night incursions by our troops in various directions.

The Headquarters of the Derajat Column were dispersed on the 7th May and their dispersal brought the operations to an end. Thus ended a Frontier campaign of unparalleled hard fighting and severity. The enemy fought with a determination and courage which has rarely, if ever, been encountered by our troops in similar operations. The character of the *terrain*, combined with trying and arduous climatic conditions, alone presented difficulties before which the most seasoned troops might well have hesitated. The resistance of the enemy was broken, and the difficulties successfully overcome by a force composed almost entirely of young Indian troops. No British troops except for the Royal Air Force, and a British Battery of Mountain Artillery were employed. This fact has without doubt, considerably raised the prestige of the Indian Army on the Frontier and increased the *esprit-de-corps* of the troops engaged.

CHAPTER XII.

Lessons of the Campaign.

The chief lesson of the campaign of 1919-1920 is that although a force may be equipped with the most modern weapons and appliances it cannot command success unless its men are well trained and its officers lead them in accordance with the time-honoured and proved principles of war as recorded in our regulations. Powerful modern weapons demand a higher standard of intelligence in their employment and a higher standard of technical efficiency in their actual use than our troops had been trained up to before their introduction. Further, it must be recognized that the rifle and bayonet are the sheet anchor of the infantryman and that all other weapons are merely auxiliary to these two. Partially, or badly, trained troops are apt to place undue reliance on these subsidiary weapons, even though they are far from expert in their use, to the detriment, in time of emergency, of the proper handling of their main weapon—the rifle.

In the initial stages of the campaign the training of the infantry left much to be desired. The special faults which led to ineffective operations and undue casualties are not new or peculiar to these operations. First and foremost there was a lack of confidence in the rifle, and power to use it efficiently. Although there were many instances of hand-to-hand fighting examples of the proper use of the bayonet were few and far between. The fire discipline was bad, resulting in poor fire effect and a waste of ammunition. The use of ground and preparation of cover was not properly understood and in many cases neither officers nor men were sufficiently trained in this important respect. In time however, these difficulties were overcome, and the infantry were trained to be keen and alert, ready to apply effective fire to any target which presented itself. As had been noted in many former campaigns the chief requirements for an efficient infantryman are physical and mental fitness, keen eyesight, supreme confidence in his rifle and bayonet, and ability to obtain cover quickly, *i.e.. sangar* making.

In operations against mobile and energetic tribesmen especially, the following very important principle enunciated in " Infantry Training " must be observed.

"The early opening of fire discounts surprise and, whether in attack or defence, often indicates the position of troops which would otherwise be unnoticed by the enemy." Rapid fire in Frontier Warfare should be the exception rather than the rule. The rifleman should depend on deliberate aimed fire, determined to place bullets very close to the spot he wishes to hit. Trained observers are indispensable not only to watch the effect of fire but to keep all ground under continuous observation, so that the slightest indication of the presence of a hostile marksman shall not be missed. For volume of fire and covering and surprise fire we should depend chiefly on machine and Lewis guns.

It cannot be impressed too strongly on young units and young soldiers that wild firing by day or night is one of the indications whereby the tribesmen gauge the moral, physical and professional standard of our troops. It is against units with indifferent day and night fire discipline that they prepare their more elaborate surprises.

Training in loading and firing with a minimum of exposure and a maximum of accuracy uphill and downhill, round and over cover, and from among rocks and boulders are some of the chief essentials for the preparation of riflemen for fighting among mountains.

Two tactical modifications of previous practice were introduced with great success—night advances and permanent piquets. Night advances were adopted in order to avoid the casualties which must have been incurred during daylight in gaining unusually difficult ground commanded by well-armed tribesmen, and also to use to the best advantage the short hours of daylight. Prior to these operations movement of troops by night was deprecated because it gave away our advantage of armament and discipline. The enemy's armament as regards the rifle being equal, and his use in it superior to that of our troops these advantages passed away from us.

The advantages we gained therefore by night movement were:—

    (a) the enemy was denied the full value from his rifle, and he disclosed his numbers and positions if he used it before daylight.

    (b) the bewildering effect on an unorganized enemy, whose lack of discipline prevented adequate piquets to watch our movements especially at night and during cold.

(c) the enemy was frequently forestalled in the occupation of important tactical points.

The system of protecting the Lines of Communication by permanent piquets had the most gratifying results and it is interesting to record that throughout the operations losses by enemy action in convoys did not exceed 26 animals. This is a remarkable result in view of the length of the Lines of Communication and of the very difficult country through which they passed.

The system has justified its institution by giving us the following advantages:—

(a) its avoidance of daily encounters to secure the march of the daily convoy; encounters which are certain to be costly with an enemy armed with a high-velocity rifle.

(b) it avoids fatigue to the troops in scaling difficult heights.

(c) if well organized this system is less expensive in the employment of troops than the daily establishment of both inner and outer lines of protection.

(d) these piquets command the main route which usually passes through the richest part of the country, and thus form an effective and constant threat to the inhabitants.

(e) it prevents all communication between separated portions of the country except during the hours of darkness, and even this can be made dangerous by the use of ambushes or offensive patrols from the larger piquets.

The dangers of the system are obvious and should be overcome by careful instruction and supervision to prevent the occurrence of regrettable incidents.

It may be possible in the future against a less enterprising and less courageous tribe than the Mahsuds to revert to longer daily advances protected by temporary day piquets. In the campaign herein described short marches and the presence of permanent piquets curtailed our losses to an extent difficult to estimate. In connection with permanent piquets the earliest steps should be taken to reduce the original strength to the lowest limits; this becomes feasible by the artificial strengthening of the position occupied by every means possible.

Tactics to mystify enemy.—The principle of daily and nightly variation in the system of protection of camps, routes, etc., cannot be known too widely : by its adoption troops are economised, longer periods of rest ensured and the tribesmen kept in a state of uncertainty.

In the case of a camp the principle is attained by providing eight inlying piquets one night, four the next night, six the third night, 3 or 4 the following night and so on, patrols round the inside of the perimeter being employed on the night when less than the maximum protection is provided.

In the case of a Mechanical Transport road, the first day may consist of maximum protection by piquets, armoured cars and Lewis guns and Ford vans, the second day parties of Cavalry and Ford Vans, the third day armoured cars and Ford vans and so on.

It is well known that the tribesmen, before carrying out a road raid, study the conditions for some days, and if there is no variation in the protection they very soon determine where the weak point or points are. Daily change of protection leaves the tribesmen guessing and that is the state of mind we desire to induce.

Ambushes.—Until the last two months of the campaign the country occupied belonged to us by day, but after dark the tribesmen were at liberty to roam at their will. This has been the history of all occupations of frontier territory. In March both in the Tochi and in the Takki Zam commanders of defence troops on the Lines of Communication were encouraged to lay ambuscades at night both on a large and small scale. Eventually there ensued a fair degree of friendly rivalry between adjacent camps. The results were very gratifying and were much beyond expectation. The tribesmen became apprehensive of night incursions and moved with much less freedom than heretofore. It is not too much to state that he became the raided instead of the raider.

Command and staff.—To demonstrate the impossible situations which arise during transition from peace to war, the following examples are given. The General Officer Commanding Bannu Brigade at Dardoni, with his communications cut except for wireless, was constantly being appealed to by the Civil Authorities and referred to by the Bannu Military Authorities to deal with incursions of tribesman in the back areas. Similarly the General Officer Commanding Derajat Brigade at Khirgi was endeavouring to control the area in his rear which is roughly 60 miles in width and 100 miles in length. Both of these commanders were deeply engrossed with the situation in their immediate neighbourhood and should have been free to attend to these matters only. This condition of affairs can be obviated by suitable command and staff arrangements in peace time : the institution of administrative commandants at Dera Ismail Khan and Bannu, in touch with local conditions and requirements, would serve the purpose. On the necessity arising for the General Officer Commanding and his staff to take the field, the Administrative Commandant is ready on the spot to deal with administrative and defence questions on the Lines of Communication, while the General Officer Commanding on moving forward has the satisfaction of knowing he has left these matters in competent hands.

For the first time in the history of the North-West Frontier, aeroplanes were employed extensively against the tribes. The aeroplanes used were Bristol Fighters, D. H. 9A's and D. H. 10's. It is impossible to overestimate the value of aircraft in tactical co-operation with other arms. Their presence alone greatly raised the moral of our troops while correspondingly decreasing that of the enemy. In order to obtain the full value of this important factor it is very necessary that the officers of the Royal Air Force should be well acquainted with the principles of Infantry tactics, and of land formations especially those employed in mountain warfare. Communication between ground and the aeroplanes in the air is essential if the fullest co-operation is to be gained. The Popham panel was found to have little value for the purpose. The positions of our troops were indicated by ground strips, but these sometimes fell into the hands of the enemy. Aeroplanes, when thus employed in tactical co-operation did considerable damage and helped in no small measure towards the success of many of the actions.

The information obtained from air photographs both vertical and oblique was of great tactical and topographical value, and officers of the land forces would find their labour well repaid if they undertook the study of this important auxiliary to the art of tactics. The study should however, be supplemented by training in observation from the air. On the other hand the results from bombing and tactical reconnaissance did not fulfil expectations. This was largely due to the nature of the country and the skill with which the tribesmen concealed themselves.

<small>Plates Nos. 30 and 31.</small>

The new 3·7-inch howitzer was used with considerable effect but the special conditions of Frontier warfare show that to obtain its maximum usefulness it must be associated with a direct quick-firing weapon. This may be a mountain gun or the Vickers machine gun. The latter, however, was not available with the Force. The Lewis gun was used in its place on occasion but it cannot be maintained that this is the proper rôle of this weapon. The Lewis gun is essentially a short-range weapon, whereas, what is required is accurate fire effect at medium and long rifle range.

Throughout the whole Force special attention was paid to the problem of sanitation and the maintenance of a pure water supply. To the efforts of the medical officers and the hearty co-operation of all ranks is due the remarkable results achieved and the immunity of the Force from the disorders that caused the heavy casualties incurred during the operations of 1917.

APPENDIX A.

ORDER OF BATTLE.

South Waziristan Field Force 1917.

Commander:—Major-General W. G. L. Beynon, C.B., C.I.E., D.S.O.

Divisional Headquarters.

Divisional Headquarters.
Headquarters Section, No. 38 Divisional Signal Company.
1 Pack Wireless Set No. 3 (Wireless) Signal Squadron.
1 Troop, 11th King Edward's Own Lancers (Probyn's Horse).

43rd Brigade.

Brigade Section, No. 38 Divisional Signal Company.
½ Squadron, 11th King Edward's Own Lancers (Probyn's Horse).
2 Sections, 30th Mountain Battery.
1 Section, 1st Mountain Battery.
No. 7 Company, 1st King George's Own Sappers and Miners.
1-25th (County of London) Battalion, the London Regiment.
54th Sikhs (Frontier Force).
1st Rifle Regiment (Nepalese Contingent).
Brigade Supply Column.

45th Brigade.

Brigade Section No. 38, Divisional Signal Company.
½ Squadron, 11th King Edward's Own Lancers (Probyn's Horse).
23rd Peshawar Mountain Battery (Frontier Force).
No. 11 Company, 2nd Queen Victoria's Own Sappers and Miners.
2-6th Battalion, The Royal Sussex Regiment.
55th Coke's Rifles (Frontier Force).
2-1st King George's Own Gurkha Rifles (The Malaun Regiment).
Mahindradal Regiment (Nepalese Contingent).
Brigade Supply Column.

Lines of Communication Defences.

1 Wagon Wireless Set, No. 3 (Wireless) Signal Squadron.
1 Pack Wireless Set No. 3 (Wireless) Signal Squadron.
1 Squadron, Alwar Lancers.
21st Punjabis.
46th Punjabis.
1-94th Russell's Infantry.
1-107th Pioneers.
Wing 1-124th Duchess of Connaught's Own Baluchistan Infantry.
127th Queen Mary's Own Baluch Light Infantry.
Brigade Section, No. 38, Divisional Signal Company.

OUTPOSTS.

1 Pack Wireless Set No. 3 (Wireless Signal Squadron).
1 Section 30th Mountain Battery.
1-4th Gurkha Rifles.
11th Rajputs.
South Waziristan Militia.
} Sarwakai.

2-67th Punjabis
South Waziristan Militia
} Khajuri Kach.

Wing 2-67th Punjabis
South Waziristan Militia
} Nili Kach.

South Waziristan Militia, Other Gomal Posts.

2 Sections, No. 154 Indian Field Ambulance
No. 25 Combined Field Ambulance (less 1 British Section).
} 43rd Brigade.

2 Sections, No. 2 Amalgamated Field Ambulance
1 British Section, No. 25 Combined Field Ambulance
} 45th Brigade

MEDICAL UNITS.

1 Indian Section, No. 12 Combined Field Ambulance
1 Section, No. 149 Indian Field Ambulance.
} 4th Brigade

1 Section, No. 2 Amalgamated Field Ambulance
1 British Section, No. 5 Amalgamated Field Ambulance.
1 Indian Section, No. 27 Combined Field Ambulance.
} Lines of Communication.

1 British Section, No. 27 Combined Field Ambulance
1 Indian Section, No. 27 Combined Field Ambulance
} In reserve.

No. 17 Combined Clearing Hospital, Jandola.
No. 1 Section, No. 2 Amalgamated Field Ambulance, Sarwakai.

APPENDIX B.

ORDER OF BATTLE.

SOUTH WAZIRISTAN FIELD FORCE.

STRIKING FORCE.

Divisional Headquarters.

Divisional Headquarters.
Headquarters Section Divisional Signal Company.
1 Wireless Station.
1 Troop, 11th Lancers.

43rd Brigade.

½ Squadron, 11th Lancers.
2 Sections 30th Mountain Battery.
1 Section, 1st Mountain Battery.
7th Company Sappers.
1-25th Londons.
54th Sikhs.
1st Nepalese.
Brigade Section Divisional Signal Company.
Brigade Supply Column.

45th Brigade.

½ Squadron, 11th Lancers.
23rd Mountain Battery.
11th Company, Sappers.
2-6th Sussex.
55th Rifles.
2-1st Gurkhas.
Mahindradal Regiment (Nepalese).
Brigade Section, Divisional Signal Company.
Brigade Supply Column.

LINES OF COMMUNICATION DEFENCES.

General Baldwin's Brigade.

1 Squadron Alwar Lancers ⎫
94th Infantry.   ⎬ Tank.
Indian Base Depôt   ⎪
Wireless Station   ⎭
Wing 124th Baluchis, Khirgi.

Garrisoned by Frontier Constabulary, Zam.
46th Punjabis ⎫
107th Pioneers ⎬ Jandola.
1 Wireless Station ⎭
21st Punjabis
127th Baluchis ⎫ Advanced L. of C.
Brigade Section Divisional Signal Company ⎭ posts.

Under Divisional Headquarters, Base, Dera Ismail Khan.

1 Flight Royal Flying Corps Depôt, Depôt and Details, Tank.

Outposts.

456 South Waziristan Militia, Wana.
25 South Waziristan Militia, Tiarza.
25 South Waziristan Militia, Karab Kot.
71 South Waziristan Militia, Tanai.
25 South Waziristan Militia, Dargai Oba.
44 South Waziristan Militia, Toi Khulia.
1-4th Gurkhas ⎫
11th Rajputs. ⎪
1 Section, 30th Mountain Battery ⎬ Sarwakai.
1 Wireless Station ⎪
186 South Waziristan Militia. ⎭
Wing 2-67th Punjabis ⎫ Khajuri Kach.
66 South Waziristan Militia ⎭
Wing 2-67th Punjabis ⎫ Nili Kach.
2 South Waziristan Militia ⎭
56 South Waziristan Militia, Spinkai.
35 South Waziristan Militia, Khuzma.
30 South Waziristan Militia, Tormandu.
20 South Waziristan Militia, Madhassan.
80 South Waziristan Militia, Murtaza.
40 South Waziristan Militia, Jatta.
66 South Waziristan Militia, Girni.
1 Troop Alwar Lancers, Hathala.
1 Troop Alwar Lancers Potah.
2 Troops, 11th Lancers, Draband.

Medical Units.

2 Sections No. 154 I.F.A. ⎫
25 C. F. A. (less 1 British Section) ⎬ 43rd Brigade.
2 Sections No. 2 A. F. A. ⎫
1 British Section, No. 25 C. F. A. ⎪
1 Indian Section, No. 12 C. F. A. ⎬ 45th Brigade.
1 Section No. 149 I. F. A. ⎭
1 Section No. 2 A. F. A. ⎫
1 British Section No. 5 A. F. A. ⎬ Lines of Communication.
1 Indian Section No. 27 C. F. A. ⎭

1 British Section No. 27 C. F. A. } In reserve.
1 Indian Section No. 27 C. F. A.
No. 17 C. C. H., Jandola.
1 Section No. 2 A. F. A., Sarwakai.
Base, Dera Ismail Khan.

Suitable cases to be evacuated from the General Hospitals to Rawalpindi as quickly as possible.

APPENDIX C.

Statement showing casualties from 10th May to 15th July 1917, by Units.

Units.	British officers.		Indian officers.		Ranks.				Followers.			
	K.	W.	K.	W.	K.	W.	M.	D.	K.	W.	M.	D.
West Surreys	...	...	...	...	...	...	...	1	...	...	...	...
2-6th Sussex	...	2	...	...	...	21	...	1	...	1	...	...
1-25th Londons	...	1	...	...	3	12	...	2	...	...	...	...
11th Lancers	...	...	...	...	...	4	...	...	...	...	...	...
23rd Mountain Battery	...	...	...	...	...	2	...	...	...	...	...	...
30th Mountain Battery	...	...	...	...	...	2	...	1	...	...	...	...
11th Rajputs	...	...	...	1	4	3	...	2	...	...	...	...
54th Sikhs	...	1	...	2	5	15	...	1	...	1	...	...
55th Rifles	...	...	...	...	2	12	...	1	...	...	...	1
2-67th Punjabis	...	...	...	...	...	...	...	1	...	...	...	...
72nd Punjabis	...	...	...	...	...	1*	...	...	...	...	...	...
94th Infantry	...	...	...	...	...	...	...	3	...	...	...	...
107th Pioneers	...	...	...	...	...	...	...	3	...	...	...	...
124th Infantry	...	...	...	...	1†	...	...	...	...	...	...	...
127th Infantry	...	...	...	...	...	...	...	1	...	...	...	...
1st Nepalese	...	...	...	3	3	10	...	...	...	...	...	...
Mahindradal Regiment	1	...	1	4	5	26	...	2	...	...	...	...
2-1st Gurkhas	...	1	...	...	37	31	4	...	...	...	...	...
1-4th Gurkhas	2	...	2	2	57	53	59‡	4	...	...	...	...
Supply and Transport Corps.	...	...	...	...	...	...	...	...	...	...	...	1
A. B. Corps	...	...	...	...	...	...	...	3	...	...	...	...
Cooly Corps	...	...	...	...	1	...	...	2	...	...	...	...
Total	3	5	3	12	118	192	63	28	...	2	...	2

Note.—

K. Killed.
W. Wounded.
M. Missing.
D. Died of disease.
* Accidental.
† Ward Orderly.
‡ Includes 2 prisoners.

APPENDIX D.

DISTRIBUTION OF TROOPS IN WAZIRISTAN ON 6TH MAY 1919.

Bannu Area.

BANNU—
  31st D. C. O. Lancers (less 1 Squadron).
  1 Section 6·3 R. M. L. guns.
  1 Section 33rd Indian Mountain Battery.
  1-103rd Mahratta Light Infantry.
  3-6th Gurkha Rifles.
  Nos. 5 & 6 Armoured Motor Batteries.

DARDONI—
  1 Squadron 31st D. C. O. Lancers.
  1 Section, 6·3 R. M. L. guns.
  33rd Indian Mountain Battery (less 1 section).
  55th Field Company Sappers and Miners.
  1-41st Dogras.
  2-112th Infantry.

KURRAM GARHI—Detachment 3-6th Gurkha Rifles.

NORTHERN WAZIRISTAN MILITIA and FRONTIER CONSTABULARY holding their usual posts.

Derajat Area.

DERA ISMAIL KHAN—
  27th Cavalry (less one Squadron).
  27th Indian Mountain Battery (less one section).
  1-76th Punjabis (less 2½ Companies).
  2-2nd Gurkha Rifles.
  No. 7 Armoured Motor Battery.

TANK—
  1 Squadron, 27th Cavalry.
  1 Section 27th Mountain Battery.
  2 Platoons 1-76th Punjabis.

MANZAI—
  75th Field Company Sappers and Miners.
  1-66th Punjabis.

JANDOLA, KHIRGI, GIRNI, JATTA—2 Companies 1-76th Punjabis.

SOUTHERN WAZIRISTAN MILITIA and FRONTIER CONSTABULARY holding their usual posts.

APPENDIX E.

Terms announced to the Wazirs and Mahsuds.

After consultation between the Secretary of State and the Government of India it was decided that no permanent policy could be formulated at that time, and that punitive operations against the tribesmen in Waziristan should be undertaken without delay. The following plan of operations was decided on:—

    (a) *Tochi Wazirs.*—Terms as hereunder to be announced at a jirga to be held at Miranshah on the 9th November 1919. Troops would advance to Datta Khel and receive a reply on November 17th, 1919. Should the terms be refused, intensive aerial bombardment and punitive measures by land force would be taken to enforce acceptance of our terms.

    (b) *Mahsuds.*—Terms as given hereunder to be announced at a jirga to be held at Khirgi on the 3rd November 1919. Reply to be given by 11th November 1919. Should the terms be refused, the whole of Mahsud country would be subjected to intensive aerial bombardment and if they still refused to accept terms, punitive operations on land would also commence, after the Tochi Wazirs had been dealt with, to enforce acceptance.

    (c) *Wana Wazirs.*—Terms and punitive measures to be held in abeyance.

1. *Tochi Wazir Terms.*—The report that an amnesty has been secured for you by the Amir is without foundation and there is no question of your country being handed over to the Amir.

2. The British Government will make roads, station troops and build posts wherever it may deem necessary or desirable in any part of the Tochi Agency, that is in any places which have been previously occupied or any places on the Bannu-Datta Khel or Thal-Idak roads.

3. The Tochi Wazirs will not interfere in any way with the construction of roads within the Tochi Agency. Such roads may be constructed with any labour the British Government may wish to employ. Should tribal labour be employed, normal rates of pay will be given, and the grant of contracts, if any, will be made on the same principle of normal rates.

4. The Tochi Wazirs will hand back all rifles, ammunition, bombs and other military equipment taken since May 1st, 1919.

5. The Tochi Wazirs will not interfere with the movement of troops or convoys within the Tochi Agency, and will not molest aeroplanes or their occupants flying over country East of the Durand Line.

6. The Tochi Wazirs will pay a fine of Rs. 40,000 (Forty thousand) and the Daurs of Tochi will pay a fine of Rs. 10,000 (Ten thousand).

7. Unpaid allowances will be forfeited and allowances will not again be granted to the Tochi Wazirs till the British Government are satisfied of their good behaviour. The allowances will then be subject to reconsideration as regards both the amount and the distribution.

8. The Tochi Wazirs will deposit as a guarantee of good faith and for the fulfilment of the above terms, 200 (two hundred) rifles which will be retained until such time as the British Government is satisfied as to their *bonâ fides*. These rifles are to be either good Pass made or of higher class. These rifles will be returnable within a period of twelve months, subject to the continued good behaviour of the Tochi Wazirs.

9. All sums already received from the Tochi Wazirs by the Political Agents are to be retained.

10. Sepoys and Sowars who deserted from the Northern Waziristan Militia will not be considered outlaws once their rifles have been handed in. All officers and non-commissioned officers must either hand themselves up for trial or will remain liable to arrest when opportunity offers.

1. *Mahsud Terms.*—The report that an amnesty has been secured for you by the Amir is without foundation and there is no question of your country being handed over to the Amir.

2. The British Government will make roads, station troops and build posts in any part of the " Protected Area " wherever the Government may deem necessary or desirable. This includes the route from Jandola to Sarwakai *viâ* the Shahur Valley.

3. The Mahsuds will not interfere in any way with the construction of roads within the " Protected Area." Such roads may be constructed with any labour Government may wish to employ. Should tribal labour be employed normal rates of pay will be given, and the grant of contracts, if any, will be made on the same principle of normal rates.

4. The Mahsuds will hand back all rifles, ammunition, bombs and other military equipment taken since May 1st, 1919.

5. The Mahsuds will not interfere with the movement of troops or convoys within the " Protected Area " and will not molest aeroplanes or their occupants flying over the country East of the Durand Line.

6. The Mahsuds will pay to the British Government a fine of Rs. 10,000 (Ten thousand).

7. Unpaid allowances will be forfeited and allowances will not again be granted to the Mahsuds till the British Government is satisfied of their good behaviour. The allowances will then be subject to reconsideration as regards both the amount and distribution.

8. The Mahsuds will deposit, as a guarantee of good faith and for the fulfilment of the above terms, 200 (two hundred) rifles which will be retained until such time as the British Government is satisfied as to their *bonâ fides*. These rifles are to be of not less value than Rs. 200 (two hundred) each in the opinion of the Political Officers. These rifles will be returnable within a period of 12 (twelve) months, subject to the good behaviour of the Mahsuds.

9. The British Government will not admit of any claims for payment owing to alleged incorrect measurements of work done on the Gomal road between October 1918 and June 1st, 1919 or for other work done for the Military Works Services within the Wana Agency during that period.

10. For the purpose of the above terms the expression "Protected Area" will comprise that country lying within the following boundaries:—

> *East.*—Bhittani protected area and Bhittani Independent territory.
>
> *North.*—From a point one mile North of the confluence of the Tank Zam with the Shahur Valley Westwards to Peak one mile South of Point 4329 on the Tsappar Garh or Nanaghara Ridge. Thence Westwards to the confluence of the Sarela Nulla with the Shahur Valley. Thence along the Ridge to Suraghar. Thence to Point 5822, three miles West-North-West of Sarwekai. Thence to the small knoll North of the Pass situated half a mile North of Wizha Ghundai. Thence North-West to Point 6150, the summit of Minchan Baba. Thence North along the Ridge to Bobai and Tiarza Post. Thence West-North-West through Point 5551 to the boundary of Wazir Protected Territory. Reference one mile to the half-inch map.

APPENDIX F.

COMPOSITION OF THE THREE ECHELONS OF THE TOCHI COLUMN ON 13TH NOVEMBER 1919.

No. 1 Echelon—
  Column Headquarters—Major-General A. Skeen, C.M.G., Commanding.
  No. 40 Divisional Signal Company, H. Q. Section.
  No. 16 Pack Wireless Section.
  1½ Squadrons, 31st D. C. O. Lancers.
  1 Section, 4·5-inch Howitzers, R. F. A.
  No. 35 Indian Mountain Battery.
  55th Field Company, Sappers and Miners.
  2-61st Pioneers.
  Northern Waziristan Militia Scouts (Cavalry and Infantry).
  67th Brigade (comprising—1-55th Coke's Rifles, 1-103rd Mahratta Light Infantry, 104th Wellesley's Rifles and 2-112th Infantry).
  Survey Section.
  Medical Units.
  Supply and Transport Units.
    Also
  2-21st Punjabis, and
  2-76th Punjabis (less 2 Companies) both from 47th Brigade. These troops were used for the defence of the L. of C. The 2-76th Punjabis were later transferred to the 68th Brigade for the Derajat operations and on 21st December joined 67th Brigade.

No. 2 Echelon—
  Lieutenant-Colonel C. R. Wilkinson, D.S.O., 2-152nd Punjabis, Commanding.
  74th Field Company, Sappers and Miners.
  3-34th Pioneers.
  2-152nd Punjabis.
  No. 6 Armoured Motor Battery.
  Medical Unit.
  Supply and Transport Unit.

No. 3 Echelon—
  Brigadier-General G. Gwyn-Thomas, C.M.G., D.S.O., Commanding.
  1 Squadron (less 2 troops), 31st D. C. O. Lancers.
  No. 33 Indian Mountain Battery (less 1 Section).
  43rd Brigade (less 2-152nd Punjabis) comprising—(4-39th Garhwal Rifles, 57th Wilde's Rifles, 82nd Punjabis, Medical Units and Supply and Transport Units).

APPENDIX G.

TROOPS COMPRISING WAZIRISTAN FORCE, 1919-20.

Commander—
Major-General S. H. Climo, C.B., D.S.O.

Headquarters, Waziristan Force—
Dera Ismail Khan.

Attached troops—
Royal Air Force.
52nd Wing, Headquarters, Dera Ismail Khan.
No. 20 Squadron, Tank and Bannu.
1 Flight, No. 97 Squadron, Mianwali.
No. 99 Squadron, Mianwali.

Details—
Draught Cable Section of 38th Divisional Signal Company.
Draught Cable Section of 40th Divisional Signal Section.
2 Mobile Pigeon Lofts.
Headquarters No. 10 Armoured Motor Brigade.
One Survey Section.
No. 4 Litho. Section.

STRIKING FORCE—TOCHI AND DERAJAT COLUMNS.

Commander—
Major-General A. Skeen, C.M.G.

Column Headquarters.

Cavalry—
*2 Squadrons, 31st D. C. O. Lancers.
†1 Squadron (less one troop), 21st P. A. V. O. Cavalry (for advance as far as Kotkai only).

Artillery—
*One Section, 4·5-inch Howitzers, R. F. A.
†No. 6 Mountain Battery, R. G. A.
†No. 27 Indian Mountain Battery.
*No. 33 Indian Mountain Battery.
No. 35 Indian Mountain Battery (joined L. of C. defences during advance of Derajat Column).
Divisional Ammunition Column.

Sappers and Miners—
55th Field Company.
*74th Field Company.
One Survey Section.
†No. 4 Photo Section.

---

* Tochi Column only.
† Derajat Column only.

Signal Units—
  †38th Divisional Signal Company, H. Q. Section.
  *40th Divisional Signal Company, H. Q. Section.
  No. 16 Pack Wireless Station.

Infantry—
  43rd Brigade (Commander—Brigadier-General G. Gwyn-Thomas, C M.G., D.S.O.)
  Brigade Signal Section.
  4-39th Garhwal Rifles.
  57th Wilde's Rifles.
  82nd Punjabis.
  2-152nd Punjabis.
  67th Brigade. (Commander—Brigadier-General F. G. Lucas, C.B., C.S.I., D.S.O.).
  Brigade Signal Section.
  1-55th Coke's Rifles.
  1-103rd Mahratta Light Infantry.
  104th Wellesley's Rifles (relieved by 109th Infantry from 68th Brigade in Derajat Column).
  2-112th Infantry.

Pioneers—
  3-34th Sikh Pioneers.
  2-61st Pioneers (remained on L of C. after Derajat Column reached Kotkai).

Militia—
  *Northern Waziristan Militia (100 Infantry Scouts and 20 Mounted Scouts).
  †Southern Waziristan Militia (100 Infantry Scouts).

NOTE—
  The 2-19th Punjabis
  ,, 82nd Punjabis
  ,, 1-103rd Mahratta Light Infantry
  ,, 2-112th Infantry
  were transferred to the L. of C. during the latter part of December. They were, later on in the operations, replaced in the force (with the exception of the 2-19th Punjabis who came from the 68th Brigade and were only with the Derajat Column for 5 days) by the following battalions who joined the Column on the dates shown. 2-5th Gurkha Rifles 5th January, 2-9th Gurkha Rifles 10th January, 4-3rd Gurkha Rifles 12th February and 3-11th Gurkha Rifles 16th February 1920.
  The 3-11th Gurkha Rifles became Column troops, while the 3 remaining Gurkha Regiments joined the 67th Brigade.

---
* Tochi Column only.
† Derajat Column only.

Administrative Units with Striking Force.

Supply Units—
No. 12 Divisional Supply and Transport Headquarters.
No. 12 Divisional Troops Supply Section.
No. 12 Divisional Supply Column Headquarters.
No. 12 Divisional Supply Park.
Nos. 7 and 34 Brigade Supply Sections.
No. 381 Bakery Section.
No. 381 Butchery Section.
½ No. 71 Bakery Section.
½ No. 71 Butchery Section.

Transport Units—
48th, 49th, 66th, 67th (3 troops) and 71st Pack Mule Corps.
3rd Government Camel Corps.
8th Patiala Camel Corps.
52nd, 53rd, 55th and 57th Silladar Camel Corps.

Medical Units—
Nos. 2 and 4 Indian Field Ambulances.
No. 42 Combined Field Ambulance.
No. 1 Bearer Unit.
5 Combined Staging Sections.
No. 3 Sanitary Section.

Post Offices—
3 Field Post Offices.

Lines of Communication—Fighting Troops.

TOCHI.

No. 1 Section, Bannu Lines of Communication Defences.

Area—
From Mianwali—Kalabagh (inclusive) to Pezu (inclusive) and Idak (exclusive).

Commander—
Brigadier-General T. R. Maclachlan, C.M.G.

Headquarters—
Bannu.

Cavalry—
31st D. C. O. Lancers (less 2 Squadrons).

Artillery—
One Section, No. 33 Indian Mountain Battery.
* 2 10-pr. Post Guns.
1 Section, 15-pr. Guns, F. G. A.
1 Section, 6·3-inch R. M. L. Howitzers, F. G. A.

---

* Later transferred to No. 2 Section, Tank Lines of Communication.

Machine Gun Corps—
    No. 5 Armoured Motor Battery
    Post Machine Guns.

Infantry—
    45th Brigade Headquarters.
    Brigade Signal Section.
    2-4th Rajputs.
    2-25th Punjabis.
    1-150th Infantry.
    2-154th Infantry.
    1 Company, Northern Waziristan Militia.

Supply Units—
    No. 9 Brigade Supply Section.
    Nos. 77 and 78 Bakery Sections.
    Nos. 77 and 78 Butchery Sections.

Details—
    Post Stokes Mortars.
    1 Wireless Station.

No. 2 Section, Bannu Lines of Communication Defences.

Area—
    From Idak to Datta Khel (both inclusive). Datta Khel was evacuated on 25th November 1919.

Commander—
    Brigadier-General W. C. Walton, C.B., C.M.G.

Headquarters—
    Dardoni.

Cavalry—
    2 Squadrons, 31st D. C. O. Lancers.

Artillery—
    No. 33 Indian Mountain Battery (less one Section).
    1 Section, 15-pr. Guns, F. G. A.

Sappers and Miners—
    74th Field Company.

Infantry—
    47th Brigade Headquarters.
    Brigade Signal Section.
    2-21st Punjabis.
    2-69th Punjabis.
    3-151st Punjabi Rifles.
    3-152nd Punjabis.
    Northern Waziristan Militia (less one Company).

Supply Units—
  No. 76 Brigade Supply Section.
  No. 110 Brigade Supply Section.
  No. 157 Bakery Section.
  No. 157 Butchery Section.

Details—
  Post Stokes Mortars.
  Post Machine Guns.
  One Wireless Station.

DERAJAT.

No. 1 Section, Tank Lines of Communication Defences.

Area—
  Darya Khan to Hathala (both inclusive), later from Darya Khan to half way between Khirgi and Jandola.

Commander—
  Brigadier-General R. B. Worgan, D.S.O.

Headquarters—
  Dera Ismail Khan (later Tank).

Cavalry—
  16th Cavalry.
  21st P. A. V. O. Cavalry (less 1 Squadron).
  27th Light Cavalry.

Artillery—
  1 Section, No. 35 Indian Mountain Battery.
  1 Section, 15-pr. Guns F. G. A.

Machine Gun Corps—
  Nos. 6 and 7 Armoured Motor Batteries.
  Post Machine Guns.

Infantry—
  62nd Brigade Headquarters.
  Brigade Signal Section.
  2-90th Punjabis.
  2-94th Infantry.
  2-102nd Grenadiers.
  2-113th Infantry (later moved up to Kotkai and joined No. 2 Section, Tank L. of C.).
  2-127th Baluchis (later moved up to Sorarogha and joined 43rd Brigade).
  2-150th Infantry (joined 43rd Brigade at Kotkai on 29th December 1919).
  Southern Waziristan Militia (less detachment with Striking Column).

Supply Units—
   No. 119 Brigade Supply Section.
   ½ No. 395 Bakery Section.
   ½ No. 395 Butchery Section.

Details—
   Post Stokes Mortars.
   1 Stationary Wireless Plant.

No. 2 Section, Tank Lines of Communication Defences.

Area—
   From Hathala (exclusive) to Murtaza and Jandola (both inclusive), later took over area from half way between Khirgi and Jandola to Ahnai Tangi (inclusive).

Commander—
   Brigadier-General J. L. R. Gordon, C.B.

Headquarters—
   Manzai (later Jandola and Kotkai).

Cavalry—
   1 troop, 21st P. A. V. O. Cavalry.

Artillery—
   No. 35 Indian Mountain Battery (less one Section).
   2 10-pr. Guns (from No. 1 Section, Bannu L. of C.).

Sappers and Miners—
   75th Field Company.

Infantry—
   68th Brigade Headquarters.
   Brigade Signal Section.
   3rd Guides (joined Striking Column on 18th January 1920).
   2-19th Punjabis.
   2-76th Punjabis (joined Striking Column on 21st December 1919 until 28th January 1920).
   109th Infantry (transferred to 67th Brigade on 17th December 1920).

Supply Units— .
   No. 37 Brigade Supply Section.
   ½ No. 396 Bakery Section.
   ½ No. 396 Butchery Section.

Details—
   Post Machine Guns.
   No. 3 Pack Wireless Station.

ADMINISTRATIVE UNITS ON THE LINES OF COMMUNICATION.

Headquarters—
   Inspector General of Communications. Brigadier-General H. C. Tytler, D.S.O.

Signal Units—

    No. 1 L. of C. Signal Section.
    L. of C. Signal Company (Indian Telegraph Department).
    Headquarters Pack Cable Section and one Brigade Section of 40th Divisional Signal Company.
    1 Brigade Section of 38th Divisional Signal Company.

Technical Units—

    Advanced Engineer Parks, Bannu, Tank and Mari-Indus.
    26th Railway Company, Sappers and Miners.
    122nd, 126th (one wing), 127th and 131st Railway Construction Companies.
    Detachment No. 9 Works Depôt.
    Detachment No. 12 E. and M. Works Depôt.
    11th Military Works Company.
    3rd Punjab, 4th Madras and 5th Madras Works Battalion.
    6th United Provinces Works Battalion.
    13th, 15th, 101st, 103rd and 120th Military Works Labour Corps.
    99th, 110th, 112th and one wing 118th Labour Corps.

Supply Units—

    No. 21 Force Supply and Transport Headquarters.
    No. 13 Divisional Supply and Transport Headquarters.
    No. 13 Divisional Supply Park.
    No. 13 Divisional Troops Supply Section.
    Nos. 33, 35, 36, 61, 62 and 63 Brigade Supply Sections.
    No. 13 Divisional Area Troops Supply Section.
    Nos. 63, 64, 384, 401, 402 and 675 Bakery Sections.
    Nos. 63, 64, 383, 384, 401, 402 and 675 Butchery Sections.
    Nos. 22, 23 and 24 Supply Depôt Headquarters.
    Nos. 162, 163, 164, 165, 166, 167, 168, 173, 174, 175, 176, $\frac{1}{2}$ of 177, 206, 207, 312, 313 and 314 Supply Depôt Sections.
    Nos. 22, 44 and 45 Supply Workshop Sections.
    Nos. 77, 79, 80, $\frac{1}{2}$ of 82, 135 and 136 Supply Tally Sections.
    Cattle Depôts at Bannu and Darya Khan.

Transport Units—

    64th, 65th, 68th (2 troops), 70th (5 troops), 72nd and 101st (6 troops) Pack Mule Corps.
    157th Pack Sub-Division.
    58th (4 troops), 59th, 60th (4 troops), 62nd and 69th (4 troops) Draught Corps.
    2nd, 5th, 6th, 7th and 71st (3 troops) Government Camel Corps.
    Nos. 7, 9, 14, 30, 36, 37, 38, 40, 42, 49, 50, 54 and 81 Bullock Half Troops.
    3rd, 4th (4 troops), 6th, 7th, 8th, 9th (4 troops), 11th, 12th, 14th (4 troops), 17th, 18th and 19th (4 troops) Bullock Corps.
    81st (6 troops), 82nd and 83rd Local Corps.
    1 Horse Transport Company.
    Nos. 7, 8, 9, 10, 11 and 12 Ford Van Companies.

Medical Units—

British Hospital, Bannu.
Indian General Hospital, Dera Ismail Khan.
Indian General Hospital, Tank.
Indian General Hospital, Bannu.
Indian Station Hospital, Dardoni.
Nos. 38, 43 and 49 Indian General Hospitals.
Nos. 7, 27, 38 and 118 Casualty Clearing Stations.
Nos. 16, 25, 27, 43 and 64 Combined Field Ambulances.
Nos. 11, 12, 13, 15, 19, 41 and 43 British and 55, 59, 60 and 66 Indian Staging Sections.
Nos. 19 and 22 X-Ray Sections.
Nos. 4, 8 and 36 Sanitary Sections.
Nos. 1, 2, 3, 4 and 5 Bleaching Powder Laboratories.
Nos. 11 and 13 Advanced Depôts, Medical Stores.
No. 3 Motor Ambulance Convoy.
No. 23 Motor Ambulance Convoy (less one Section).

Veterinary Units—

Nos. 5, 14 and 21 Field Veterinary Sections.
Nos. 26 and 27 Field Veterinary Sections (Camels).
No. 4 Base Depôt Veterinary Stores.

Remounts—

Remount Depôt, Dera Ismail Khan.
Remount Depôt, Bannu.
Remount Depôt, Tank.

Ordnance—

Advanced Ordnance Depôt, Bannu.
Advanced Ordnance Depôt, Tank.
Ordnance Transit Depôt, Mari-Indus.
No. 34 Ordnance Mobile Workshop, Bannu.

Post Offices—

3 Field Post Offices.

APPENDIX H.

DETAIL OF TROOPS ADVANCING THROUGH THE AHNAI TANGI ON THE 14TH JANUARY 1920.

Advanced Guard—

    Commander—Lieutenant-Colonel H. Herdon, C.I.E. (1-55th Coke's Rifles).
    1-55th Coke's Rifles.
    2 Companies, 2-5th Gurkha Rifles.
    1 Section, No. 27 Indian Mountain Battery.
    Advanced Party, No. 38 Divisional Signal Company (H. Q Section).

Special Flank Guard—

    Commander—Lieutenant-Colonel J. D. Crowdy, D.S.O. (2-5th Gurkha Rifles).
    2-5th Gurkha Rifles (less 2 Companies).

Main Body—

    Commander—Major-General A. Skeen, C.M.G.
    1 Troop, 21st Cavalry.
    No. 6 Mountain Battery (less 1 Section).
    No. 27 Indian Mountain Battery (less 2 Sections).
    2-76th Punjabis.
    2 Companies, 109th Infantry.
    3-34th Sikh Pioneers.
    55th Field Company, Sappers and Miners.
    No. 38 Divisional Signal Company H. Q. Section (less Advanced Party).
    No. 16 Pack Wireless Station.
    Survey Section.
    Photo. Section, 2nd Sappers and Miners.

Rear Guard—

    Commander—Major A. E. Mahon, D.S.O. (attached 109th Infantry).
    109th Infantry (less 2 Companies).

Covering move of Transport on road in rear of Column—

    Commander—Brigadier-General F. G. Lucas, C.B., C.S.I., D.S.O.
    2-9th Gurkha Rifles.
    57th Wilde's Rifles.
    1 Section, No. 6 Mountain Battery, R. G. A.
    1 Section, No. 27 Indian Mountain Battery.

APPENDIX I.

Statement showing casualties in the Waziristan Force from 26th October 1919 to 1st May 1920.

	Average strength (whole Force).	Admissions.		Deaths.	
		Sick.	Wounded.	Sick.	Wounded.
Operation Areas.					
British officers	1,094	72	41	...	8
British other ranks	939	40	1	...	1
Indian officers	1,294	55	64	...	4
Indian other ranks	41,843	3,915	1,501	20	74
Non-combatant ranks	37,870	1,360	39	7	8
Total	83,040	5,442	1,646	27	95
Lines of Communication Areas.					
British officers	...	540	12	14	2
British other ranks	...	586	4	6	1
Indian officers	...	334	14	8	1
Indian other ranks	...	14,690	290	441	57
Non-combatant ranks	...	16,943	26	792	7
Total	...	33,093	346	1,261	68

APPENDIX J.

Statement showing casualties in the Derajat Column from 11th December 1919 to 8th April 1920.

	Killed.	Missing.	Wounded.	Total.
British officers	28	1	40	69
British other ranks	...	...	1	1
Indian officers	15	4	68	87
Indian other ranks	323	232	1,574	2,129
Total	366	237	1,683	2,286

APPENDIX K.

ORGANISATION AND WORKING OF THE LINES OF COMMUNICATION OF WAZIRISTAN FORCE, 1919-20

1. Plan of Operations

1. Briefly the plan of campaign was to concentrate a force of 2 Brigades at Dardoni early in November 1919 which would move on Datta Khel and operate in the upper Tochi as eventualities demanded.

After the conclusion of these operations a large portion of the Force was to move to the Southern Line by road and operate against the Mahsuds.

2. The following reserves were to be laid in :—

  At Bannu 25 days for all troops at Bannu and beyond.
  At Tank 15 days for the garrison.
  At Dardoni 15 days for the Tochi Column and the garrison.

The numbers on which reserves of supplies were to be calculated were :—

  Bannu—
    British 25,000
    Indian 43,000
    Animals 20,000
  Dardoni—
    British 700
    Indians 25,000
    Animals 13,000

Sub-Appendix I shows Reserve of Rations, held on 1st March 1920.

3. On the 15th November the column marched to Datta Khel. On 17th November, the Tochi Wazirs conceded to our terms. On the 25th November the transfer of troops to the Southern Line was commenced, last Echelon reaching Tank on the 5th December.

2. Lines of Communication.

1. The lines of communication for Waziristan Force comprised two lines (*see* map No. 6) :—

  (i) the line from Kalabagh *viâ* Bannu to Dardoni (and later to Datta Khel) which provided for the requirements of the Forces which operated against the Northern Wazirs. There was also a post at Mianwali to meet the requirements of the Royal Air Force.

  (ii) (a) the line from Kalabagh *viâ* Tank to Piazha Raghza which served the Force operating against the Mahsuds.

  (b) Subsidiary to (ii) (a) was a line from Darya Khan to Tank.

(iii) an offshoot of *(ii) (b)* to provide for the requirements of the Force operating against the Sherannis was organised *via* Saggu to Draband.

The above lines were organised with sections as follows:—

1. NORTHERN LINE.

Sections and Posts.	Administrative Commandants and Staff.
Kalabagh Section.	Administrative Commandant (graded as D. A. Q. M. G.).
Kalabagh to Laki Marwat including Mianwali post	1 Staff Captain.
Bannu Section.	Administrative Commandant (graded as A. Q. M. G.).
Laki Marwat (exclusive) to Saidgi (exclusive). It also included Latambar	2 Staff Captains.
Idak Section.	Administrative Commandant (graded as D. A. Q. M. G.).
Saidgi (inclusive) to Idak (inclusive)	1 Staff Lieutenant.
Dardoni Section.	Administrative Commandant (graded as D. A. Q. M. G.).
Idak (exclusive) to Dardoni (inclusive)	2 Staff Captains.
Datta Khel Section.*	Administrative Commandant (graded as D. A. Q. M. G.).
Dardoni (exclusive) to Datta Khel (inclusive)	1 Staff Captain.

*After the conclusion of operations against the Tochi Wazirs the head of the Line of Communication was withdrawn to Dardoni.

2. SOUTHERN LINE.

Kalabagh Section.	As above.
This Section was common to both Northern and Southern Divisions.	
Darya Khan Section.	Administrative Commandant (graded as D. A. Q. M. G.).
Railhead to left bank of the Indus including post at Karlu and Steamer Point	2 Staff Captains.
D. I. Khan Section.	Administrative Commandant (graded as D. A. Q. M. G.).
Left bank of the Indus (exclusive) including posts at D. I. Khan, Potah, Hathala.	1 Staff Captain D. I. K.
	1 Staff Captain, Draband.
Saggu, Draband	1 Staff Lieutenant, Saggu.
Tank Section.	Administrative Commandant (graded as D. A. Q. M. G.).
Tank (inclusive) to Jandola (exclusive) with posts at Tank, Kaur Bridge, Manzai, Khirgi.	1 Staff Captain, with an administrative Commandant, (graded as Staff Captain) and 1 Staff Lieutenant at each post.
Jandola Section.	Administrative Commandant (graded as A. Q. M. G.).
Jandola (inclusive) to Piazha Raghza (inclusive) with posts at Jandola, Kotkai, Sora Rogha, Piazha Raghza.	1 Staff Captain. Posts being administered as in the Tank Section.

3. The establishment sanctioned for I. G. C. Headquarters was as follows:—

 One A. A. and Q. M. G., D. A. A. G. . . . D. A. D. V. S.
 Two D. A. A. and Q. M. G. . . . . A. D. Remounts.
 Two Staff Captains A. D. S. and T., A. D. W., A. D. R. T., A. D. M. S.

Clerical establishments were completed from civilian clerks. Provost and Rest Camp establishments were filled as far as possible by convalescents.

3. *Characteristics of the L. of C. in Waziristan Railways*

1. Certain characteristics of the communication by rail and road in Waziristan militated against simplicity of working. Goods reaching Mari-Indus have to be transferred from broad to narrow gauge and ferried across on flats or else transported across the Indus by barge or boat and loaded into narrow gauge trucks on the right bank. One line of supply had to be fed at the expense of the other and that side where active operations were not in progress was consistently cut down to a bare minimum. Except for a period in June and July when ferries cannot carry deck loads, the limiting factor as regards carrying capacity is the K. B. Railway whose daily average carrying capacity is 650 tons. The average carrying capacity of the ferry except for a portion of June and July is approximately 800 tons.

2. *Roads.*—The main road to Tank runs from D. I. Khan, a place which is not served by the narrow gauge railway at all. Matters here were alleviated to some extent by laying the Decauville railway along the D. I. Khan-Tank Road, thus increasing the tonnage at the expense of the road. Lateral communications are also deficient, in that the Advanced Bases and railheads of Bannu and Tank are not connected directly either by road or rail. The necessity for transferring stores from Bannu to Tank by rail *via* Lakki Marwat seriously affected the tonnage available for maintaining the forces from Kalabagh.

3. Movements of troops from Bannu to Tank on the conclusion of operations in the Tochi were carried out *via* Pezu and thence alongside the railway to Tank. The going from Pezu to Tank is sandy and heavy and water difficulties are great. Wheeled transport cannot use the road, but must proceed *via* D. I. Khan involving a detour of 80 miles.

4. Kalabagh, the principal railway centre for Waziristan cannot be reached by road at all.

5. Forward communication in the Tochi beyond Bannu consists of a road for wheeled traffic as far as Datta Khel, beyond which place no operations were undertaken.

The road is inadequate as a military road, and there is no alternative route. A track for pack transport was made clear of the metalled road, from the Baran river 4 miles out of Bannu, to Dardoni, and later to Datta Khel.

6. Forward of Tank, there are alternative routes as far as Khirgi, which consist of a metalled M. T. road *via* Kaur Bridge to Khirgi in two stages, and a cross country camel track *via* Chaisan Kach to Khirgi in one stage. In addition the Tank-Kaur railway extension has been successfully used for the carriage of war material of all sorts.

7. Beyond Khirgi there was a double camel track only, which followed the Tank Zam for the greater part of its course.

8. Telephonic communication was established throughout the area with the exception of a trunk line to Kalabagh.

4. *Position of I. G. C., H. Q.*

1. The Headquarters of the L. of C. was at first located at Kalabagh but owing to the poor communication by road and rail from Kalabagh, and the absence of telephonic communication with Force Headquarters, the L. of C. headquarters was transferred to D. I. Khan on 8th October.

5. *The position of depôts.*

1. The base for the Force was at Lahore and the requirements of the Force were forwarded *via* Mari-Indus (where a Base Transit depôt was established) Kalabagh and to a minor degree *via* Darya Khan to advanced Depôts within the Force as follows:—

- (*i*) *Supplies.*—Main Supply Depôts were located at Bannu for the Northern and at Tank for the Southern Line.

  From the above Depôts Reserves of rations, grain, fodder and fuel were stocked at Posts as shown in Appendix I attached.

- (*ii*) *Ordnance.*—Advanced ordnance depôts were established at Bannu and Tank.

  From these, Ordnance Dumps were established at Dardoni, Jandola and Sorarogha to meet the requirements of advanced troops. In addition an officers' shop was opened at the latter place.

  Ammunition Parks were established at Dardoni and Jandola with ammunition refilling points at Datta Khel and Piazha Raghza.

- (*iii*) *Engineer Field Parks.*—Advanced Engineer Field Parks were established at Bannu and Tank and from these Engineer Dumps were located at Dardoni and Datta Khel on the Northern Line and at Jandola and Sorarogha on the Southern.

- (*iv*) *Remounts.*—Remount Sections were established at Bannu and D. I. Khan with advanced Sections at Tank and Kotkai.

- (*v*) *Medical Stores.*—Medical Store Depôts were located at Bannu, D. I. Khan and Khirgi.

Forms of Transport employed.

Line.					
Northern line	Kalabagh to Bannu.	Bannu to Idak.	Idak to Dardoni.	Dardoni to Datta Khel.	
	Kalabagh Bannu Railway (narrow gauge)	Draft animal (mule, pony and bullock) Transport.	Mechanical Transport (Ford vans on the road. Pack Animal Transport (mule and camel) on camel track.	Mechanical Transport (Ford Vans on road and Pack Animal Transport (mule and camel) on camel track.	

Southern Line	Kalabagh to Kaur Bridge.	Darya Khan to Dera Ismail Khan	Dera Ismail Khan to Tank.	Kaur Bridge to Khirgi.	Khirgi to Piazha Raghza.
	Kalabagh Bannu Railway (narrow gauge).	Draft animal Transport pony and bullock).	Decauville Railway (60 centimetre gauge)	Mechanical Transport (Ford Vans).	Pack Camel Transport.

N.B.—1. Draft Animal Transport (pony and bullock) and hired pack camels were employed between Dera Ismail Khan and Draband.
2. Camels were usually worked on a 6-7th basis and draft Corps on a 9-10th basis.
3. Forward of Datta Khel and Piazha Raghza the $\frac{\text{Tochi}}{\text{Derajat Column}}$ operated with their own Transport (pack mule and camel).

(vi) *Veterinary Stores.*—Base Veterinary Stores were located first at Bannu for the Tochi Operations and later at D. I. Khan for the Derajat Column.

(vii) *Postal.*—Base Post-Offices were located at Bannu and D. I. Khan.

(viii) *Stationery.*—A Stationery Depôt was established at Kalabagh.

(ix) *Red Cross.*—Red Cross Depôts were located at Bannu and Dera Ismail Khan, with advanced Depôts at Tank and Jandola.

(x) *Live Stock.*—Cattle Depôts were located on the Northern Line at Bannu, on Southern Line at Darya Khan with a Sub-Depôt at Tank. (Two thousand sheep were received at Darya Khan daily by special trains from Rawalpindi and Lahore.) The Depôt on the Northern Line was filled by local purchase.

6. Transportation.

1. The Forces on both the Northern and Southern Lines were supplied mainly through Kalabagh through which an average of 600 tons and 200 personnel and a maximum of 680 tons and 180 personnel were transported to Bannu and Tank.

Owing to the limited receiving capacity at Mari-Indus only 60 broad gauge wagons could be discharged daily by direct transhipment or into the small transit dumps.

Small reserves of supplies (fodder and grain) and military works stores were maintained but the lack of regular reserve depôts with sidings caused an uneven flow on the narrow gauge, especially of fodder, and hence it was often found that less urgent military works stores were forwarded to avoid congestion or the narrow gauge ran below its full capacity.

It is to be noted that the Kalabagh-Bannu Railway is not equipped to take the same amount of tonnage to Tank as to Bannu, Vacuum stock being essential in the Tank section.

2. The Decauville was able to carry from Dera Ismail Khan to Tank a daily average of—

    160 tons supplies.
    1,600 sheep.
    100 personnel.

3. The daily average delivered by rail to Kaur Bridge was 250 tons. A maximum of 300 tons was reached.

4. The average tonnage delivered at the Head of each Line of Communication was as follows:—

    Datta Khel . . . . 200 maintenance and reserve.
    Piazha Raghza . . . . 100 tons maintenance.

5. On the Southern Line 'going' in the Tank Zam was particularly bad for pack transport and it became necessary to work camels on a $\frac{3}{4}$ basis (instead of the normal 6/7th basis) and to allow 18 per cent. for casualties and lameness.

6. The following M. T. (Ford Van) Companies worked on the L. of C. Against each is shown the approximate percentage of vans which were in workshops daily:—

	Per cent.
No. 7 M. T. Company	40
„ 8 „ „	29
„ 9 „ „	14
„ 10 „ „	65
„ 11 „ „	15
„ 12 „ „	12

All M. T. Companies were worked on a basis of 75 per cent. of fit cars. Deficiency of personnel in Transport units both in numbers and efficiency when judged on pre-war standards increased considerably the strain upon the Transport Service.

But despite the difficulties which had to be contended with this Transport performed very valuable service.

7. *Control of Railway tonnage.*

The supplies by rail to Mari-Indus and Darya Khan were regulated through decade tonnage demands on the Base Lahore and allotments by the Base.

8. *System of Supply to the Striking Force.*

1. As the Striking Force advanced it laid in at each place destined to be a post on the Line of Communication 10 days supply for itself and the eventual garrison.

2. When a further advance was made, the column lifted forward, the 10 days reserve, leaving at each Post 10 days reserve for the garrison.

3. After the completion of the above arrangements the Line of Communication was extended to include each post in succession and an administrative commandant was placed in charge.

9. *Improvements to Communications and Rolling Stock.*

1. *Railways.*—Additional sidings were placed in the Depôts at Mari-Indus, Darya Khan, Bannu and Tank.

A Decauville Railway was laid between D. I. Khan and Tank.

Narrow gauge and Decauville trucks were cribbed for fodder.

In addition a proportion of Decauville trucks were converted for evacuation of the sick, for carriage of sheep and also for personnel

2. *Roads.*—The road Darya Khan-D. I. Khan was grassed.

The road Hathala-Draband was improved so as to take ambulance motors.

A motor road was constructed from Manzai to Khirgi and later extended to Jandola. The track from Jandola to Piazha Raghza was also improved.

10. Reinforcements.

1. A daily average of 200 personnel including civilian traffic was conveyed by the K. B. Railway to Bannu and Tank.

The Decauville Railway was capable of carrying 100 personnel in addition to supplies and live-stock thus doing away with the route march from D. I. Khan to Tank.

Thus it was found easy to forward expeditiously all reinforcements even at the greatest time of pressure.

2. Advanced Base Camps were situated at Bannu, D. I. Khan and Tank where all deficiencies in clothing and equipment reinforcements were made good.

Rest, Reinforcement and Convalescent Camps were located as shown in Sub-Appendix II attached.

11. Sanitation.

At all places on the L. of C. sufficient arrangements were made for incineration and bathing but on account of the great number of transport animals employed, sanitation was difficult. The difficulty was partly met by employing local labour and splitting up Sanitary Sections to supervise. Early in the year a considerable reinforcement of sweepers was received from India and sanitation was placed on a satisfactory basis.

12. Water Supply.

It was found necessary in all places to improve the water supply to enable troops to obtain pure water. Force pumps, pulsometers and engines were installed, tube wells sunk and all water was chlorinated in masonry or iron tanks provided for the purpose. Where an extensive pipe system was not laid and where it was possible to use water carts, these were employed to facilitate a pure supply of drinking water for the troops. The existing supply of drinking water for the echelons at Shah Baz Khel and Abizar during their march from Bannu *viâ* Pezu and Abizar to Tank, was the most precarious but this was supplemented by water being run out in tanks from Tank along the K. B. Railway.

13. Medical.

1. The means of evacuation employed were camel kajawah, motor ambulance, ambulance train (both narrow and broad gauge) and Decauville (in specially converted trucks). Hospital accommodation proved adequate for the troops whose health as a whole was good.

2. Owing to an epidemic of Influenza, congestion did arise, and a further congestion arose as the echelons marched from the Tochi to the Derajat. Cases were not usually evacuated from the Forces to Rawal Pindi unless the number of cases increased to such an extent as to congest hospitals. Indian General Hospitals were never unduly empty but were kept as full as safety allowed.

14. Canteens.

1. Monro Canteens were located at Mari-Indus and Kalabagh and proved of great value.

2. At Darya Khan, Bannu, Tank and Kaur Bridge all troops arriving by rail were served with hot tea before marching to Rest Camps.

3. Branches of Madan's Canteen were opened under the direction of the S. and T. at

Kalabagh	(Headquarters with one month's reserve.)
Bannu	⎫
D. I. Khan	⎪
Tank	⎪
Manzai	⎬ Endeavour was made to keep up one week's supply.
Jandola	⎪
Kotkai	⎪
Piazha Raghza	⎭

There was also a Canteen with the Derajat Column at Ladha.

15. Messes and Clubs Library.

1. Standard messes with folding furniture, crockery and servants complete were established at places mentioned in Appendix F. attached and contributed greatly to the comforts of B. Os. and B. O. Rs.

A convenient unit was found to be:—
 A mess for 12 B. Os. (expandable to 18 B. Os.).
 A mess for 20 B. O. Rs.

Soldiers' Clubs were located at D. I. Khan, Bannu and Tank.

2. A circulating Library for Indian Troops existed at D. I. Khan.

16. Dairies.

Dairies were located at Kalabagh, Bannu, D. I. Khan, Tank and Jandola which sufficed for Hospital requirements, the surplus (if any) being sold to B. Os. and B. O. Rs. messes.

17. Labour.

The labour organization was not altogether satisfactory, as no labour control either as a separate directorate, or as a branch of the

S. and T. control was established. The D. A. and Q. M. G. or the I. E. S. had no one of technical knowledge or whole time officer, to study the economical use of labour. (*Note.*—The future labour organization now specified provides for this and for the general principles of labour organization as a Q. M. G.'s Service.)

18. Miscellaneous Personnel.

The want of employment companies and followers' companies was much felt, a unit is required by which the many miscellaneous requirements in personnel outside organised services, can be furnished. (*Note.*—This is being organised.)

SUB-APPENDIX I.

RESERVES OF RATIONS.

Held on 1st March.

Tank line	Ladha	10 days.	
	Piaza Raghza	10 ,,	
	Sorarogha	10 ,,	
	Kotkai	10 ,,	
	Jandola	30 ,,	for its garrison and all posts beyond.
	Khirgi	30 ,,	
	Manzai	30 ,,	
	Kaur Bridge	30 ,,	
	Tank	30 ,,	for its garrison and certain minor constabulary posts and 10 days for its garrison and all posts up to Ladha.
Bannu line	D. I. Khan	40 ,,	
	Dardoni	30 ,,	
	Idak	30 ,,	
	Saidgi	30 ,,	
	Bannu	40 ,,	for its garrison and 10 days for all posts beyond.

N. B.—Lately reserves have been increased to 60 days across the Indus, the surplus being kept at Tank and Bannu and at Dera Ismail Khan for that Post.

Sub-Appendix II.

The following table shows the accommodation provided in Rest, Reinforcement and Convalescent Camps at the various posts on the Line of Communication:—

Place.	Nature of Camps.	Accommodation.		
		B. Os.	B. O. Rs.	I. A. O. Rs.
Mari Indus	Rest	20	40	950
Kalabagh	Rest	60	18	824
Bannu	Rest	32	140	420
Bannu	Reinforcement Convalescent.	...	...	300
Idak	Rest	...	6	100
Dardoni	Rest	...	50	300
Darya Khan	Rest	14	80	760
Darya Khan	Reinforcement	28	400	1,480
D. I. Khan	Rest	40	200	900
D. I. Khan	Reinforcement	...	...	900
D. I. Khan	Convalescent	...	...	900
Tank	Rest and Reinforcement.	50	48	920
Tank	Convalescent	...	...	140
Kaur Bridge	Rest	...	...	190
Manzai	Rest	12	20	200
Manzai	Convalescent	...	...	100
Khirgi	Rest	40	16	600
Jandola	Rest	40	32	500
	Reinforcement	...	...	300
	Convalescent	...	...	388
Kotkai	Rest	10	18	300
Sorarogha	Rest	15	25	200
Piazha Raghza	Rest	14	30	200

Sub-Appendix III.

List of Messes administered by Inspector of Messes.

Place.	B. O.	B. O. R.
Tank line.		
Darya Khan	24	20
D. I. Khan	24	20
Tank	12	20
Tank	24	...
Kaur Bridge	12	20
Manzai	12	20
Khirgi	12	20
Jandola	12	20
Jandola	12	...
Kotkai	12	20
Sorarogha*	12	20
Derajat Column	12	...
Draband	12	...
Bannu line.		
Mari-Indus	12	20
Kalabagh	12	20
Kalabagh	24	...
Bannu	36	40
Dardoni	12	...

* For the use of British Service officers attached to the Column.

APPENDIX L.

Main sub-divisions of Darwesh Khel Wazirs and Mahsuds with fighting strengths.

UTMANZAI (Tochi) WAZIRS.

Tribe.	Sub-tribe.	Place of residence.*
Ibrahim Khel (5,600)	Madda Khel (2,000)	Khaza Valley. Maizar and Sheranni.
	Manzar Khel (400)	Between Datta Khel and Mami Rogha, head of Khaisora.
	Tori Khel (3,200)	Spinwam on Kaitu, across Tochi and Khaisora Valleys to mouth of Shaktu.
Wali Khel (5,000)	Bakka Khel (1,000)	Majority in Bannu District near mouths of Tochi and Khaisora. Some in Shawal Plain (S. of Maizar).
	Jani Khel (1,000)	Bannu District near mouth of Khaisora with grazing lands near Shawal.
	Kabul Khel (including Malikshahi) 3,000).	In winter on Kurram between Thal and Zarwam. Summer in Birmal (Afghanistan).
Mohmit Khel (2,880)	Bora Khel (1,000)	Sheratala Plain and Palosina plain in Kaitu. Summer quarters – head of Khaisora.
	Wuzi Khel (800)	Head of Khaisora.
	Khaddar Khel (680)	Tochi between Datta Khel and Sheranni.
	Hassan Khel (400)	Kaitu Valley. Migrate to Laram Range on Khost border in summer.

* The great majority of both Tochi and Wana Wazirs are nomadic and migrate every year with their families to their summer grazing grounds, which are in some cases in British territory.

AHMADZAI (Wana) WAZIRS.

Tribe.	Sub-tribe.	Place of residence.
Kalu Khel (8,500)	Isperka (1,300)	Bannu District. Summer quarters Shakai Plain and head of Khaisora.
	Nasradin (7,200)*	Wana Wazirs. Have settlements N. of Bannu.
Shin (Sani) Khel (3,400)	Hathi Khel (2,000)	N. E. of Bannu. Possess land in Wana and Shakai.
	Sirki Khel (800)	Bannu and Wana.
	Umarzai (600)	Bannu District. Shaktu Valley near Mandanwam. Graze their flocks near Razmak in summer.

* Nasradin (main sub-divisions):—
  Shadi Khel—
    Khojal Khel (170).
  Bomi Khel (3,350)—
    Zalli Khal (1,200).
    Tojiya (or Taji) Khel (1,600).

MAHSUDS.

Tribe.	Sub-tribe.	Place of residence.
Mahsuds.		
Alizai (4,500)	Manzai (3,000)	Mostly between the two branches of the Tank Zam and along Shahur.
	Shabi Khel (1,500)	
Bahlolzai (4,500)	Nana Khel (1,500) *	
	Aimal Khel (2,000)†	
	Shingi (1,000)	No separate settlements—scattered over Mahsud country.
	Band Khel (300)	
Shaman Khel	Chahar Khel (600)	
	Khalu Khel (300)	
	Galeshai (700)	
	Badanzai (300)	

* Nana Khel (main sub-divisions):—
  Abdur Rahman Khel.
  Nekzan Khel.
  Haibat Khel.
  Jalal Khel.
  Kikarai.
  Gigar Khel.
  Umar Khel.
  Urmar Khel.

† Aimal Khel (main sub-divisions):—
  Abdullai.
  Malikshahi.
  Nazar Khel.

Sketch Map A
OF
WAZIRISTAN

Scale of Miles

Administrative Boundary
Boundary of Afghanistan
Railways, Narrow Gauge
M.T. Roads in existence on 1.12.36
Cart Tracks

No. 4 GENERAL MAP.

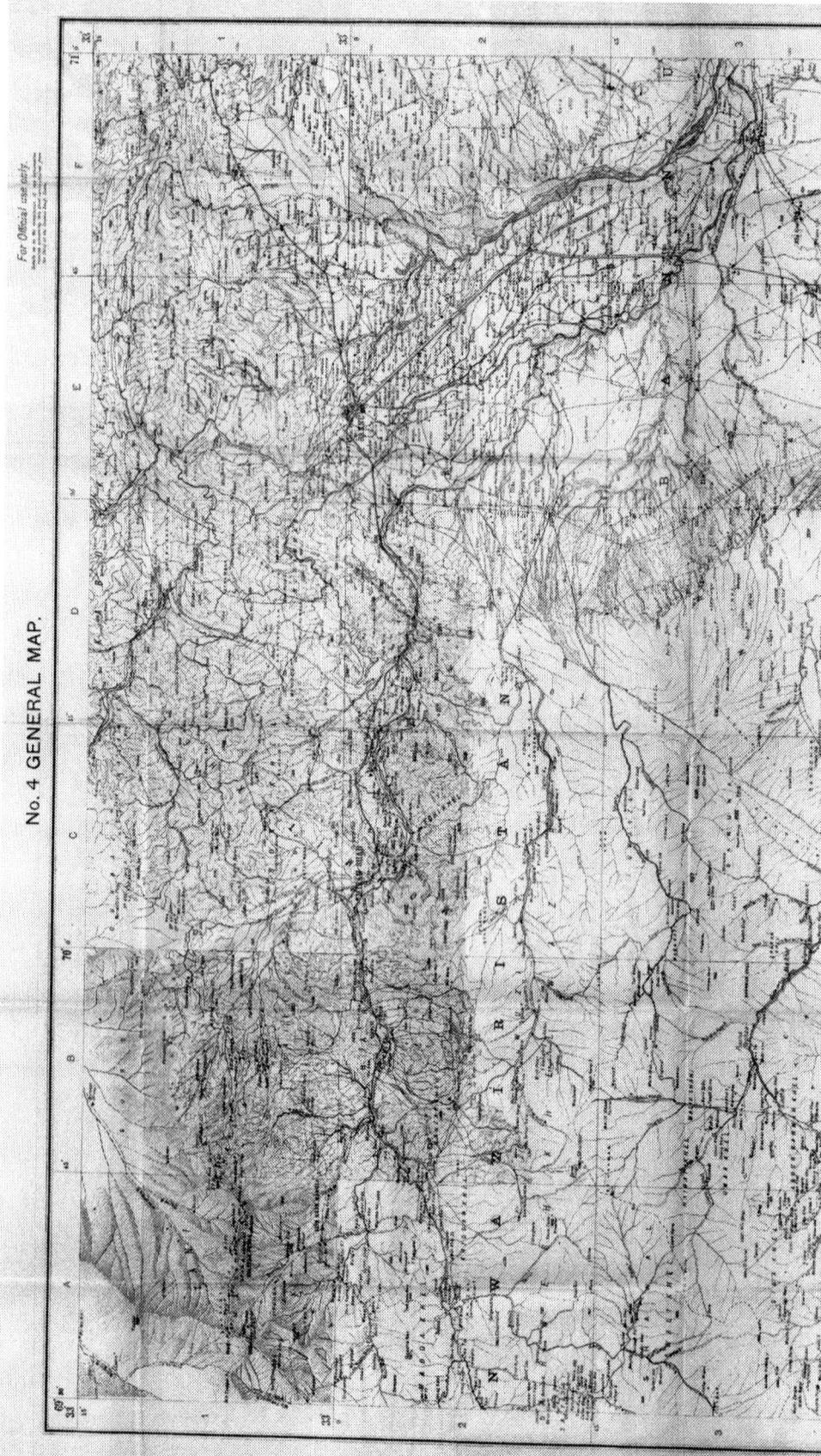

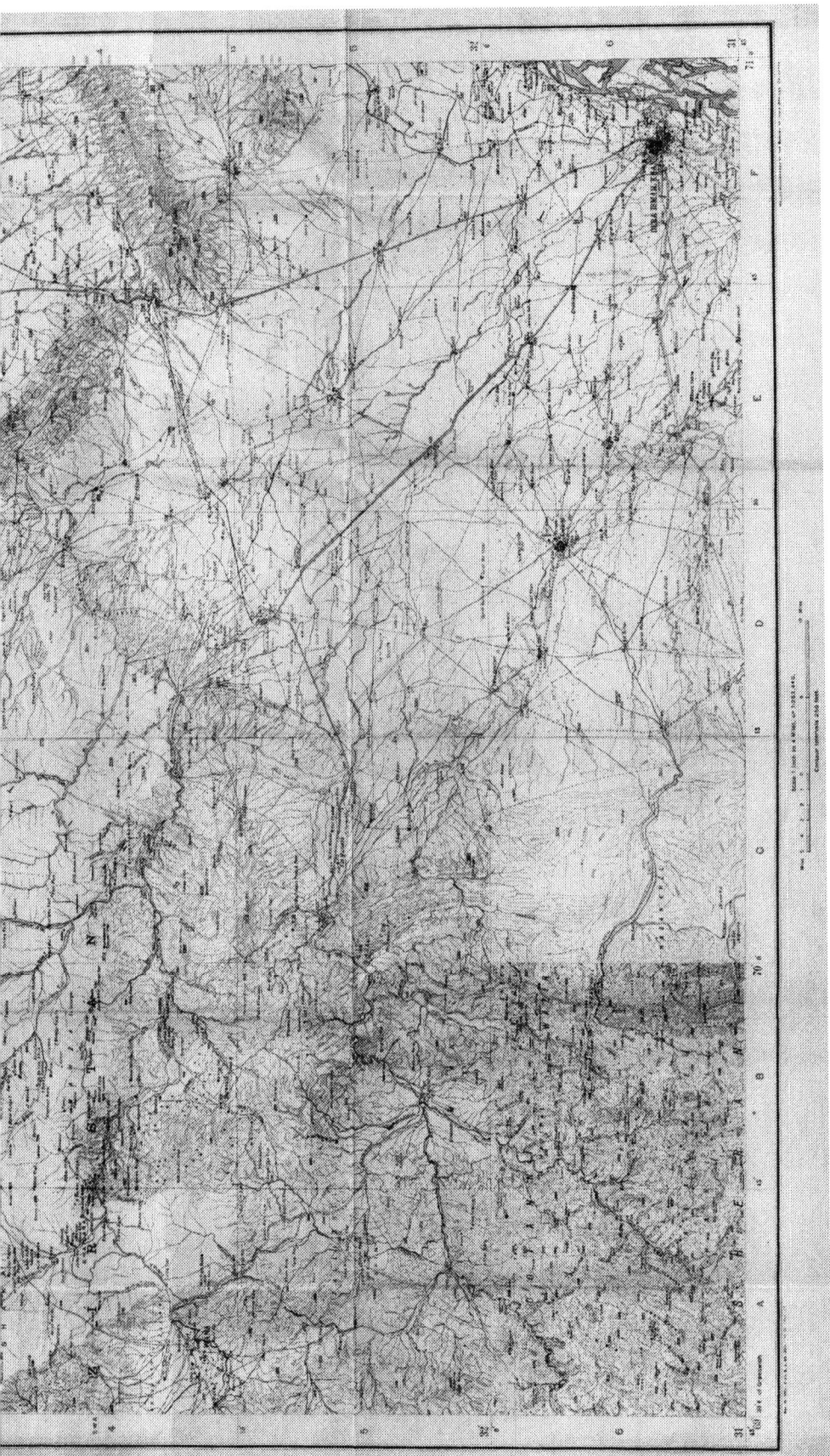

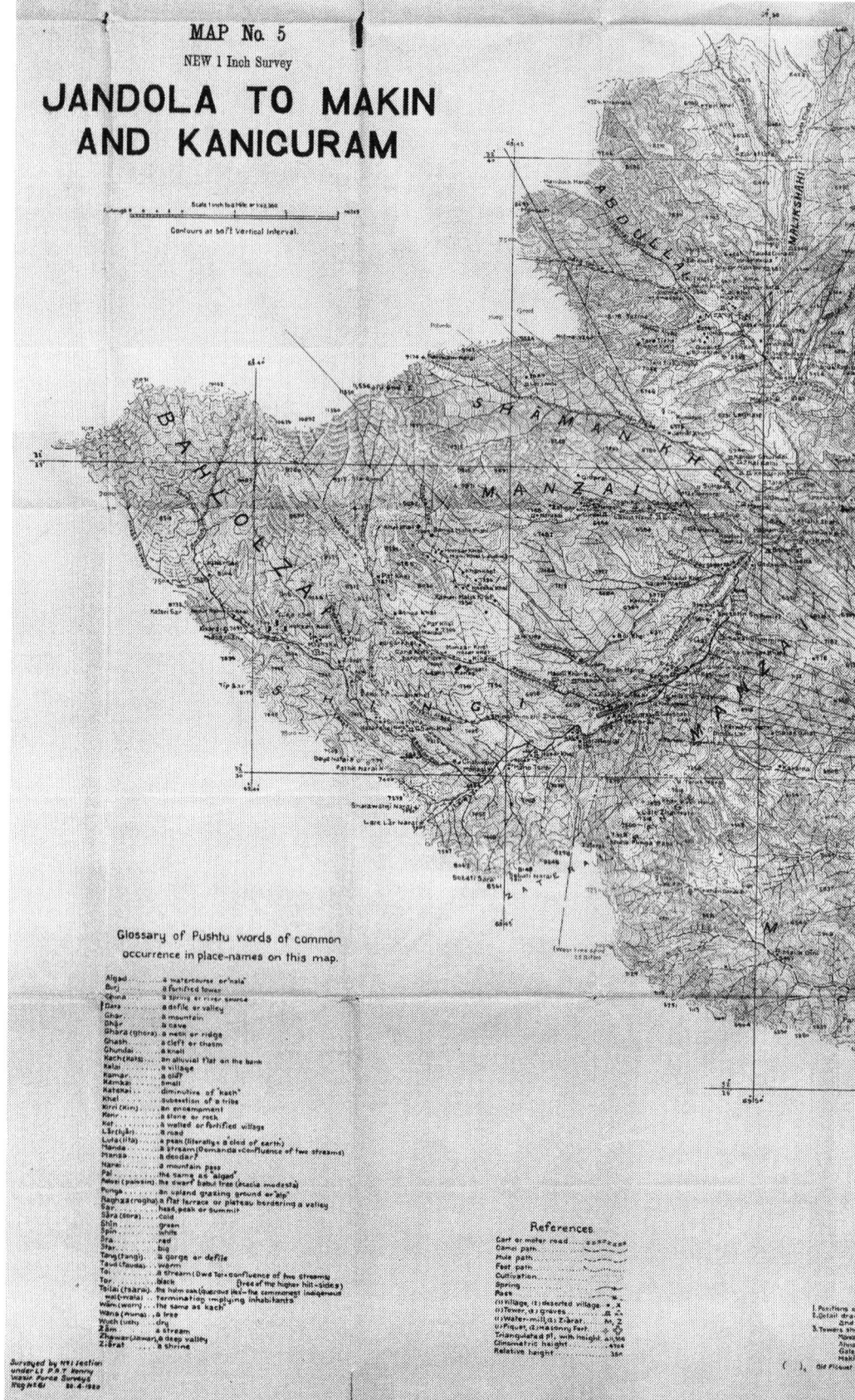

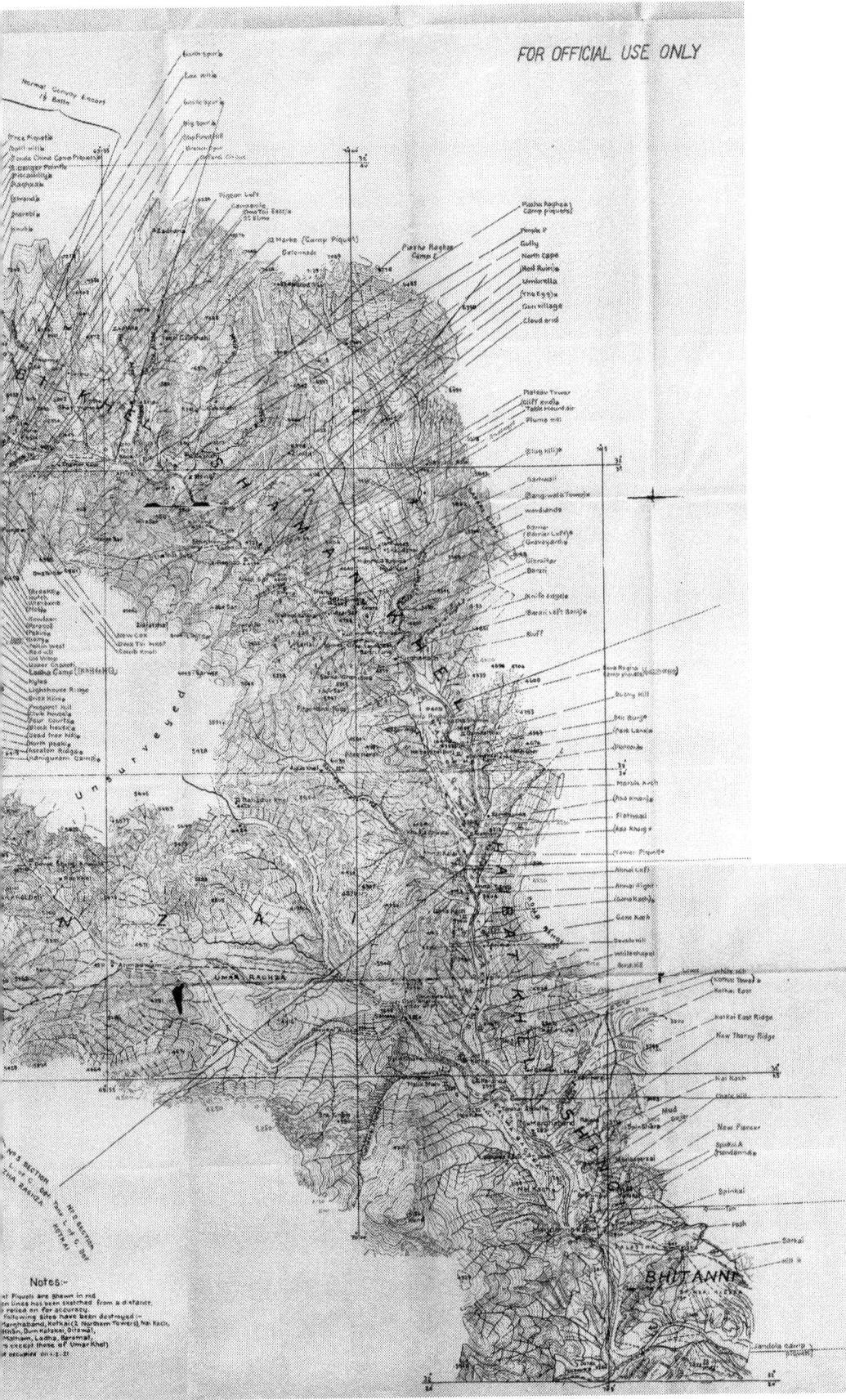

www.ingramcontent.com/pod-product-compliance
Lightning Source LLC
Chambersburg PA
CBHW051051160426
43193CB00010B/1149